Murder and Mayhem

Number Six:
Sam Rayburn Series on Rural Life
Sponsored by Texas A&M University–Commerce
James A. Grimshaw, Jr., *General Editor*

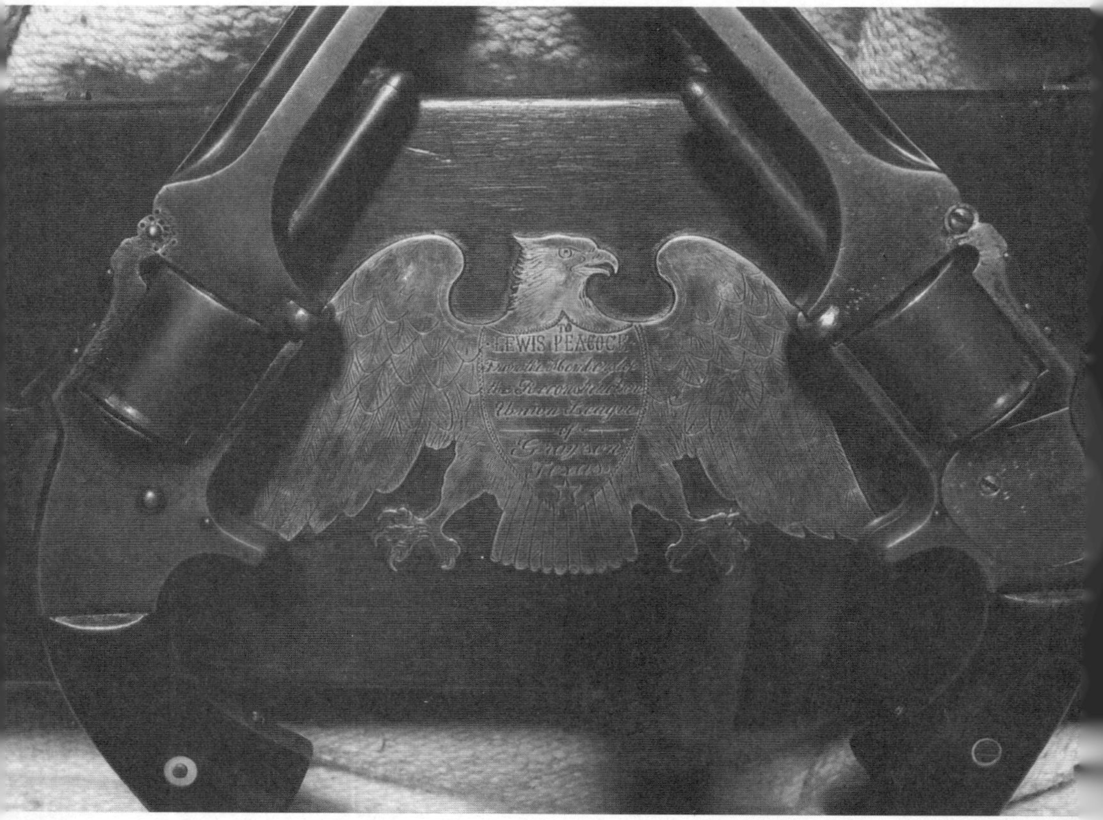

A brace of Smith and Wesson #2 Army Revolvers, .32 rimfire caliber, given to Lewis Peacock circa 1866 for his service as head of the Reconstruction Union League. Now in possession of coauthor Larry Peacock. Photo by Timb Hamilton.

Murder and Mayhem

The War of Reconstruction in Texas

By
James M. Smallwood, Barry A. Crouch,
and Larry Peacock

Texas A&M University Press
College Station

Manufactured in the United States of America

First edition

The paper used in this book meets the minimum requirements of the American National Standard for Permanence of Paper for Printed Library Materials, Z39.48-1984.
Binding materials have been chosen for durability.
♾

Library of Congress Cataloging-in-Publication Data

Smallwood, James.
Murder and mayhem ; the war of Reconstruction in Texas / by James M. Smallwood, Barry A. Crouch, and Larry Peacock.—1st ed.
p. cm. — (Sam Rayburn series on rural life ; no. 6)
Includes bibliographical references (p.) and index.
ISBN 1-58544-280-1 (cloth : alk. paper)
1. Reconstruction—Texas. 2. Reconstruction—Social aspects—Texas. 3. Violence—Texas—History—19th century. 4. Lee, Bob, d. 1869. 5. Peacock, Lewis, d. 1871. 6. Vendetta—Texas—History—19th century. 7. Texas—History—1846–1950. 8. Texas—Social conditions—19the century. I. Crouch, Barry A., 1941– II. Peacock, Larry, 1948– III. Title. IV. Series.
F391 .S6297 2003
976.4'061—dc21

2003005002

For
Loyd Guy Peacock, Charles Lewis Peacock, and the late Barry A. Crouch

Contents

Illustrations

Series Editor's Foreword

Judy Falls and the late David Pickering's *Brush Men and Vigilantes,* the first book in the Sam Rayburn Series on Rural Life, provided revealing details on the violence that was prevalent in Northeast Texas during the Civil War. In a sense, this current volume by James Smallwood, Barry Crouch, and Larry Peacock continues the story of *Brush Men* by following the violent history of Northeast Texas into the Reconstruction era.

As Falls and Pickering point out, during the Civil War conflicts arose between the "brush men," who opposed the Civil War in general and slavery in particular, and vigilante "safety" groups, who supported the Confederacy and its "peculiar institution." Texas history is replete with such conflicts: the Early-Hasley feud in Bell County, the Horrell-Higgins feud in Lampasas County, the Mason County War, the Shackelford County mob, and the Stafford-Townsend feud in Colorado County, though gone, are not forgotten. Some of those conflicts, sometimes labeled as "feuds," became the stuff of legends in Texas history. But many of those legendary stories relied heavily upon memories, sometimes biased, sometimes merely misinformed, sometimes just forgetful of the details. Revisionist historians now know that many such stories contained as much myth as fact.

This study concentrates on Northeast Texas, most especially Corners Country, the area where the county lines of Grayson, Fannin, Hunt, and Collin counties converge. This work analyzes the conflict between former Confederates, joined by some outright brigands, and white Unionists and their allies, the new freedpeople. The former group was committed to upholding the deeply rooted antebellum Southern traditions and values that included white supremacy and suppression of the new freedpeople. The latter group was committed to giving at least a modicum of freedom to the ex-slaves. The struggle grew out of four long years of war, death, and destruction, hatred fanning the flames in the hearts of the Rebels following their bitter defeat in the Civil War. Despite the lost war, ex-Confederates were determined to win the War of Reconstruction in Texas as in the rest of Dixie. Reconstruction became an irony mixed with tragedy, as C. Vann Woodward has noted in *The Burden of Southern History.* American pretensions, categorized as illusions of innocence and virtue, and the larger issues plagued the Reconstruction era; and the ensuing hostilities created animosities that passed from one generation to the next.

Murder and Mayhem: The War of Reconstruction in Texas closely examines a conflict that is sometimes misnamed the "Lee-Peacock Feud." The word "feud" suggests that only personal and familial factors caused the conflagration in Corners Country and the larger region of Northeast Texas. That is far too simplistic an explanation for the widespread violence that played out in the region. In fact, the Lee-Peacock fight, seen in the larger perspective, was part of the struggle between ex-Confederates and Unionists to control Northeast Texas and—when coupled with similar struggles elsewhere—to control the entire state as well. Northern newspapers called the violence committed by ex-Confederates "The New Rebellion." Indeed, it was. It amounted to a second Civil War, a war won by the late Rebels. Consequently, the drive to give blacks at least "surface" equality under the law had to wait another one hundred years to achieve a delayed victory. The ex-Confederates like Bob Lee won the struggle, and Union men like Lewis Peacock were sacrificed along the way. In short, the authors bring to light previously untold, well-documented evidence in a captivating narrative and present a compelling argument for a different interpretation of the Lee-Peacock fight.

This volume, then, adds a sixth snapshot to the Sam Rayburn Series on Rural Life album, a series established on the Texas A&M University-Commerce campus under the auspices of the Texas A&M University Press book-publishing program. The Series promotes original research on diverse subjects related to northeast Texas and the surrounding region. When viewed collectively as a montage, these Series snapshots will provide information that may lead to a better understanding of this dynamic region as an entity unto itself and also as a part of a much larger picture.

James A. Grimshaw, Jr.
General Editor

Preface

At some point in everyone's life, he or she may wonder about ancestry. That curiosity came into my life in 1978 while I was visiting my father's parents, George Lewis and Goldie Whitley Peacock. Both of my grandparents were born in Texas in the late 1800s, and like their forebears, they made their living by farming. Hardworking, honest, Christian people, they raised three children on their Johnson County farm. During my early childhood, I spent time with them on the farm, but I was never able to extract much information about our family's roots.

My grandfather was named after his grandfather, Lewis Peacock, one of the subjects of this book. George Lewis Peacock was born late in his father's life and never knew anything about his grandfather. My grandfather told me only that Lewis Peacock was killed as a result of the War Between the States and that a distant cousin had an old picture of him. I obtained a copy of the tintype, and I hung it in my office, where it has remained. Every day I looked at the likeness of him and wondered how he met his death.

It was 1997 before I started any serious research into my family's history. It started with a conversation at a coffee shop where I talked with Clifton Earl "Buddy" Peacock. Buddy informed me that his brother Donald Lewis Peacock was the secretary of the Peacock Family Association of the South, a genealogy group formed in the 1970s. I called Donald, and he shared with me his years of research on the extended Peacock clan.

Many articles and a book have been produced about the Lee-Peacock Feud, a saga that occurred during the Reconstruction era of Texas. I never dreamed that the Lewis Peacock in these writings was my great-great-grandfather until Donald shared his knowledge with me. Lewis was portrayed as an outlaw and a killer in various writings, but I had to learn more, to learn if it was really true. I had to start my own journey into the past.

I learned that my great-grandfather John Edgar Peacock was eighteen years old when his father Lewis was killed. He moved west to Parker County, Texas, after his father was murdered. John married and raised a family there but apparently never told his story to anyone. As I researched, I learned why John Edgar never talked of Lewis's murder. Confederate sentiment was so prevalent in the South that if he had told the truth to anyone, he might have brought trouble, perhaps even violence, upon his immediate family. From what I learned, I also believe that John Edgar had reason to believe that the infamous outlaw John

Wesley Hardin was looking for him. Hardin and his numerous cousins lived in the "Corners" area of Northeast Texas where the borders of Grayson, Collin, Hunt, and Fannin counties converge. Most of the ex-Confederates with whom Lewis Peacock had trouble with were related to the Hardins.

After three years of work and many miles of travel, I uncovered enough evidence to know that the traditional views of Lewis as a renegade were false. Courthouse research, for example, showed that Lewis was a target of the Bob Lee gang and other former Confederates and that several attempts had been made on Lewis's life before the last attempt was successful in ending his days. I felt that previous researchers who had depicted Lewis Peacock as a mere gunman were wrong. He was a loyal citizen of the United States, a fact that made him most hated by former Rebels.

Around Christmas of 1998, I contacted James Smallwood, a professor in the history department at Oklahoma State University. Smallwood and I had a visit, and we went over the material that I had collected. He saw possibilities for a book on the so-called Lee-Peacock Feud. In his own work on Texas during Reconstruction, Smallwood had encountered the infamous Bob Lee and also had other research material that directly or indirectly related to the struggle. Smallwood also saw the larger context in which to place the events. It really was not a traditional feud at all. "Feud" suggests that personal animosities and personality clashes were the causes of the trouble. In fact, the Lee-Peacock war was a story about a handful of Texans loyal to the United States and the ex-Confederates who went after them.

Smallwood and I decided that we needed a third party to help with the proposed manuscript: Professor Barry A. Crouch of the history department at Galluadet University in Maryland. A prolific researcher and writer on Texas' Reconstruction era, Crouch shared all his research that related to the Lee-Peacock fight, made suggestions for revisions, and helped with the final editing.

Many earlier writers who looked into the feud stood history on its head by condemning Lewis Peacock and idolizing Bob Lee as the great champion of the Lost Cause. Many writers penned stories that reversed the actural roles: The "good guys" became "bad guys" and the "bad guys" became the "good guys." The three of us have produced a book that sets the record straight, as well as one that will contribute to our knowledge of Reconstruction in Texas and in the wider South.

Larry Peacock

Acknowledgments

We have incurred many debts in researching and writing this volume. First, we would like to thank the extended Peacock family for their assistance with this project. Thanks also go to the many residents of Leonard and Trenton, Texas, two towns near the sites where much of the action mentioned in this study took place. We appreciate their sharing the history and legends surrounding the lives of the major characters in this book.

We would like to thank the archivists at the Greenville Public Library for allowing us to use their collection of primary materials. We appreciate, too, James Conrad and his staff at Texas A&M–Commerce for giving us the use of all collections there that helped round out our study. The staff at the National Archives gave us great assistance as we worked through several record groups in their holdings. We are grateful for the efforts of the record clerks of the four county courthouses (Grayson, Collin, Hunt, and Fannin) who helped us as we searched for more primary material. Donaly Brice of the Texas State Library also deserves notice for finding and sending us various materials from the library that related to our subject.

Thanks go to the staff of the Texas A&M University Press and to Tracy Row, who helped make this work a better book. We also had four anonymous readers who evaluated our manuscript and found it acceptable. Each reader made constructive suggestions that helped us revise and improve our material.

Oklahoma State University's History Department secretaries Susan Oliver and Diana Hover typed the many drafts of the study as it was revised again and again, and we are grateful for their hard work.

James M. Smallwood
Larry Peacock

Murder and Mayhem

East-Northeast Texas. Map by Donald S. Frazier.

Introduction

Prelude to a Nightmare

Four years of Civil War engendered animosities, hatreds, and resentments that lingered and often erupted into violent encounters even decades after the end of the war. Southerners who made the commitment to remain loyal to the Union found themselves persecuted and perceived as outcasts, while their beliefs were denigrated and dismissed as treason to the homeland. Most returning Confederate veterans found it difficult to accept the results of the late war and the South's capitulation. Whether they owned slaves or not, many resented the intrusion of new ideals that Reconstruction Congresses imposed and new laws that attempted to bring about equality between whites and blacks.

Across the former Confederacy, Unionists and those who supported secession or fought for the South in the conflict clashed in open warfare after the peace at Appomattox. These imbroglios, in fact, had begun while war still raged and became increasingly more hateful and murderous with the end of hostilities. The emotions had a long gestation period, involved the very foundations of the Southern culture, and could not be easily disregarded or dethroned. This warfare was probably inevitable due to the deep-seated ideals felt and experienced by the opposing forces. It could not have been otherwise. Honor and duty played a major role during the bloody years of Reconstruction, and a host of individuals were caught up in this drama. Reconstruction really amounted to a Second Civil War, one that pitted whites who had supported Confederacy against loyal white Union men, the freedmen, and the Northern forces who occupied Texas. It was a guerrilla war that the ex-Confederates were determined to win at any cost.

What has been termed the Lee-Peacock Feud was an important chapter in the South's Second Civil War. It played itself out in the Corners of Northeast Texas, the area where Grayson, Fannin, Hunt, and Collin counties converge. It was a struggle wherein Unionists led by Lewis Peacock and former Confederates led by Bob Lee had at each other until blood ran in the streets. Because he refused to accept the results of the late war, the Southern loyalist Lee became a Ku Klux Klansman and an outlaw raider and took the fight to the Southern Unionists, Yankee soldiers, and the newly freed slaves. More than 200 white and black men and women may have been killed in the struggle while hundreds more may have died because of an indirect link to the fight. Events of the feud have been told and retold in countless newspapers, by local and regional historians, and by lay writers who accepted Confederate myths about the Reconstruction era or the South's Second Civil War. Thus, most writers have viewed the Lee-Peacock fight as a simple, clear story of good versus evil. But most accounts have stood history on its head, to say the least, by denigrating the freedpeople and loyal white Unionists of any stripe—North or South—and by practically deifying the Ku Klux Klan, other terrorist groups using different names, and assorted outlaw raiders like Bob Lee, a cut-throat who called the Corners home. Lee was a man who tormented and killed so many people that he became known as "The Man Eater."[1]

According to Reconstruction myths, Northern carpetbaggers, traitorous Southern scalawags, and the ignorant freedmen of Dixie united to inflict barbarous political, economic, and social rule on the noble, white, honor-driven Southern patriots who had fought a war for the justifiable reason of upholding honor and the states' rights political philosophy. Perhaps without realizing it, writers who continued to advance old myths were still following the now discredited Dunning School of Reconstruction historiography that glorified the South and the Lost Cause and vilified the North, including everything associated with that region. Dunningites idolized ex-Confederate Democrats and condemned scalawag and carpetbagger Republicans. Dunning's followers also exalted the Ku Klux Klan, other terrorist groups, and outlaw gangs while degrading the Loyal Union League—and men like Lewis Peacock, the most prominent Unionist in the Corners.[2]

But a major problem exists. The Dunningites of yesteryear wrote about a past that never was. Many modern scholars know that the traditional view of Reconstruction is a myth. Many of today's scholars know that, for example, few carpetbaggers came to Texas, and most who did were young white women that the American Missionary Association recruited to teach the newly freed African Americans. Most agree that the Republicans were not really devils in human form. Instead most Republicans were sincere Union men, like E. J. Davis, who were loyal to the Union before, during, and after the war. Nor was there "Negro domination." At most, the black voting bloc was the swing vote that helped Republicans come to power. Throughout Reconstruction, the great majority of officeholders were white. Even among revisionists one question still needs to be answered, however: Did violence and intimidation play a major role in the Democrats' drive to redeem Texas in the 1870s? How important were groups like the Ku Klux Klan and former Confederates who became social bandits because they could not accept the Civil War's outcome and the freeing of former slaves? Today's serious researchers do not glorify the Klan and former Confederates who became outlaw raiders, but scholars disagree on questions regarding the overwhelming importance of the violence.[3]

Revisionists' views about Reconstruction in Texas since the 1960s and 1970s have been slow to reach the public. Often, when general readers encounter books that advance new interpretations, they tend to reject these volumes out-of-hand because such interpretations do not conform to the myths that they have embraced all their lives—myths amounting to spurious stories that were passed down from generation to generation. Perhaps this book will help reverse the trend and capture the attention of the reader.

Within the context of recent scholarship, it might well be that the Lee-Peacock Feud should not be presented as a feud at all. "Feud" implies that a struggle existed between families or individuals for familial or individual reasons or personal grudges wherein ideas about right or wrong become lost as one family battles and retaliates against another. Instead, the Lee-Peacock disturbance is the saga of white Southerners who were Unionist before, during, and after the Civil War, and a story about the persecution that they faced during Reconstruction.

In East-Northeastern Texas, early in the Reconstruction era, criminal guerrilla bands, whose members were mostly ex-Confederates, coalesced to challenge the verdict of the Civil War or to use the verdict for their own ends. Some joined societies like the Ku Klux Klan. Others became raiders who were intent on punishing or killing freed blacks, white Unionists, and occupying federal forces. Such groups killed discriminately; they seldom went after former Confederates unless those ex-Rebels had developed Unionist leanings after the conflict. Some violent groups had much support in the Lone Star State. In that, the former Rebels in Texas were like many people across the wider South. Many of Dixie's white citizens believed that they had not really been defeated; rather, they had been "overwhelmed" by superior numbers. They would not accept Yankee rule after the close of the conflict. Bob Lee of the Corners was one such Southerner, and he soon became the bane of Unionist Lewis Peacock's existence. Lee fits the definitions of both outlaw and Confederate. He believed in the Lost Cause, a belief that led him into his horrific life of crime.

Chapter 1

Texas and the Second Civil War

Late at night on June 13, 1871, Dick Johnson, Joe Parker, and an unidentified man rode to Unionist Lewis Peacock's place in the southeastern part of Grayson County. The unidentified man may have been John Wesley Hardin, a teenager who was already a hardened killer. Or he could have been Mace Bowman, a professional gunman. The three stalkers intended to kill Peacock because they held him personally responsible for the death of their friend, the notorious outlaw "Captain" Bob Lee, who had earlier spread terror throughout Northeastern Texas as he fought and killed white Unionists and the freed slaves who supported them.[1]

Peacock's farm was near the Corners, the closest little town being Pilot Grove. After the threesome reached the Peacock place, they secured their horses some distance away, crept through the woods, and hid in the bush near Peacock's backyard. After positioning themselves so that each had a clear line of sight to the yard, at least one climbed an elm tree for better vision. About sunrise, Peacock emerged from his back door and may have headed toward his woodpile to retrieve logs for his breakfast fire. More likely, he had earlier followed the nineteenth century approach by getting his wood the day before. Once outside, he probably headed for the outhouse. Reportedly, he was wearing red longjohns and had strapped his gunbelt around his waist. As he walked through the yard, Johnson, Parker, and the other man opened up with double-barreled shotguns at point-blank range. Even as he was shot, Peacock tried to defend himself. He grabbed for both of his six-guns, but he slapped empty leather. Incredibly, with his early drowsiness, he had forgotten to load the holsters. With Peacock defenseless, the three assassins continued to fire with their handguns, shooting Peacock to pieces. The Union man never reached his outhouse. He collapsed in the yard, probably dead before his body hit the ground. Peacock's wife Emaline may have seen him die, or she certainly knew there was trouble afoot when she heard the gun shots. Terrified and fearing for her own life, she stayed in the house, no doubt praying that the gunmen would not kill her. If she thought of her teenaged son John Edgar, she was probably glad that he was away, working at a temporary job; he would have tried to defend his father and would likely have died in the effort.[2]

Lewis had earlier been wounded several times as the ex-Confederate fight ran its course during Reconstruction. So, to make sure that they had finished the job, the killers reloaded their weapons, and they came into the yard. They gathered over their quarry. At such a close range that left powder burns on Peacock's long-johns, each fired two more rounds from their shotguns. Dick Johnson later said that one of Peacock's feet kept shaking, so they shot him until that foot was still. They mangled Peacock's body so terribly that he was practically unrecognizable when the killers finished.[3]

Lewis Peacock (1824–71). A principal character in the Lee-Peacock struggle, Lewis was murdered in 1871 as a result of his participation in the politics of the Civil War and Reconstruction. He was killed by Dick Johnson, Joe Parker, and an unidentified third party. Photo courtesy Larry Peacock.

Dick Johnson, who escaped into Missouri, lived to a ripe old age and returned to the Corners at least once—in the 1920s to visit his surviving relatives and old friends. He talked with J. C. "Red" Smith, a descendant of Reverend Martin Smith, who was Bob Lee's brother-in-law. Johnson admitted being in the party that killed Peacock and gave the grizzly details of the shooting. Further, G. W. King was a contemporary of Dick Johnson, and King later remembered that Johnson gave him and others a first-hand account of the murder. Many years later, John Gentry, son of Parson Martin W. Gentry, confirmed that there were three men and that they admitted to killing Peacock. Another contemporary said that Johnson bragged and jested about the way he and the two other men killed Peacock. Johnson's words and demeanor made one listener's blood run cold.[4]

Parson Gentry and his family, whose farm was adjacent to the Peacock place, were having their breakfast when Lewis met his end. They heard the assassins' guns report rapidly a number of times. All at the preacher's table sat silently for a moment, stunned as surprise and fear gripped them. The parson broke the silence with six simple, and in this case deadly, words: "There, they've got Peacock, I figure." The killers knew that Parson Gentry doubled as the area undertaker. They rode up to his place, stopped at the edge of his front yard, and shouted out: "Hello! Hello, in there! Parson Gent, you can go and dress the fowl. We've killed it!"[5]

Gentry and his son John roused themselves, left their house, hitched their team, and drove Martin's wagon to the Peacock place. There, they found Emaline in a state of shock over losing her husband and over seeing the gruesome way that he was killed. The sight was sickening. After advising her to leave the area, Martin Gentry and son John helped her pack and hitch her team. Afterwards, with John's help, the parson loaded Lewis's body in his wagon and, with Emaline following, he drove to the nearby graveyard. After a short service, Gentry buried the body in an unmarked grave, whereupon Emaline left for parts unknown and got word to her son not to return to the Corners. Never again would Emaline be seen in Corners Country, and neither would John Edgar. As far as Lewis's enemies were concerned, his wife and son just vanished. Such action was necessary because the men who murdered her husband likely would have also killed John Edgar if they had ever found him.[6]

Galveston's *Flake's Daily Bulletin* Pilot Grove correspondent almost made a joke of reporting the death of Peacock. In his words, "Last evening a squad of men, three in number, arrived with double-barreled shotguns, revolvers, et cetera." They "rode leisurely into our burg," but "their colloquial powers were limited." After they stayed a few minutes, "they mounted their horses and rode off in an easterly direction. Since their departure," the editor continued, "we are creditably informed that the famous Lewis Peacock, formerly chief-in-command of the Peacock party, was shot to atoms this morning at sunrise in his yard."[7]

Thus ended the so-called Lee-Peacock War. Like Peacock, hundreds, if not thousands, of men (and some women) in East-Northeast Texas died because of animosities between Unionists and former Confederates, and countless others were wounded by the frequent gunfire that erupted as the conflict intensified.[8]

The significance of the Lee-Peacock struggle can best be measured when it is seen as a momentous chapter in the off-and-on Reconstruction-era guerrilla war that many supporters of the Lost Cause, including outlaws and terrorist groups, waged against white Unionists—who joined the Republican party and the Loyal Union League—and the freedmen who supported those white Union men. The political, social, and economic stakes were high. They included nothing less than who would win political control (and therefore economic and social control) of the Lone Star State—Unionists or supporters of the defeated Confederacy. A second issue was also most important: Would white Rebel sympathizers be allowed to control completely and to suppress the former slaves? Would the blacks be returned to a state of semi-slavery, or would they be given the rights of a free people? Would national Republican party policies—including those that sought to protect and to uplift the South's black community—prevail in Texas, or would the former secessionists fight off Republican control?

For a time, the answers to such questions were not at all clear. The absence of those answers allowed near chaos to flourish in many parts of Dixie, including regions like East-Northeast Texas, an area that became one of the most violent parts of the South during the Civil War and Reconstruction. To fight the white Unionists and their black allies, defeated Southerners founded "Democratic clubs," some members of which tried to intimidate both white and black Unionists by using threats and economic coercion. Terrorist groups also formed, and die-hard Rebels who joined them did whatever was necessary to reestablish Democratic control of the state. Some of those things that they were willing to do included violence and outright murder. In fact, a "New Rebellion," a Second Civil War developed.[9]

The larger story of the Reconstruction era in Texas history is the backdrop against which the Lee-Peacock struggle played itself out. If the Civil War brought chaos to Texas, the immediate aftermath of the war caused even more. In April of 1865, after Gen. Robert E. Lee surrendered in the Eastern Theater of the war, Texas' local, county, and state governments collapsed. Courts were disrupted while armed, violent bands of Southern soldiers, deserters, and common criminals roamed East and Northeast Texas. Under the cover of darkness, in the middle of the night of June 11, 1865, unknown parties even looted the state treasury in Austin. Statewide, mobs, including both men and women, overran Confederate commissaries, confiscating whatever they wished. Men also descended upon arsenals, looting them for arms and munitions. Some broke into and robbed private homes. Many Texas towns experienced such incidents.[10]

In Tyler, home of a number of Confederate installations, for example, mobs stormed the quartermaster's warehouse and the pharmaceutical laboratory. As well, looters tried to steal a horse herd belonging to the dissolving Confederate command. Desperate women with hungry families attempted to loot the commissary but failed. Civilians later attacked the armory, intending to seize arms and ammunition. Many area women were afraid to leave their homes. When they did go out, they traveled only by day. They were armed and usually went in groups of at least two, three, or more. The timely arrival of one hundred federal troopers in Smith County averted worse developments.[11] But even as the Union soldiers were trying to restore order, one observer noted that "there have been four or five men shot or hanged within a few miles of us [Tyler] in a week."[12]

Shortly after the sacking of the state treasury, Union occupation of Texas began. On June 19, 1865, General Gordon Granger and 1,800 men occupied Galveston. He announced that the slaves were free. Granger then paroled all Texans who were in the Confederate Army. Knowing that the Lone Star State was out of control, he tried to reestablish order. But he could send only small detachments to Austin, San Antonio, Tyler, and Marshall. This was precisely the problem that Granger and the commanders who followed him faced in Texas—

they never had adequate troop strength to police the state thoroughly. The number of Union forces rose to a high of 51,000 through 1865, but by mid-1866, the number had fallen to approximately 3,000, as massive demobilization took place, leaving few men to patrol the interior of the state. Some troopers had to serve on the frontier, further depleting the number available for service in East-Northeast Texas. Terrorist groups like the Ku Klux Klan and outlaw gangs—all claiming that they were fighting for the Lost Cause—exploited the shortage of federal manpower to the fullest. Refusing to accept the results of the late war, they plundered and looted their way across East-Northeast Texas, spreading mayhem wherever they went.[13]

Two days before Granger landed in Galveston, United States President Andrew Johnson appointed Unionist Andrew Jackson Hamilton as provisional governor of the Lone Star State. Hamilton's charge was to implement the president's Reconstruction plan which, vaguely based upon Abraham Lincoln's tenuous "10 percent plan," was most forgiving of the Confederates. Texas could reorganize its civil government by accepting a three-step process: declare secession null and void, repudiate Confederate war debts, and ratify the Thirteen Amendment, which abolished slavery. The president barred only high-ranking Confederates and extremely wealthy men from participating in the political process; and no Southerner was to be punished further. There would be no war crimes trials (save one—the commandant of Georgia's Andersonville Prison), and Southerners would not lose their civil or political rights. Nor would the government confiscate Southerners' property. Hamilton arrived in Texas on June 21, two days behind General Granger, and immediately began fulfilling his duties. By appointing Unionists—and some men who had remained loyal to the South—to state, county, and local government offices, Hamilton restored civil rule in eighty counties within a month. Included were the four counties whose borders comprised the Corners.[14]

Grayson originally made up the northeast corner of the old Peters Colony land grant. It is bordered by the Red River and by Fannin, Collin, Denton, and Cooke counties. After the surveying of the Peters Colony in the 1840s, American settlement of the area rapidly expanded as the Dixie frontier exploded westward. Organized as a county in 1846 with Sherman as its county seat, Grayson had a population of 2,008 in 1850. Ten years later, the count stood at 8,184. Other than Sherman, small settlements included Preston Bend on the Red River, Warren, and Pilot Grove in the Corners.[15]

Like Grayson, Collin County was part of the old Peters Colony. Its northern border only twenty miles south of the Red River, Collin became a county in 1846 with Buckner as the county seat, which was moved to McKinney in 1848. By 1850 the county's population stood at 1,950, a figure that had risen to 9,264 by 1860. The founding white families included those headed by Collin McKinney, a signer of the Texas Declaration of Independence, and George W. Throckmorton, the father of James W. Throckmorton, who became a noted Texas politician. In addition to McKinney and Buckner, small hamlets included Highland, Millwood, Plano, Rock Hill, and Roseland.[16]

Created in 1837, Fannin County is one of the oldest counties in Texas. Its northern border is the Red River. By 1850, small settlements included Bonham, the county seat, Honey Grove, Old Warren, and a few other tiny villages. By 1860, the county's population was 9,217.[17] Created in 1846, Hunt County slowly attracted settlers—350 when organized as a county. Greenville became the county seat. Other early settlements included Bean Creek, Shiloh, and Timber Creek. By 1850 Hunt County had a population of 1,520, a figure that had grown to 6,630 by 1860.[18]

In all four counties, lush farmlands attracted settlers. The region's growing season varied slightly by county, the average being about 330 days a year. Adequate rainfall guaranteed that growers would have bountiful seasons. Yeoman farmers harvested great fields of corn, beans of different varieties, sweet and Irish potatoes, pumpkins, onions, tomatoes, and squash, in addition to some wheat and a few other eatables. Small orchards bore different kinds of fruit that added delightful variety to the people's diets. Most farmers had a few dairy cows as well as small cattle and horse herds. The everpresent pigs were legion, for pork was the dietary mainstay of Dixie. Men supplemented their families' daily fare by hunting the white-tailed deer, rabbits, squirrels, and other small game. They also fished in a number of rivers and creeks. All four counties were heavily forested, and the first great cash industry was the lumber business. Farmers strove for self-sufficiency and had little or no interest in the cotton culture, for the counties were settled primarily by people from the Upper South and even had a sprinkling of Yankees. Where horse trails often took the place of roads, farmers had limited access to outside markets. Most growers had to haul their goods all the way to the East Texas metropolis of Jefferson to secure a trade outlet. Cotton was far too bulky to haul, and most farmers put their work into other crops. There were a number of plantations, however, where landowners grew cotton and other crops. Indeed, one of the wealthiest planters in the state came from Corners Country. Originally from South Carolina, J. E. Hudson of Grayson had developed a showplace plantation. According to the census of 1860, his 105 slaves grew 150 bales of cotton and 3,000 bushels of corn, along with other crops. But plantation agriculture involving large numbers of slaves was the exception. Most slaves were held by yeoman farmers each of whom had relatively few. Other slaves were hired out to work in the various towns in Corners Country.[19]

The Corners counties continued to evolve during Reconstruction. Increasingly, politics occupied the attention of residents, some of whom were loyal to the Union, some of whom were not. Although it did not immediately touch the Corners counties, on September 5, 1865, the Freedmen's Bureau began to function in Texas. However, from its inception until its withdrawal in 1870, the agency was woefully under-manned and under-funded, and it never had enough military manpower to implement fully the federal Reconstruction policies. Further, since its general charge was to help the state's black community make its transition from slavery to freedom, it incurred the downright hatred of the residents who had supported the Southern war effort. Often even those who had favored the Union and opposed secession did not help the bureau for fear of retaliation by the ex-Confederates.[20]

Along with freed slaves and Union soldiers, bureau agents became a symbol, the embodiment of the Confederate disgrace during the war and during the Reconstruction era. Unarmed freedmen and bureau men, who usually had only a small personal guard, were particularly easy targets for the wrath of the defeated because they were seldom protected by troops. Local hatred of the bureau personnel—soldiers, blacks, and white Unionists of any stripe, North or South—has been institutionalized by demonizing Union men like Lewis Peacock and by deifying the cutthroats like Bob Lee and his men.[21]

General Oliver Otis Howard, national commissioner of the Freedmen's Bureau, named Gen. Edgar M. Gregory as Texas' first Freedmen's Bureau assistant commissioner. Reportedly, Howard did so because he had to send his best man to the Lone Star State, for he identified Texas as the worst area in the South regarding the extreme hatred many whites had for blacks and regarding the violence that such hatred spawned. Gregory did his work as best he could and wanted freedmen to receive equal rights. However, he was so limited in money and manpower that he could extend the bureau's reach only to the coastal region of the state.[22]

Gregory coped—but with mixed results. In time, he established sixteen sub-stations in East Texas, appointing military men or loyal civilians as sub-agents. Although Gregory was short-handed, he did his job too well. Because he insisted on decent treatment for the freedmen and for white Unionists and because he refused to deal with the old master class, a constant stream of criticisms from Confederate sympathizers gushed into Washington. In the face of so many complaints, President Andrew Johnson finally ordered Gregory's recall. Following in turn as Texas assistant commissioners were the generals Joseph B. Kiddoo, Charles Griffin, and Joseph J. Reynolds. They expanded the bureau to include more sub-stations, but even at its peak in 1867, the agency counted only fifty-nine sub-agents and ten assistant sub-agents, numbers too small to administer Texas satisfactorily. The decline of bureau activity in Texas (except for some functions related to education) began in 1868. The bureau was phased out altogether in 1870, but not before beginning a permanent school system for the black community. That system was later absorbed by the public school system that radical Republicans gave the people of Texas. The agents also promoted the legal rights of black Texans.[23]

In Austin and around the state, leaders began reacting to Reconstruction in 1865. In the politically complex, explosive twelve months after Governor Hamilton reached Texas, the white majority—including old secessionists—refused to follow moderate Unionists like Hamilton and former Governor Elisha M. Pease. Instead the majority aligned with the forces of Collin County's James W. Throckmorton, a "semi"-Unionist who voted against secession but who fought for the Confederacy and who detested blacks. In the early political struggle, race relations became a major issue. Leaders like Hamilton and Pease advocated basic civil rights for the freedmen but not full equality, while Throckmorton adamantly opposed giving any rights whatsoever to blacks, beyond recognizing their freedom under the Thirteenth Amendment. His political strength was such that his forces managed to control the Texas Constitutional Convention that convened on February 7, 1866. The convention extended no basic rights to the freedmen and denied them the right to vote, to hold office, or to serve on juries. In the statewide elections that followed, voters chose Throckmorton for governor over Pease by a landslide majority of 49,314 to 12,694.[24]

In the new administration, old secessionists, including Southern diehards, wielded predominant power. They believed in white supremacy and intended to reduce the new freedmen to semi-slavery or peonage. Toward that end, the legislature passed the infamous "Black Codes" that regulated many aspects of the freedpeople's lives. As part of this legislation, in October of 1866 the solons passed an apprenticing provision that gave whites control over the labor of under-aged black children. In November five more sections followed, the most heinous of which was the Contract Labor Code that created a second type of slavery for black adults, who were destined to be treated worse than the serfs of Europe's Medieval era. Blacks had to find an employer and sign labor contracts, with the usual contract period being one year. The signature or "mark" of the head of a household bound the entire household. Workers could not quit during the period that the contract was in force. Further, employers could fine workers for many infractions, including breaking tools and missing work. Employers were also given the right to administer corporal punishment. Many such employers resorted to the whip when it suited their whim.

Next, the Texas Homestead Law specifically excluded blacks from the list of people eligible to claim farm land in the state's public domain. That exclusion guaranteed that the great majority of freed slaves would remain landless peasants who could become but sharecroppers or tenant farmers. Other codes dealt with convict leasing, with vagrancy, and with severely limiting the blacks' rights in courts.[25] Thus, because of President Johnson's lenient Reconstruction plan, Texas, like most Southern states, passed codes that virtually re-enslaved the black community. Although supporters of the codes emphasized the nondiscriminatory or color-blindness of the legislation, all people realized that the laws were intended to apply only to the former slaves. Equally disturbing, many whites—former Confederate soldiers and outlaws—were emboldened to take justice into their own hands and continue their persecution of blacks, white Unionists, agents of the Freedmen's Bureau, and others who stood in their way. Lewis Peacock became an early target in Corners Country because he was so outspoken in the defense of white Unionists and blacks. The War of Reconstruction in Texas was about to intensify.

Chapter 2

Pandemonium's New Home

With a certain gift for hyperbole, a correspondent of the *Cincinnati Commercial* wrote in 1869, after touring Eastern and Northeastern Texas:

> You cannot pick up a paper in East Texas without reading of murder, assassinations, and robbery . . . and yet not the fourth part of the truth has been told; not one act in ten is reported. Go where you will, and you will hear of fresh murders and violence. . . . The civil authority is powerless—the military insufficient in number, while hell has transferred its capital from pandemonium to Jefferson, and the devil is holding high carnival in Gilmer, Tyler, Canton, Quitman, Boston, Marshall and other places in Texas.[1]

Perhaps not equally gifted with words, Gen. Phillip Sheridan, who commanded the Fifth Military District, nevertheless was heard to mutter that if he owned both hell and Texas, he would rent out Texas and live in hell. Both the correspondent and the general were, of course, referring to the inordinate amount of violence that accompanied Reconstruction in the Lone Star State. And neither missed the mark by much. Contemporary observers and later historians alike held that Texas was among the most lawless, the most violent of all the states in the Reconstruction South.[2]

In East and Northeast Texas, disgruntled former Rebels did all they could to resist federal control and to harass freedmen and white Unionists with impunity, often with public participation and approval. As one local author wrote, "This was the first war in the total history of humanity in which the conquered have enjoyed the fruits of victory, bought with the blood of the victor. . . . The United States [government] has shown that it invariably generated more contempt than gratitude."[3]

In all of settled East Texas, not many areas went so completely out of control as the land known as Corners Country. The area's oldest settlement was Grayson County's tiny Pilot Grove, also called "Lickskillet," a reference to the poverty and hunger that the area experienced during the Civil War. Some of the earliest pioneers to settle near Pilot Grove were the families of Buford Clement,

Dick Brewer, C. W. Batsell, Frank Stinnett, Simon Sivells, W. A. Kuykendall, W. D. Hoard, and the physician W. H. Pierce.[4]

Surrounded by fertile black farmland that lies in the headwaters of the Sabine and Sulphur rivers and the East Fork of the Trinity, the Pilot Grove area attracted agrarians who grew great stands of corn and hills of potatoes, and different varieties of beans, along with squash, tomatoes, pumpkins, onions, and other crops. The vicinity had numerous freshwater springs, a must for Indians who first frequented the area and for the American farmers who moved in later. Wide bands of timber grew along the waterways, thereby giving settlers ample raw materials out of which to build their homes, barns, and other out structures. Wildlife appeared everywhere. Deer, rabbits, and turkey were plentiful; even black bears and black panthers roamed the area. The daytime skies often darkened as covies of black birds and pigeons took flight. Most pioneers loved pigeon pies. The rivers teemed with fish, allowing settlers to supplement their diets.

In the far southeastern corner of Grayson and within a few miles of all four corners, Pilot Grove early on became the home of a general store, established by a Mr. Bartee. The hamlet also had a post office by 1858 and lay on the stage route running through Clarksville to Jefferson and thence south to Waco. Even though a few other hamlets were near, Pilot Grove was still located in a relatively isolated area. It was about twenty-five miles from any county seat: Sherman (Grayson); Bonham (Fannin); Greenville (Hunt); and McKinney (Collin). Other than the main stage route, transportation was poor. Cow paths and horse trails sometimes replaced roads. Bridgeless creeks also meandered about, while the entire region was heavily forested.[5]

Moreover, the whole area was rural with a sparse population; those demographics contributed to isolation even though the Corners counties had relatively substantial populations. By 1870 Fannin was home to 10,721 whites and 4,681 blacks; Hunt was home to 9,213 and 1,078, respectively; Grayson, 12,237 and 2,145; and Collin, 12,348 and 1,653. The largest towns were Sherman, which had 1,439 residents by 1870; Bonham with 928; McKinney, 503; and Greenville which was so small that the census taker of 1870 did not list it as a town.[6]

The rural nature of the area and its transportation problems made the job of law enforcement a major difficulty. Many contemporaries and later researchers have reported that whenever blacks and Unionist whites were the farthest removed from federal troops, murders of those blacks and those white Unionists increased as supporters of Dixie's cause were determined to do all that was necessary to reestablish their control. Unionists did not lose the War of Reconstruction in larger cities and towns, especially if those places had military garrisons; they lost it in countryside areas like the thickly wooded Corners.[7]

Residents of the isolated Corners called the most inaccessible part of their

Road near Lee homestead and Lee Cemetery. Note the density of what is left of Wildcat Thicket. Photo by David Carter. Courtesy Larry Peacock.

area Wildcat Thicket, near the present towns of Trenton and Leonard (just a few miles northwest of Leonard). A solid, thick mass of trees, bushes, thorn vines, brambles, saplings, briar patches, and other plant growth made the thicket almost impossible to get through and indeed impossible to see through except in winter. It was elliptical in shape and was approximately seven miles long and four miles wide. Also in Corners Country and near Wildcat Thicket were Jernigan's Thicket, a circular mass whose center was the place where the county lines of Fannin, Lamar, Hunt, and Hopkins converge; Black Jack Grove; the Big Thicket; Mustang Thicket just south of Leonard; Black Cat Thicket just northeast of Greenville; and Choctaw Bottoms.

Other smaller natural masses included Tidwell Thicket, north of Greenville, Hobbs Thicket, near Enloe, and Big Creek Thicket, a bit north of today's Cooper. All were similar, and all were contained in an approximate sixty-mile square of the Sulphur Forks watershed. Once the tangles within each thicket became established, they were most resistant to fire and tended to expand ever outward, engulfing the land of prairies and forests. Alfred Howell visited Black Cat Thicket in 1854. He later informed his brother that if one were to get lost in it that one might never find his way out, adding that the thicket was home to panthers, wolves, bears, and wildcats. In their isolation and vastness, the area thickets became havens for all sorts of malefactors during the Civil War, including

Confederate deserters, irregular troops like those who followed William Clarke Quantrill, Union loyalists who were oppressed in their own communities, and draft dodgers in addition to common lawbreakers wanted for offenses ranging from simple robbery to murder.[8]

Jernigan's Thicket, the largest, spilled into two of the Corners counties—Fannin and Hunt. It was about ten-miles square with the length a little longer than the width. It was a jungle so thick that in places a person needed a knife to cut through all the tangles. At different times, Bob Lee and his raiders hid in one or the other of the area thickets including Jernigan's. It was named for Curtis Jernigan who in 1843 shot and wounded a deer near the thicket and then followed the animal as it disappeared into the maze. For the next four days, the woebegone hunter spent his time wandering around, lost in the overwhelming brush. Later, near the thicket, Curtis's brother Bill opened a store at Cow Hill in Hunt County, a place that evolved into present-day Commerce.[9]

Postbellum violence and murder seemed foreordained to occur in Corners Country because Unionism was so prevalent in the area before the Civil War. In February of 1861 more than seventy percent of the electorate in Collin County voted against secession. The count was 948 (against) to 405 (for). Aside from little interest in preserving slavery, residents apparently listened to long-time leaders Collin McKinney and James W. Throckmorton, a state senator who lived in McKinney. Both were among the founding families of the county, and both were temporary Unionists although Throckmorton served with the Confederacy once the Civil War began; he rose to the rank of brigadier general. McKinney, for example, lectured his neighbors about the folly of secession. Both the *McKinney Messenger* and the *Sherman Patriot* supported Collin McKinney's position and helped hold the county for the Union. E. Junius Foster, editor of the *Patriot,* continued to publish his Unionist views until the fall of 1862 when an assassin's bullets silenced him. Like the people of Collin County, residents of Grayson County also rejected secession and did so by a vote of 901 to 463. The town of Whitesboro, however, held one of the first rallies in support of secession.[10]

In Fannin County, Unionist State Senator Robert Taylor was one of the signers of the 1861 anti-secessionist "Address to the People of Texas." He made impassioned appeals to his constituents, asking them to stay true to the Union. He, and others like him, succeeded. Fannin's people voted against secession by a majority of 656 to 471, but settlers in Hunt County were more deeply divided. Brothers Martin D. Hart and Hardin Hart, later a Reconstruction era Freedmen's Bureau agent-turned-federal-district judge, became spokesmen for the anti-secessionists. But they could not corral a majority. Thus, Hunt became the only Corners county to go with the Confederacy, doing so by a vote of 416 to 339. Majorities in the nearby counties of Cooke and Lamar also voted to reject secession, thus leaving Hunt as the only area county where a majority supported the Confederacy. Indeed, at one point, some of the counties on the tier adjacent to the Red River tried to secede from Confederate Texas and join the Union.[11]

Although there were complex reasons why the majority in Corners Country voted against secession, local historians Graham Landrum and Allan Smith surmised that loyalty to Sam Houston, hero of the Texas Revolution and the first president of the Republic of Texas, may have been the major factor accounting for the pro-Unionist majorities. A Unionist, "Old Sam" was the sitting governor in 1861, and he vociferously condemned the secessionist movement. He even gave an accurate prediction about the outcome of a war with the North. Union armies, he explained, would take control of the Mississippi River and divide Dixie while a naval blockade would starve its people. A war of attrition would follow, said Houston, and much of the South would become a vast wasteland. Old Sam also correctly predicted that slavery would be abolished. He was right in all his musings—Dixie lost, and slavery was no more.[12]

Many historians have noted that the Corners vicinity was a land of small yeoman farmers, a majority of whom held no slaves and did not have the zeal for war of others. Beloved area-resident Collin McKinney, who had a town and the county named for him, even asserted that not one man out of ten in the Corners region would favor secession if it came to an uninfluenced vote, thereby voicing his suspicion that secessionists' threats intimidated some area Unionists before the statewide referendum on secession took place. Perhaps symbolic of the divisions in the area, there was a "flag flap" in Sherman. Although a majority in Grayson County were Unionist in sentiment, succession enthusiast T. C. Bass raised the first Confederate flag at the courthouse where it waved majestically in the wind. Surreptitiously, a Union man decided not to truck with Bass's flag, preferring, instead, to act for the majority. Under the cover of darkness, he hauled down that flag and ran up the Stars and Stripes. Thereafter, the Bass-led Rebs, in the minority, had to post an armed guard to keep Dixie's banner flying.[13]

A similar event occurred in Fannin County's Honey Grove. After secession, the tiny town's populace was divided: Some favored raising the Southern banner, others wanted the Stars and Stripes. William Gambill, Jr., a hearty Unionist partisan, settled the matter in the fastest, most direct way he could. No doubt seized by heartfelt emotion, he led the Unionists who hauled down the Confederate symbol, grabbed it, and set it ablaze, after which Gambill and comrades raised the United States' escutcheon. In 1867 Gambill wrote General Charles Griffin detailing the story of Honey Grove's flag flap and commenting on his wartime experiences. Drafted, he was forced into the Confederate army but resolved to never fire his gun in battle, adding that had he the power, he would have "crushed the Rebellion." Accused of being a traitor and an abolitionist, he was robbed of his property during the war by being forced at gunpoint to sign away his wealth. Gambill concluded by asking for Griffin's help in bringing the culprits to justice and in restoring his property.[14]

Geography and demographics help explain why the tier of counties in North Texas largely opposed succession. Farmers in the Corners counties depended on Indian Territory as a market for their surplus wheat, corn, and other crops. Government agencies there did a hearty business with North Texas growers who believed they would lose their primary market if war came. Further, they also feared that their very homes would be in danger, for Indian raids or even a Union invasion from Kansas were possibilities that threatened to destroy all that they had worked so hard to build. Demographic trends were also important. While people from the Deep South settled much of East Texas, like the counties of Harrison, Smith, and Rusk, pioneers from the Upper South settled Northeast Texas. They were from such states as Tennessee, Kentucky, Missouri, and Arkansas. The simple yeomen never relied as heavily on slave labor and the cotton culture as did many other areas of East Texas. Further, in the northern tier a sprinkling of Yankees from Ohio, Illinois, and Indiana claimed land in the area. They had no interest in slavery. By 1860 people from the Upper South comprised between 50 and 65 percent of the populations of the Corners counties.[15] As historian Walter Buenger notes: "North Texans in 1859 were Unionists of varying hues, but they were almost universally Unionists."[16] Only the arson and slave insurrection panic of 1860 dampened Union resolve, but the majority still held for the United States and supported "Old Sam" in his efforts to save Texas for the Union. Further, the region remained "racked by [Unionist] dissension" even after secession.[17]

As anyone might suspect, the fact that a majority in Corners Country voted against secession led to much trouble during the Civil War and Reconstruction. The majority who identified with Unionism had to contend with the violent minority who identified with Dixie and whose leaders controlled the state and its military forces in addition to having pro-Confederate officials at the county and local levels. During the war itself, the conflict was most notably observed in Cooke County, where Gainesville became the scene of the "Great Hanging." Confederate authorities there convened a Kangaroo court and hanged more than forty Unionists whose only crime appeared to be talking about—but not acting upon—resisting the Confederate draft. Later, a Rebel band, led by the son of a Confederate officer believed to have been killed by Unionists, swept the county and murdered another eighteen people (perhaps more) who were loyal to the United States. Although not as dramatic, there were also wartime clashes in Hunt, Collin, Grayson, and Fannin counties, especially where their boundary lines converged at the Corners. During the fall of 1862, while the Gainesville trials were taking place, Rebel soldiers swept through other counties of Northeast Texas, killing at least 200 more suspected Unionists. In Hunt County the extensive hatred the secessionists had for people loyal to United States resulted in a particularly gruesome murder. The Rebs killed one Unionist, a Mr. Wilson, stripped his corpse, cut it asunder, and fed the pieces to grateful hogs.[18] In most confrontations, Southerners from the Deep South comprised the vigilantes while Unionists from the Upper South or from the North furnished most of the victims, many of whom were poor or were men of moderate means. Most also belonged to the anti-slavery wings of various Protestant church groups.[19]

Another incident between Unionists and Confederates involved John Honeycutt from Hunt County. With friends he originally joined the Confederacy, but some of the men remained sympathic to the Union. Home on furlough, Honeycutt led the men who now proclaimed their Union sentiments and left, heading south, hoping for safe haven in Mexico. There ends their story. Honeycutt and his comrades simply vanished, just disappeared, never again to contact even their closest relatives. They were probably killed either by Indians or by a Rebel patrol. The only survivor of their group was a little pony that eventually appeared in Greenville, the place from whence it had come.[20]

During and after the Civil War, outlaw bands and guerrilla fighters—now developing a culture of violence—frequented the counties that the Corners called home. None was more notorious than William Clarke Quantrill, an Ohioan born in 1837. As a young adult, he taught school in Illinois, sold his father's *Tinman's Guide,* and worked as a bookkeeper. Later, he adopted the alias Charley Hart. Quantrill accompanied three other men to Kansas in 1857 in the hopes of obtaining a land claim. Encountering difficulties with his companions, he turned to theft and eventually traveled to Utah and Colorado. Not a proponent of slavery, Quantrill believed that pro-slavery Democrats were rascals, who had attempted to constitutionally swindle Kansas.[21]

On the eve of the Civil War, Quantrill was back in Kansas, but his politics had radically shifted to the pro-slavery faction. He associated with "border ruffians," returned escaped slaves to their owners for bounties, betrayed abolitionists, and rustled both cattle and horses. In short, he was a freebooter. When war broke out, he briefly sojourned in North Texas and in the Cherokee Nation and later fought for Gen. Sterling Price in various battles. By January of 1862, Quantrill was back in Missouri, where he formed a group of irregulars, which included such infamous notables as Cole Younger and Frank and Jesse James. His raiders looted towns and engaged federal troops in both Kansas and Missouri, doing serious damage and enhancing Quantrill's reputation as a killer. Some of the men later known as Bob Lee's guerrillas rode with Quantrill, thereby getting experience in murder and mayhem and later descended upon Corners Country.[22]

More noticed nationally was the gang's August 21, 1863, guerrilla attack on Lawrence, Kansas, a town of 3,000 to 4,000 residents. In the attack, the malefactors killed 200 and left behind 85 widows, 250 orphans, and two million dollars worth of property destruction, which included 182 buildings and 100 homes gutted by fire. At Baxter Springs, Kansas, two months later, the group murdered ninety-eight men of the personal escort and headquarters train of Maj. Gen. James G. Blunt. The infamous Quantrill and his band often donned Yankee garb or just Yankee bluecoats before their attacks.[23]

For a time the gang operated in the area of Little Rock, Arkansas, committing various depredations. Because authorities there finally mounted a campaign against him, Quantrill returned to the vicinities of Sherman and Bonham in October of 1863 to hide out. He may well have crossed the Red River and hid in the area just north of Preston Bend. Or he may have established his headquarters in one of the thickets in the Pilot Grove vicinity. After receiving intelligence that Quantrill's gang was in the area, Gen. Henry E. McCulloch worried much about the carnage that the guerrillas might inflict on Northeast Texans. He expressed his alarm when he wrote Capt. Edmund P. Turner. McCulloch averred that Quantrill practiced a "savage inhuman warfare in which men are to be shot down like dogs, after throwing down their arms and holding up their hands supplicating for mercy."[24]

The general had good reasons to worry. On one occasion the gang "treed" Sherman (shot up the place), even firing into the local Methodist Church. The raiders added robbery to the list of their crimes before leaving Sherman behind when Confederate regulars chased them into the Indian Nations. Alarmed civilians—and soldiers, too—declared that the entire area was infested with absentees and deserters from the army and with other renegades as well. Many of the villains committed thefts, robberies, murders, and other dark crimes. Chaos and unruliness claimed the day. Indeed, conditions became so horrible that a number of Sherman's leading citizens petitioned Governor Pendleton Murrah, asking him to send troops to protect their lives. Specifically, the Shermanites asked for the regiment commanded by Col. L. M. Martins, for many local men were in that unit.[25]

What of Quantrill himself? McCulloch's men eventually found and arrested him in Bonham. However, the killer quickly subdued four guards, jumped atop his mount, and made a fast getaway. He rejoined his gang and headed for Colberts Ferry on the Red River. McCulloch then ordered Colonel Martins and his charges to find Quantrill and his men, telling the colonel to bring them back dead or alive. But all the outlaws escaped by crossing the Red and again hiding out in Indian Territory.

By 1864 Quantrill was having increasing problems with his men. One,

"Bloody" Bill Anderson, broke with him over a personal matter. Bill had become enamored with a local Sherman belle and had thoughts of marriage. Quantrill strongly objected, thus leaving Bill an either-or situation. Bloody Bill chose the young woman and carved his own gang out of Quantrill dissidents. Bill lived on until 1864 when he was shot and killed in Missouri (or Kansas). Lieutenant George Todd also broke away later, leaving Quantrill virtually without support. Nevertheless, with a diminishing band of followers, he participated in more raids into Missouri and later into Kentucky, where federal guerrillas finally ended his reign of terror when Edwin Terrill shot him in the back. From May 10 until June 6, 1865, Quantrill lingered in the Louisville Military Prison hospital before he died, but while he lived, he had done much to destabilize the Corners counties and to accustom citizens to repeated rounds of violence.[26]

Just as Grayson County had trouble with the likes of Quantrill, Collin County also had its share of turmoil. As conditions worsened, Collin County leaders, like those in Grayson, petitioned Governor Murrah for reliable troops who could protect lives and property. The petitioners asserted that many people were packing up and leaving the county because conditions were so unsafe. Like Grayson's leaders, those in Collin asked specifically for Colonel Martins and his men to protect their area, including the contiguous counties. Explaining their troubles, Collin's finest said that "last Spring after Colonel Martins left . . . lawless men prowled over our farms and prairies and held our county terror-stricken. Decrepit age and helpless innocence were alike the subjects of the most brutal indignities. . . . The county was powerless to protect itself."[27]

Another petition coming out of Collin County asserted that Confederate soldiers caused much of the trouble. Holding that the "debris of the retreat of General [Sterling] Price [of Missouri] are already pouring into these [Northeast Texas] counties," the petitioners contended that "only bayonets can control them," adding that "many of them are lawless characters that have been 'jayhawking' in Mo [Missouri]."[28] The noted James W. Throckmorton confirmed that the petitioners were correct. Also referring to Price's men, Throckmorton said they were nothing but "a mob and a set of robbers" who "took money and all sorts of private property" from citizens.[29]

Throckmorton also reported that observers had seen Price's "whole army" loaded with plunder. They held up a train in the area, thereby collecting yet more loot. Destitute women and children from Arkansas were also streaming into Northeast Texas, since Price would not help them. Throckmorton referred to "deserters, dodgers, and traitors" who caused trouble as well as to "Kansas Jawhawkers and Indians." He said that renegade Indians had recently raided the Collin County countryside and made off with a sixty-five-head horse herd. In all,

Another part of Wildcat Thicket. Photo by David Carter. Courtesy Larry Peacock.

Throckmorton gave a most negative assessment of the general conditions of the Corners' counties.[30]

General Henry McCulloch took command of the Northern Sub-District of Texas in 1863, and his main charge was to deal with deserters, draft dodgers, and the riff-raff that infested Corners country. Writing Maj. Gen. John Bankhead Magruder in October of 1863, McCulloch estimated that at least 1,000 such men could be found in the thickets of his district. Secessionist and future governor O. M. Roberts added that in Hunt County, alone, 200 to 400 deserters hid in three camps in three different thickets. All were about ten miles of each other and could concentrate within a couple of hours if threatened by authorities. Consequently, authorities left the deserters alone.[31]

The Unionist Henry Boren of Corners Country, who later became a major figure in the Lee-Peacock struggle—in fact, he led the patrol that found and killed Bob Lee—commanded one of the groups about whom McCulloch and Roberts complained. Born in 1828 in Arkansas (probably in Hempstead County), Henry never wavered in his task of trying to restore Northeast Texas to the Union. Knowing Boren's identity, Henry McCulloch tried to negotiate with him. The general sent two Confederate officers—Maj. Throckmorton of Collin County and Col. Robert H. Taylor of Fannin County—to talk to Boren. Both officers had originally opposed secession. McCulloch was hoping that Boren might identify with them and reach some agreement with the Confederate authorities. The general believed that Boren would be likely to listen to them. Asked to surrender, Boren had conditions. He said that he and his men would fight on the frontier to control the Indian menace but first demanded arms, ammunition, supplies, and a brief time to see their families and put their business and personal affairs in order before leaving. When Colonel Taylor and Major Throckmorton reported Boren's terms to McCulloch, the general rejected the offer. An informant later told the general that he had made a wise decision, for Boren had no intention of going to the frontier. He intended to use the arms and ammunition to seize Bonham and other towns in the Corners counties and to "wipe out secession in this part of Texas."[32]

Later, Unionist Boren and his "bush men," including his brothers Israel and John, moved southeastwardly until they found a Confederate camp where they tried but failed to secure more arms and ammunition. Eventually, Boren and his followers moved into Lamar County and lived in open defiance of Confederate authorities there. According to the *Clarksville Standard,* General McCulloch had been too pacific in negotiations with Boren, the editor, in fact, saying that the military should launch a campaign to drive them out of the bush. They were "traitorous scoundrels," the editor of the *Standard* exclaimed, forgetting that he, like all Confederates, was the real traitor for trying to destroy the United States Constitution and to do so by violent means.[33]

On December 9, 1864, Throckmorton again wrote Governor Murrah, complaining about the area's state of affairs. The Northeastern part of the Lone Star State, Throckmorton said, was "becoming the most miserable point in Texas, both on account of its easy access to Kansas Jayhawkers and Indians." Continuing, he held that horse thieves, cattle rustlers, robbers, and "deserters and dodgers and traitors" seemed to be everywhere.[34] The future Reconstruction-era governor agreed with other area leaders that Confederate soldiers also committed dastardly deeds. "Price's whole army [is] nothing but a mob and a set of robbers. . . . They [take] money and all sorts of private property from the citizens," declared Throckmorton.[35]

Living with violence and death all around them, the people of Northeast Texas including the Corners counties may well have become anesthetized to the turmoil. Given the split between Confederates and Unionists and all the other travail, some people anticipated that the violence would continue long after the war. They were correct.

Chapter 3

Murder and Mayhem

Soon after the Civil War, Unionists in Northeast Texas convened a meeting in Paris, Lamar County, guided by B. W. Gray of Titus County. On July 17, 1865, the delegates reaffirmed their loyalty to the United States. They pledged their willingness to "submit to the Constitution" and the laws of the federal government. Several men represented the Corners counties—Fannin's Robert H. Taylor and Sam G. Galbraith along with Hunt's Hardin Hart and M. H. Wright.[1] Despite the auspicious gathering and the meaning of the Paris pledge, peace did not come to Northeast Texas. Instead, Union men and Southern devotees had at each other, both sides determined to win the War of Reconstruction. The drama played itself out in many places like the Corners. And after the war, Lewis Peacock emerged as the most prominent Unionist in the vicinity of the Corners, a fact for which he was later murdered.

The son of John Peacock and Delilah Hayworth Peacock, Lewis was born on April 23, 1824, in Guilford County, North Carolina. The family soon moved to Washington County, Georgia, where Lewis grew up and attended school. Lewis was intelligent and proved to be a good student. It was in Washington County that he met his future wife, Emaline Benson, born in Florida to parents Lewis and Sarah Benson, who also eventually moved to Sandersville in Washington County. After the appropriate courtship and its rituals, Lewis Peacock and Emaline Benson married on December 15, 1846. They eventually had a family that included two beloved children: Melinda Catherine, born in 1848, and John Edgar, born in November of 1852. According to the 1850 census of Sandersville, Lewis had become a hard worker. He was a farmer, a blacksmith, a wheelwright, and a wagon-maker, and he worked long hours to support his family. Although Georgia was a slave state, Lewis's extended family owned no slaves, and he had no interest or stake in the South's "peculiar institution."[2]

Some secondary sources suggest that Lewis and his family may have migrated to Kansas in the 1850s although primary records are silent on the subject. If the family did spend time in Kansas, they found nothing but trouble after 1854, the year that Illinois Senator Stephen Douglas pushed the Kansas-Nebraska Act through Congress. A local civil war developed in the Jayhawker region between the pro-slaveryites, mostly from Missouri, and the anti-slavery and free-soil settlers, most of whom were Northerners. Even if the Peacock family indeed lived in Kansas for a time, for safety's sake, Lewis had moved to Texas by 1858 and settled in Grayson County, near Pilot Grove. His wife's parents also migrated to the Lone Star State but headed farther south, settling in Limestone County. The 1860 census reveals that Peacock was still prospering by plying his trades and farming while also reporting that he had real estate worth $480 and a personal estate valued at $900.[3]

The tall, husky, blond-haired, and gray-eyed wheelwright homesteaded 160 acres of land about three miles southeast of Pilot Grove near the Grayson-Fannin county lines. Near the Tate place, Peacock's land formed one border of Parson Gentry's farm. A good farmer, Lewis grew great stands of corn, along with sweet and Irish potatoes and other crops such as beans, squash, pumpkins, tomatoes, and onions. He also had a few pigs and cattle, including dairy cows, but he never owned a slave. Even when he was a relatively young man, he decided that the South's "peculiar institution" was barbaric. Like the majority in the Corners area, he had no interest at all in slavery nor in a war to protect human bondage; rather, he followed politicians like Sam Houston, the old hero of the Texas Revolution and the state's sitting governor when Texas seceded from the Union. Peacock did not support leaving the Union and did not support the war. He managed to escape the Confederate conscription law because his job as a blacksmith and wheelwright exempted him from service. He remained a civilian and continued to work supporting his family as the war ran its course. He also became a cow hunter, a job that should not be equated with the term rustler. He sometimes caught wild, unowned, unbranded cattle that he later butchered or sold. For his times, Peacock was a hearty yeoman who strove for self-sufficiency.[4]

After the war, Lewis became one of the most outspoken political leaders in the vicinity of the Corners. Indeed, he became the local area leader of the Union (or Loyal) League, headquartered in Pilot Grove. He was not an unprincipled Southern opportunist who intended to take advantage of the results of the late war. Rather, he remained consistent in his political views. Like many other Texans who did not support the conflict, he was a Sam Houston Unionist before the war, during the war, and after the war. Under his leadership, the Loyal League of the Corners area held regular meetings in Pilot Grove and in other nearby places. Peacock always supported the policies of the federal government, including the Thirteenth, Fourteenth, and Fifteenth Amendments once they were proposed. He and his following also strongly supported the Texas Republican party and its platform once it was organized in 1867.[5]

Among loyal men, Pilot Grove became known as a place where civilian Unionists, federal soldiers, and Freedmen's Bureau agents could receive assistance with assorted problems. It was also a place where newly freed slaves could get help if they were being cheated out of crop shares, or assaulted, or terrorized. Further, as Klan terrorist groups and various outlaws increased their activities, Peacock rode with Union troops, serving them as a guide or scout. He also recruited other Unionists to form posses when it became necessary to help the federal troops in the area. Because loyal men made up the political majority in Corners territory—and in three of its four counties—Peacock had much informal political power, a fact that some Rebels could not tolerate. As one writer mentioned, Peacock "ran things" in the Corners. That statement was an exaggeration but one headed in the direction of truth, for he was most important in helping give the Corners what little stability it had in the aftermath of the war. Further, he was willing to fight, to risk his life repeatedly, because he wanted to see the Union cause prevail.[6]

Lewis Peacock's son John Edgar Peacock, his wife Janie Eubanks Peacock, and two oldest daughters, ca. 1885. Photo courtesy Larry Peacock.

Peacock had many Union supporters in Corners Country, but less is known about them than about their leader.[7] At least the names of some Union supporters are known. Most were independent farmers who were either born in Texas or migrated in from the Upper South. One supporter was James Maddox, the son of area farmer Nicholas Maddox. Along with Bob Lee, Bob's younger brother James, and many other men in the Corners counties, young Maddox joined the Confederacy's army. The Lees, Maddox, and most of the others served in the Ninth Texas Cavalry. However, after the bloodbath, Maddox could not support Southerners like Bob Lee who virtually declared war on the free blacks and white Unionists, robbing them and murdering them almost at will. On at least one occasion, young Maddox criticized Lee for Lee's unjust treatment of the freedmen. Their exchange led to violence.[8]

Other Peacock followers included John Vaught, L. D. "Dow" Nance, "Doc" Wilson, Hugh Hudson, John and Levi Baldock, Elijah Clark, Bunk Alexander, Reuben Hogue, Tom and Dolph Waters, and William Thompson, along with the brothers Dan and Clay Saunders. Also close to the Peacock faction were Judge Hardin Hart, Bill Smith, John D. Coffee, Sam Bier, Hardy Dial,

Bud Favors, and brothers Israel, John, and Henry Boren, Henry being the wartime Unionist gang leader who caused Gen. Henry McCulloch such wartime agony. Other noted Unionists of the area included the circuit-riding preacher Stephen Marshal, J. D. Ivey, John Sinclair, G. M. Wisdom, H. C. Saunders, Charles Saunders, Robert K. Brewer M. L. Boling, D. L. Lewis, R. P. Tarleton, John Milican, James H. Morrisson, and others.[9] Not one left an account of the Lee-Peacock struggle.

In November of 1865, Bvt. Maj. Gen. William E. Strong, inspector general of the Freedmen's Bureau, submitted a report that divulged what Unionists like Peacock and his supporters were up against. Strong toured East and Northeast Texas including Corners Country. What he saw and heard shocked him. Although neither he nor Peacock could know it, what the general observed helped explain why Peacock would later be murdered in the backyard of his place in the Corners. Strong was amazed at the "most intense hatred" that committed secessionists and their sympathizers held toward the newly freed slaves, white Unionists like Peacock, Yankee soldiers, and the national Republican government. Strong asserted that "there is more of it [hatred] in Texas than any other southern State that I have visited." Both sickened and angered by what he saw, Strong averred that a "campaign of an army through the eastern part of the State, such as was made by General Sherman in South Carolina, would improve the temper . . . of the people."[10] Strong concluded that East Texans were so hateful and so resistant perhaps because the state had never been successfully invaded during the war and that the only fighting in the Lone Star State had occurred along the Gulf Coast and in select parts of South Texas. As a result, Strong said that the Rebel Texans and their sympathizers did not feel defeated, had not directly felt the power of the federal government, and intended to resist Reconstruction with all their strength. Some whites even believed that a new form of slavery could be instituted.[11] Strong probably exaggerated in singling out Texas as a defiant state, for in other parts of the South, ex-Confederates hated their enemy and refused to truck with the white Unionists, with the Yankee army, or with the freedmen.

Yet, Strong's judgement of affairs in East and Northeast Texas was most accurate, especially when applied to the Corners. Die-hard Southerners showed more rebelliousness than they did in some other areas—perhaps because the place was so isolated, so hard for regional authorities to reach. Further, the fact that a majority in the area had been pro-Union before the war made the ex-Confederates more extreme, for they were originally in the minority. Perhaps they had to be aggressive because they were outnumbered. And in the Corners most people had to fend for themselves. The closest Freedmen's Bureau agents in 1867 were in Sherman and Greenville, not in Pilot Grove. At the time, the closest federal troops were even farther away. After bureau agents arrived in Sherman and Greenville, Peacock became their man in Corners Country, and Pilot Grove continued to be a control point. Lewis helped white and black refugees find food, shelter, and jobs so that they could begin building new lives. He was also a politician. He invited freedmen to join the Union League and to vote Republican—to vote for the party that had freed them. Lewis was one of the most committed Unionist in Texas, one who operated on the principle that all people, even blacks, deserved decent treatment.[12]

Peacock's work was dangerous and was made more so because of the Corners' isolation. Writing in 1867 after Congress had seized control of Reconstruction and after more federal troops began their occupation of Texas, the editor of the *Sherman Courier* reported: "Were it not that we are continually reminded by the newspapers that we are under military rule, we could forget that such an institution exists as far as Grayson County is concerned, although about a hundred troops are quartered [here] in [Sherman]."[13] Even as those troops were occupying the Grayson county seat, they were still twenty-five miles from Pilot Grove. They were not capable of delivering the kind of protection that Union men in the Corners needed. Thus, Peacock and his followers not only had to protect themselves, they also had to try to protect other people, white and black, who were loyal to the Union.

Bob Lee. Drawing by Toni M. Beyl.

As for Peacock, who originally had no military protection, his major antagonist was Confederate veteran Robert Jehu "Bob" Lee whose farm, which he established in 1859, was in Hunt County seven miles east of Pilot Grove. As a mature man, Lee stood five feet-eight inches. He had dark black hair and dark eyes. His complexion was sallow, and he was clean shaven except for a slight, thin black moustache.[14]

Bob's father, Daniel W. Lee, born in 1810, was originally from Tennessee. Daniel migrated first to Virginia and then to Missouri before settling in Arkansas for a time. He married Polly Davis, and the couple had three children: Robert Jehu Lee, Minerva Lee, and William M. Lee. Daniel and his family came to Texas in the 1830s and settled in the Corners where Bob was born in 1835, the year the Texas Revolution began. Forty-nine years old in 1860, Daniel was well-to-do for his times, a fact noted by the census of that year. After Polly died Daniel remarried. His second wife Elizabeth—then thirty—was originally from Illinois. The census also reported that there were ten others in Daniel's household, ranging from two to twenty-one years of age. All were born in Arkansas or Texas.[15]

Robert J. Lee's farm was adjacent to his father's holdings. Born in Arkansas, he was twenty-five years old in 1860 as was his wife Melinda Lee who was also born in Arkansas. In the census of 1860, Bob listed himself as a farmer and claimed $700 in real estate. Bob and Melinda had three children, all Texas-born: Daniel C. (four years old); Mary E. (two years old); and Thomas L. (a newborn only one month old).[16]

In 1861, Bob Lee and his younger brother William joined the Confederacy's fighting men as privates. Bob, now twenty-seven years old, and William were in a company of volunteers in the Texas State Troops, captained by Jackson E. McCoole, in a regiment commanded by Col. W. B. Sims of Sherman. After training at Camp Reeves in Grayson County for about six weeks, Lee's unit was ordered to move into Arkansas to become Company C of the Ninth Texas Cavalry in an army commanded by Gen. Ben McCulloch. Later transferred east of the Mississippi River, Lee's unit saw service in such battles as Chusto-Talash in Indian Territory, Pea Ridge in Arkansas, Iuka in Mississippi, and many other engagements including one at Nashville, Tennessee, in 1864, wherein Union forces destroyed General John Bell Hood's Army of Tennessee. Some sources paint a dark picture of Bob Lee's Civil War career. According to at least one contemporary account, Lee was guilty of war crimes. Among the alleged atrocities was murder. Any time Yankee prisoners fell into Lee's hands, he apparently killed the defenseless men unless eye witnesses were around to stop him. According to John Gentry, Lee probably also robbed the bodies, for he returned to the Corners with a lot of money, much more than he made as a sergeant.[17]

After returning to the Corners when the war ended, the gallant cavalier "Captain" Bob Lee—who had once ridden with the famed Gen. Nathan Bedford Forrest—boasted that he never surrendered to Union forces. That fact was correct. He was still in what was left of the Army of Tennessee and stationed near Memphis, Tennessee, when the end was near. He simply deserted his unit and headed home well armed and atop his dappled gray mare. According to several local historians, when "Captain" Lee reached the Corners, the residents became euphoric, shouting "BOB LEE'S HOME, BOB LEE'S HOME" in every hamlet in the area while all the little children ran to worship the returning hero as he passed by. Although local authors were full of hyperbole regarding Lee's return, "Captain" Lee came home wearing a cavalier's plumed hat and had gold in his coat pockets. He also had several revolvers in his belt and both a shotgun and a rifle swinging from his saddle horn. Indeed, Bob Lee was home. But once there, he embellished his war record greatly, hoping to become the leader of the anti-Union faction in his region. One thing was sure: like most white Texans, Lee embraced white supremacy and intended to keep free blacks in their place even if violence and murder were necessary. He collected a band of other former Confederates and had early run-ins with area Unionists, thereby coming to the attention of Peacock who watched Lee's activities closely.[18]

In addition to being a deserter who may have committed war crimes, Lee was never a "captain." He only passed himself off as one when he returned to the Corners. Confederate military service records in the National Archives in Washington, D.C., verify that Lee went into the Southern army as a private and won promotion to sergeant, but he was never an officer and was absent without leave when his unit surrendered. At some time, he informally changed his middle name from Jehu to "Jackson." The real Robert Jackson Lee was indeed a Confederate captain, but he was in the Twenty-seventh Texas Cavalry. Both men shared some campaigns and battles together. Both were in the Corinth campaign, the siege of Vicksburg, and General Hood's campaign in Tennessee near the end of the war. Robert Jehu probably knew Robert Jackson. Apparently, Robert Jehu was trying to assume Robert Jackson's identity or at least to some way muddle the past and hide it from curious people. He also wanted the home folks to believe that he was something he was not. He was apparently interested in status among ex-Confederates after the war. A Lee family Bible verified that Jehu was Bob Lee's real middle name. Because he spun so many untrue tales and even tried to adopt someone else's identity, Lee's account of the beginnings of Lee-Peacock imbroglio and of the events that followed simply can not be believed. Lee, of course, blamed Peacock and other Unionists for starting the troubles in the Corners, but he simply told self-serving falsehoods about the beginning of the struggle just as he lied about his entire military career.[19]

While Lee greatly exaggerated his wartime career and only postured as a great Southern hero, one thing was certain: He had grit. When he returned to the Corners, the area's military veterans and their supporters hailed him as a leader—one who exhibited courage and determination. Many young hotspurs—especially the "sporting" element—gladly followed him after he vowed to continue the Civil War "from the thickets and canebreaks of Texas for a hundred years if necessary."[20] As one writer put it, Lee did not come home a "defeated penitent."[21] He was still willing to continue the Civil War and to carry the fight to the Yankees, to the beleaguered Southern white Unionists, and to the unfortunate blacks. It was Lewis Peacock's fate to lead the Unionists who opposed Lee.

As Bob Lee began his reign of terror, he had many allies, including the members of his own family. The Lee clan and their supporters were a rough

Historical marker, Pilot Grove. Marker incorrectly states that Lee was killed in 1865. Lee was in fact killed on May 24, 1869. Photo by David Carter. Courtesy Larry Peacock.

bunch. In 1860, Daniel reported to census takers that he had $800 in real property and $3,000 in a personal estate. According to local lore, however, the Lees were already rich before they arrived in Texas. When they migrated, they supposedly brought a fortune in gold with them, a sum of at least $14,000. The wartime profits that Daniel enjoyed in raising horses and beef cattle and selling them to the Confederacy added to the family's riches.[22]

The story of Lee gold was likely a fabricated tale, one designed to explain why the Lee men were seldom seen working. Fact was that Daniel made part of his living by stealing horses. Likely, he was a cattle rustler, too. Called a "wicked man" by Reverend John Gentry, Daniel proved the old adage: "Man will not work for what man can take." Before, during, and after the Civil War, he was in and out of trouble with area authorities. The other Lees were thieves, too. About their leader Daniel, one writer said that a "trusty black snake whip" and a 10-gauge shotgun were part of his "everyday dress." He used the whip to teach "freedmen and white trash proper respect." He reserved the shotgun for "more worthy opponents." In 1877, several years after the Peacock-Lee fight ended, Dan stole one horse too many. It belonged to Will Smith who shot and killed the thief on March 19 while Daniel was sitting atop Smith's stolen mount. After

Smith reclaimed his horse and reported the incident, authorities investigated the incident and put Smith on trial. A jury cleared him of any wrong doing.[23]

While the struggle between the ex-Rebels and Unionists was ongoing, allies flocked to Bob Lee's banner. John Hugh "Irish Jack" Dixon—who called himself a "full-blooded Irishman"—and his family was close to the Lees. Like them, the Dixons were "100 percent" Southern sympathizers, and Irish Jack's farm was only about five miles northwest of the Lee place. Born in 1808, Jack was an Indianan, who came to Texas in 1858 by way of Illinois and Missouri. He bought a quarter section from John Sloan and built a sturdy home atop a little rise that became known as "Dixon Mound," a hill actually built for religious rituals by the Caddo ancestors of the Hasinai Indians who once inhabited the area. During the war, Irish Jack developed a profitable overland freight business, Dixon Lines. His wagons hauled sundry local items, including massive amounts of goods destined for the Confederacy, to Jefferson, then a thriving East Texas metropolis. On return trips, Dixon Lines hauled assorted merchandise, including food and manufactured items. Wagoneers made deliveries all along the route and in the Corners area as well.[24]

Grave of Daniel Lee (1810–77), Bob Lee's father. Will Smith killed Daniel Lee because Daniel stole Will's horse. Photo courtesy Larry Peacock.

Jack's oldest boy, Simpson "Simp" Dixon, may have been active in the war. According to one researcher, Simp sometimes rode with Quantrill who made Northeast Texas his home away from home. After the war, when Simp returned to Dixon Mound, he quickly fell in with Lee's bunch, which soon numbered at least thirty young guns. Simp also worked alongside the other Dixons who were trying to develop the Dixon Lines freight business. He drove for Irish Jack, hauling goods to and fro between the Corners and Jefferson, some 150 miles away. He occasionally became a trail boss, supervising wagon trains bound for the East Texas entrepot.[25]

Simp's mother died when the Dixons still lived near Springfield, Illinois. Soon, Jack married a young widow, Sarah Anne Rickets Johnson. Her son, Richard "Dick" Johnson, and Simp Dixon were about the same age. Dick also worked for Dixon Lines. The two young boys became close friends. Younger still was Billy Dixon, Jack's son by Sarah. Billy also helped in the business and worked on the family farm. Fourteen years old when the war ended, Billy was a good wagoneer. He became close to Simp and Dick. Jack and Sarah had six other children, including four girls approaching their teens in 1865: Hester Anne, Susan, Lydia, and Sallie. Hester Anne later played an important role in the Unionist-Confederate struggle by spying on the Unionist faction for Bob Lee. The girls had a younger brother, Ennis, who, as local lore had it, could do a great Rebel yell, and a baby brother, Robert Lee. Word around the Corners was that Irish Jack and his family would stick with Bob Lee to the end.[26]

Two other Dixon families, headed by first cousins, settled in the Corners vicinity in the area's fertile river valleys. They also sympathized with the Lees. "General" Dixon and family reached Texas in the late 1850s and established their residence in far northern Collin County at Blue Ridge near the Corners. Also, a "Doctor" Dixon and family settled at Black Jack Grove in nearby Hopkins County, the home of desperado Ben Bickerstaff and his gang, who at times joined forces with Lee in the War of Reconstruction. While the Civil War still raged, Charles "Charlie" Dixon, Doctor Dixon's son, moved to the Corners and joined cousin Billy as a teamster for Dixon Lines. Many times the two boys traveled the route to Jefferson, hauling goods, and then became best friends.[27]

Another Lee partisan was young William Perry "Bill" Penn whose home was in Kentucky-Town, a fast-growing hamlet six miles north of Dixon Mound. A cousin of the noted outlaw John Wesley Hardin (as were the Dixon boys), Bill was born in 1847. He was the third child among the eight children of Sanford R. Penn and Elizabeth Hardin Penn, both originally from Kentucky. Arriving in Northeast Texas in the 1850s, the Penns became a founding family of Kentucky-Town. Bill Penn grew up much like other boys in the region. He loved to hunt and in time became an expert with firearms, be they handguns, shotguns, or rifles. He would later be one of the best killers among the Lee raiders. He was also a good horseman. Fourteen years old when the Civil War began, Bill served with the Home Guards for the duration of the conflict. Tragedy struck the Penn family in 1862 when Sanford died in battle, giving his life for the Confederacy. Bill, only fifteen or sixteen, had to help support the rest of the family. To that end, he redoubled his efforts to see that the family farm produced all it could.[28]

Bill developed a small freighting business, its route including Kentucky-Town to Bonham to Cypress Bayou and on to Jefferson. He first met Billy and Charlie Dixon in Jefferson. The three became good friends, and all became committed Lee men as the Second Civil War developed. While working as a teamster during the war, young Penn met many of the men in Quantrill's gang who spent at least one winter camped near Kentucky-Town. Penn went over to the Lee gang soon after the Civil War. He had an altercation with freedman Henry Scales when he returned to Kentucky-Town from one of his trips to Jefferson. Penn's hatred of blacks was well known, and the beating that he gave Scales seemed to prove it. Authorities from Grayson County arrested Penn, charging him with assault and battery. A friend posted Bill's bond, but the young hotspur failed to appear in Sherman on the day of his trial. A fugitive for the rest of his life, Penn fought and killed freedmen, white Unionists, and Yankees while also adding robbery to what would become his bloody resume.[29]

Told by a friend that if he stayed in Corners Country he would be hunted down and killed by the authorities, Penn responded: "No I'm not leaving here. And I'm going to kill every ——— Yankee who crosses me and every ——— Negro who won't tip his hat to me."[30] Thus, Penn was like most of the men who joined Lee or other Northeast Texas raiders. They killed but did so discriminately.

The Benjamin Pierce family also sided with the Lees once the troubles in the Corners began. Originally from Tennessee, patriarch Benjamin was a veteran of the War of 1812. He fought alongside General Andrew Jackson at the Battle of Horseshoe Bend and in the epic Battle of New Orleans, a victory that made a national hero out of Jackson and ultimately helped propel "Old Hickory" into the White House in 1828. After the war, Benjamin returned to Tennessee. In the 1850s he moved his family to Texas, settling first at Cannon, a tiny village about five miles west of Pilot Grove itself. During the Civil War he moved again, this time to Pilot Grove. His family included his son, the physician William H. Pierce, William's wife, their two children, and Benjamin's eighteen-year-old daughter Dorinda Anne who began teaching school even as the Civil War continued to rage. Later, both William and Dorinda Anne played key roles in assisting Bob Lee once he began his errant ways.[31]

Parson Martin Gentry and family tried to stay neutral in the local ex-Confederate-Unionist struggle. After migrating to the Republic of Texas in 1844, Gentry patented 160 acres of wilderness, cleared it an acre at a time, and developed a showplace farm that was adjacent to the Lewis Peacock place. Gentry also became a circuit-riding preacher who spread the word to many congregations in the counties whose boundaries converged at the Corners. The parson and his wife had thirteen children, two of whom—John and William—fought for the Confederacy but came home alive and well. When they returned, they heard the sad news that their mother had died during the conflict. Soon, Gentry married Elizabeth whose maiden name is lost to history. She was a young woman who had three children of her own. Gentry and his sons John and William were staunch supporters of the Confederacy and offered morale support for Lee and his supporters, but, apparently, they were peaceful and committed none of the violence that made the Corners famous. They even maintained a distant friendship with Lewis Peacock and his family.[32]

Others close to Lee included Dow Witt, who eventually terrorized northern Collin County and the entire Corners region; a mysterious man known only as "Hayes" (who may have been either William or Perry Hayes who had ridden with Quantrill during the war), also of Collin County; J. A. Drye of Pilot Grove; Elijah Clark; the Soloman and Robert "Bob" Fitzhugh clan of Collin County; and John Marshal and William Beard, both also of Collin County. Other Lee men included the Clements clan, Billy, Rial, Levi, Manning, and J. W.—all cousins of Simp Dixon; Napper and Ben Connally; a man named Harshaw; "Indian" Bill English; Fletch Everhart; Ellis Harper; men named Chaney and Rollins; George Williams; Ike Dodson, who was especially close to the Dixons; Joel Webb of Hunt County; Parson Martin Smith,(Bob Lee's brother-in-law); and Bill Boren, one of the notable Boren clan whose members were divided, some supporting Lee, others identifying with Peacock and the Unionists.

Further, Jack Dixon's sister Elizabeth married James Gipson Hardin, a circuit-riding preacher and land speculator. On May 26, 1853, Elizabeth gave birth to a boy. The happy parents named their infant John Welsey, who was a first cousin to Simp and Billy Dixon and a nephew of Irish Jack. The Hardin place was twenty-two miles south of the Red River on the edge of the North Texas blackland prairie at Blair's Spring on Bois d'Arc Creek near Orangeville. South of Bonham, it was three miles north of present-day Trenton in Fannin County, close to the Grayson County line. Although John Wesley was still young when the struggle in Corners Country began, he may well have had a hand in the fight, for he became good friends with Simp and Billy Dixon and Dick Johnson. By 1867, the teenaged Hardin had already joined a band of what some people referred to as "nigger" killers, lawless men who terrorized free blacks and white Unionists. Much later, after Unionists killed Billy and Simp, John Wesley swore revenge.[33]

The professional gunman Mace Bowman, later a noted lawman, probably rode with Lee for a time. A former Confederate, who once fought in the same brigade as the Lee boys and who became friends with them, Bowman felt a certain kinship—born in battle—with the Lees. He might have been the unidentified third man who waited by the Peacock woodpile (if the third man was not Hardin) and killed the Unionist when he emerged from his back door. The only document that directly connects Bowman with the war in the Corners, however, is his obituary in New Mexico's *Raton Comet.* The obituary was rather inconsistent with known facts and known chronology. For example, the Lee-Peacock, Unionist-Confederate fight that lasted several years was telescoped into four months in the obituary and had Bowman and Lee "exterminating outlaws," a description that hardly described the redoubtable Peacock and other loyal men. Still, it is possible that Bowman could have been the third shootist, for he was in the Corners vicinity when Peacock was murdered but, then, so was young John Wesley.[34]

The cast of the major characters in the Lee-Peacock Feud was complete. Now violence began as the Corners exploded in an orgy of pistol shots, shotgun blasts, rifle fire, and blood.

Chapter 4

The "Man Eater" and Other Northeast Texas Desperadoes

In 1865, shortly after the war, the United States Army assigned Lt. Col. George A. Custer to a command that included Northeast Texas. He and his subordinates had some knowledge about Lee and other desperadoes. Custer's cavalry patrol leaders noted that—already at an early date—in Northeast Texas ruffians had organized guerrilla bands and had no fear of Union troops who were trying but failing to reestablish law and order. According to Custer, the raiders ambushed patrols and robbed wagon trains, while sheriffs and judges loyal to the Southern ideal protected the gang members. Custer added that many men in the public-at-large also protected the raiders, perhaps because such men claimed that they represented the Lost Cause. The colonel further believed that three renegade holdouts were the most dangerous of the ruffians and that they formed an unholy triumvirate: Cullen Montgomery Baker, Benjamin F. Bickerstaff, and Bob Lee. Custer believed that the outlaws sometimes joined each other for nefarious purposes. He was correct. Further, families close to the Lees had relatives in Freestone, Limestone, and Navarro counties who were involved in attacks on army personnel, civilian Unionists, and the freedmen.[1]

According to one Freedmen's Bureau agent, Lee, Baker, and Bickerstaff represented the continuing Southern resistance and the refusal of the Rebels to accept the results of the late war, making the implementation of Reconstruction laws and new ideals more difficult to enforce. The outlaws cared nothing for life, nothing for the law, and nothing for the stability of their region. Death and destruction characterized their world, one that they, themselves, made. Another bureau man added other renegade holdouts to the list: Jack English, Dick Johnson, and Simp Dixon, the latter two belonging to the Lee partisans in the Corners' counties.[2]

By the winter of 1865–1866, while Peacock gave food to blacks and helped them survive the cold, Bob Lee was attracting more attention. In Bonham, loyal Union men raised the American flag when he and his friends were in the town at a local saloon getting drunk and celebrating their misspent lives. When he learned of the doings outside, Lee became enraged as did his men, all of whom got ready for a fight by checking their guns. Lee refused to let the local Union men have their small victory. Instead, backed by the guns of his friends, Lee stumbled out of the saloon, staggered to the flag, lowered it, and personally tore it to shreds while engaging in a verbal harangue against the United States government and anyone who supported it. Outnumbered Union men could do nothing. Further, the local civil authorities, most Southern adherents, did not have the nerve nor the inclination to arrest any of the Lee bunch who, again, could afford to be defiant because of their superior numbers. A short time later, Lee ventured into Wise County, pursuing a Unionist whom he had marked as his enemy. While there, he found and murdered the man.[3]

In addition to his other criminal actions, Lee kidnapped a young black boy near the end of Civil War and enslaved him. When Lee returned to Texas, he forced the boy to come with him. like many whites in Texas, Lee refused to free the child on Juneteenth; rather, he held the young boy in bondage until July of 1866. Further, the Lee family men contracted with some of the new freedmen to work Lee land. After crops were in, the Lees' refused to give their laborers their share of the harvest. Lee intimidated his workers and forced them to continue working for the family without receiving crop shares or wages. In effect, Bob Lee held them unlawfully in a situation much like slavery. The Freedmen's Bureau agent for Hunt County Hardin Hart (noted Unionist and later a district judge) learned of Lee's refusal to obey the terms of the contracts and his refusal to let the workers go. Hart also learned of the kidnapped youngster after which the bureau man led a small detachment of the Twenty-sixth United States Infantry to arrest Lee and liberate his workers, including the child. The detachment secured the release of the trapped blacks, but Lee drew two revolvers and put up a fight, firing his weapons while screaming that he would kill Hart. Outnumbered, Lee quickly took flight and avoided arrest. Forever after, he was a fugitive from justice, a fugitive who hated Hardin Hart for the rest of his life. Later, Lee and his men tried repeatedly to ambush and kill Hart. Lee simply refused to accept the outcome of the Civil War and the end of slavery. He also hated the people who abolished the South's "peculiar institution," especially the Union occupying forces and white Texas Unionists. Likewise, he believed in white supremacy and had no sympathy for or mercy upon the newly freed slaves. Like many other whites, he intended to rule the freedmen in Corners Country and in all other places he happened to find himself. If blacks did not submit to him, their lives were forfeit.[4]

Lee had trouble with more people than Hardin Hart. In the summer of 1866, Bob pilfered the goods of a Unionist, and authorities in Fannin County issued a warrant for his arrest on the charge of theft; thereafter, Lee spent much time in hiding. A renegade on the run from the law, Lee refused to give up, refused to let the late war end. He was determined to out-wit and out-shoot his foes, including Lewis Peacock who condemned Lee's outrages. Lewis knew the people of the Corners and knew that chaos would soon erupt. He also knew that he was the only person in the area who could effectively lead those who prayed for peace.[5]

Now a wanted man, Lee went into hiding and sometimes stayed at Joel Webb's house located on "Webb Hill" in Hunt County. During the late summer of 1866, nine-year-old Pauline Wilson traveled by horse and buggy to Webb Hill to visit Joel Webb's daughters, Lutie and Mattie. After the three girls conversed and played on the porch for a time, one of the Webb girls asked in hushed tones if Pauline would like to meet Bob Lee. Pauline later recalled that "I was delighted. I was about nine years old. He was Bob Lee, the hero to some[,] and Bob Lee, the desperado[,] to others."[6] All three girls went down to the end of the porch, and one of the Webbs knocked on a door. Presently, the door opened, and there stood the fugitive. He had a handsome, agreeable face, to hear Pauline tell it. According to W. Walworth Harrison, local historian of Hunt County: "Joel Webb was obviously harboring Bob Lee at this time[,] and Lee had probably been using Black Cat Thicket, south of Webb Hill, as a hiding place."[7]

While the outlaw was on the run, significant political events occurred. In the summer of 1866, the state was still in the hands of those who had lost the war. The former Confederates were flying high, very much in control of the state. That year the legislature passed the infamous "Black Codes" to control the freedmen and to reduce them to semi-slavery and economic peonage. In the governor's race, conservative James W. Throckmorton, once a high-ranking Confederate officer, defeated the Unionist Elisha M. Pease by an overwhelming majority in the election of 1866. The governor's chair was thus occupied by someone sympathetic to Dixie's Lost Cause. Southern loyalists also controlled both houses of the Texas legislature. Lee, then, did not begin his fight just to save the Lost Cause. He had come home a deserter and a renegade who had committed violence before the war and who was disposed to continue on that path. Yet, he also viewed himself as loyal to the South's cause. As for Throckmorton, the new governor did nothing to aid hard-pressed freedmen and their white Unionist allies. Indeed, Throckmorton even denied that those two groups had reason to complain. He accused Union loyalists and Yankee soldiers of spinning falsehoods. He wanted the Freedmen's Bureau dismantled, for its agents had documented that hundreds if not thousands of blacks had been murdered by whites in the immediate postwar years.[8]

About the governor's attitude and his failure to enforce law and order and therefore to let chaos reign, Gen. Phillip Sheridan said that the condition of freedmen and white Unionists in the remote, rural areas of the state was "truly horrible." He told Gen. Ulysses S. Grant as much, saying that "the [American]

Government is denounced, the Freedmen are shot, and Union men are persecuted."[9] Sheridan also wrote Throckmorton, charging that "there are more casualties occurring from outrages perpetrated upon Union men and freedmen in the interior of the state than occur from Indian depredations on the frontier." The general next accused the governor of refusing to enforce the law when the only victims were white and black Unionists. In answering Sheridan's charges, the governor denied that any problems existed, while calling Unionists a "howling crowd of canting, lying scamps." Throckmorton's response led John L. Haynes of the Texas Loyal League to condemn the governor, charging that "whilst red handed murder stalks abroad in every county in the state, there he [Throckmorton] sits at Austin like an old hen on a bad egg, clucking away about only an 'occasional crime.'"[10] Meanwhile, Peacock and other Unionists in the Corners could but wish that they had some protection from the authorities.

In addition to a government that was favorable to the South's antebellum ideals, the Freedmen's Bureau had not established many stations in Texas, nor had the Union military established many posts. Certainly, the Corners Country was isolated, having no military or bureau presence. That development would only come later. Although he had no justifiable reason to take on the authorities in 1865 and 1866, Lee had already become known as a lawbreaker and as one of Texas's premier "nigger killers." That attracted the attention of the authorities even before Republicans took control in 1869. People in Northeast Texas could have believed that Lee had gone over the edge. Indeed, Unionists and Confederates, alike, came to call him the "Man Eater," thus attesting to his lethal nature.[11]

General Sheridan, Haynes of the Loyal League, and others like them confirmed in their complaints that a Second Civil War was being fought. In fact, in all Southern states complaints were similar—white Unionists and freedmen being killed out-of-hand, along with implementations of Black Codes that shackled African Americans with semi-slavery and along with the rise of terrorist groups like the Ku Klux Klan.[12]

Such complaints prompted national Republicans to seize control of Reconstruction and implement a reform plan that included giving military commanders the authority to remove hostile, unreconstructed civilian officials. For one, Sheridan wasted no time. He removed Throckmorton as an impediment to Reconstruction in July of 1867 and named the Union-friendly ex-Governor Elisha M. Pease to take his place. By the end of November, Sheridan had also removed thirteen of seventeen district judges, while another ex-Confederate judge resigned just prior to his certain removal. Peacock and other Unionists in the Corners applauded Sheridan's decision to clean out a good number of the former Confederates.[13]

The political shake-up affected Lee not at all, except that it gave him a grand excuse to continue his violent attacks on the black and the white Unionists in the Corners. He could now posture as a faithful Southerner trying to uphold the Lost Cause, protect white womanhood, and win the Second Civil War. He continued his violent activities that he had begun when the state and county governments were favorable to those of his sort. A local historian claimed that Lee led a band of "young hellions" who robbed travelers and highjacked freight wagons on the road to Jefferson, then the major commercially driven center in East Texas. They also rustled cattle and horses. The historian added that during Reconstruction Lee and his guerrillas killed freedmen and white Unionists practically for sport. Army Lt. H. E. Scott added that Lee and his minions "lived in open defiance of the law." Civil authorities, the lieutenant added, did not have the "nerve to attempt to arrest them."[14] Yet, Lee and his supporters were more than common outlaws; they continued to discriminate whenever they listed their targets, and they never attacked people loyal to slave-holding Dixie.

In late 1866 and early 1867, Lee continued to attract more notice and came to the attention of United States President Andrew Johnson. The president knew about all the violence in Northeast Texas and attributed most of it to leadership coming out of Lee Station, about three miles from present Leonard. Johnson's reference to the Corners' Lee family was obvious. That Bob had come to the attention of the sitting president was astounding, for Texas was a long way from Washington, D.C., and Corners Country was only a small, remote, isolated area of the Lone Star State. According to one source, President Johnson averred that in Texas the Civil War had not ended. He was correct. The war still raged and would continue to do so unless law and order could be reestablished in East-Northeast Texas. Lewis Peacock's leadership was much needed if Unionism was going to live. He redoubled his efforts to monitor the Lee bunch and to offer help to any white Unionists and freedmen who asked for assistance.[15]

By early 1867, Freedmen's Bureau Sub-Assistant Commissioner DeWitt C. Brown was stationed in Paris, Lamar County, and he had a farm in Fannin County where he spent part of his time. He was well qualified to testify about the chaos of the Corners counties. Brown reported that all of Northeast Texas was out of control, that the area was home to some of the state's worst characters. Civil officers could not maintain law and order. Mrs. L. E. Potts of Paris confirmed that Brown was correct. In an open letter to Congress, she described the pitiful condition of freedmen in the region. In addition to the Ku Klux Klan, outlaw gangs roamed the area, committing violence against blacks before running to hide out in another place where they used aliases to confuse authorities. Along the way, the raiders were helped by whites with Southern sympathies or by whites who had been terrorized by the gangs and were afraid to inform the authorities about the outlaws' whereabouts. Many such people were probably afraid *not* to help outlaws and Klansmen for fear that they would be attacked next. Bob Lee and Elijah Clark, for example, murdered the Unionist Wiley Tabor in Farmersville, Collin County, in April of 1867, but authorities were powerless to arrest the desperadoes who were housed and protected by area whites. In August of that year, Lee also attacked army commissary wagon trains and seized United States mailbags along with many other items. Lieutenant Thomas Tolman, who would later be a leader of "Chaffee's Guerrillas"—a military unit that hounded Lee and other malefactors—led a scout into Corners Country to dog Lee. With Tolman giving the orders, the troopers staged the first of their several raids on Lee's home. There Tolman discovered two of the mailbags with the locks broken and their contents rifled and partially removed. He also found other property taken from the wagon train, but Tolman's quarry, the "Man Eater," was nowhere in sight.[16]

Meanwhile, Bureau Agent Brown identified the most notorious of the raiders. According to him, the worst were Bob Lee, Cullen Montgomery Baker, Benjamin F. Bickerstaff, Ben Griffith, Elisha Guest, Dick Johnson, Sam (Simp) Dixon, and George "Indian Bill" English. On another occasion, Brown amended his list to include Henry Farrar, John Henderson, and John "Pomp" Duty. Brown said that English, for example, boasted of killing many freedmen, white Unionists, and Northern soldiers. Mostly roaming in Titus County near Mount Pleasant but also seen frequently in the Corners in the company of Bob Lee, English once had the pleasure of allowing a soldier to buy him a drink while the federal explained that he had been sent to Mount Pleasant to arrest George English. After the Yankee asked if English knew the man, the badman introduced himself before casually shooting the questioner to death. When English killed blacks, he sometimes flayed them and nailed their skins to trees. In addition to English and the rest, Brown could have included the name of the young teenager John Wesley Hardin on his list, for Hardin was also active in the Corners' area and was helping his kinsman Bob Lee. Further, guerrilla leaders like Lee, Baker, and Bickerstaff frequently acted in concert, a development that swelled their ranks. When they worked together, they often had numerical superiority over the Yankees and area Unionists like Peacock whom they bedeviled.[17]

Brown was accurate when he named Baker and Bickerstaff as comrades of Lee. Both Baker and Bickerstaff led guerrilla bands during and after the war, and both were staunch Lee friends. The former, a native of Tennessee born in 1835, came to Cass County in 1839 with his parents. As he grew into his teenage years, he became a bully. In 1854 he flogged a younger boy, an orphan named Stallcup, almost whipping the boy to death. Later, authorities arrested Baker who was tried and convicted of assault. Area farmer Wesley Bailey, fifty-two years old, bravely served as the chief witness at the trial. The same day that Baker paid his fine, he got even. He went to Bailey's farm and murdered the old man as he was coming out of his barn where he had just finished feeding his horses. When Bailey walked out into his yard, Baker cut loose with a double-barreled shotgun, even as the old farmer begged for his life.[18]

Earlier, Baker had been just a troublesome pest who occasionally hurt others, "but by shooting Bailey, he had crossed the line dividing mean from criminal."[19] Baker made Boston, Bowie County, his headquarters from whence he periodically conducted raids and spread terror throughout Northeast Texas and Southwestern Arkansas. Baker and his men robbed Union supply trains, killing federals in the process. Baker also became known as another of the "nigger killers" who intended to keep blacks in their place. Whenever he was in Corners Country, he found Lee and rode with him.[20]

William P. "Bill" Longley, another noted teenage criminal who was sometimes called "Wild Bill," probably rode with Baker for a time. Born on October 16, 1851, in Mill Creek, Austin County, young Longley first attracted the attention of authorities when he killed a black soldier. Using the Lost Cause and the supposed excesses of Reconstruction as his excuse, he was soon committing more crimes, including thefts and murders. Finally on the run, Longley—still not much more than a boy—headed north where he found and joined Baker's gang. Later, after Baker's death, some sources hold that Longley joined Lee's wild bunch.[21]

Born on a farm in Titus County, Bickerstaff also became a Lee friend and a terror who punished freedmen and white Unionists. In the words of former slave Lee Pierce, Bickerstaff was "one of the main leaders of the [ex-Confederate] whites. They [Bickerstaff and members of his gang] killed several of the colored militia and wounded lots more."[22] Like Baker, he roamed all of Northeast Texas and often cooperated with Lee and his men. Having fought as a guerrilla during the war, Bickerstaff was most proficient with arms. He came to the attention of the regional authorities in 1865 when he was returning home after the Civil War. A hater of the free blacks, he murdered a former slave when he was passing through Louisiana headed for his home in Titus County. Now on the wrong side of the law, he became a man determined to resist the Reconstruction process and refused to tolerate the new freedom of the ex-slaves. He became known as a Southern hotspur who would shoot first and ask questions later. In the first few months after his return, Bickerstaff murdered several blacks in the Gray Rock area. He recruited about twenty men and set up a camp in the bottoms of White Oak Creek. At some point he moved his center of operations from Titus to Hopkins County and headquartered near Sulphur Springs from whence he was often in communication with both Lee and Baker.[23]

Another "nigger killer," Bickerstaff continued to rob and execute blacks. He attacked Union army supply trains and supply depots, killing Union troopers, taking what he could, and burning what he could not. He cloaked his deeds by claiming to be one of Dixie's patriots who, like Baker and Bob Lee, was willing to fight for the lost honor of the South. Despite his crimes, Bickerstaff developed a wide popular following because he cast the War of Reconstruction as a great noble struggle wherein Dixie's boys, oppressed Rebels all, were forced to do battle with evil Northerners, dastardly Southern scalawags, and the uppity freedmen who were industrious enough to try to rise above caste. For a time he got away with his depredations. As was true with Lee, Baker, and other desperadoes, Bickerstaff had supporters who helped him and his men as best they could by serving as spies, by warning them when authorities were near, by hiding them, by feeding them and their mounts, by buying guns and ammunition, and by performing whatever other services that the raiders needed.[24]

Different observers noted that other outlaws, who joined or led gangs, also occasionally roamed about the Corners vicinity and cooperated with Lee. They included Bill Bateman, Wade Anderson, Phillip Simpson, Bill Taylor, Charlie Hodges, Bill Parrish, and Thomas Nichols. Lee knew all of them and often cooperated with them when they were in Corners Country. One Freedmen's Bureau sub-agent called the whole sorry lot "general murderers, miscellaneous robbers, and cut throats" who would "kill a freedman for 75 cents," adding that Hodges killed one black child because the boy "had his hands in his pockets and didn't stand at attention when Hodges rode past."[25]

By 1868, then, if not earlier, various terrorists in Northeast Texas had formed a loose alliance and often helped each other. Baker, Lee, Bickerstaff, and Longley—and their men—often joined each other for nefarious purposes. More and more people reported that they were confirmed "nigger killers." By mid-1868 other sources listed the following men who conspired together: Bickerstaff, Baker, Jack and George English, Lee, and two of Lee's men—Dick Johnson and Sam (Simp) Dixon—as well as others who had recently killed six or seven white Unionists and "who roamed the Northeastern Texas countryside" and its towns without fearing "negative consequences."[26]

Meanwhile, in the Corners the Lee bunch was becoming braver, so much so that Peacock became more concerned for the safety of all area people, black and white, who remained loyal to the federal government. Lewis also feared for his family, afraid that Emaline, John Edgar, or Cathy might become targets of vengeance. Peacock started a petition drive, asking for the commander at Sherman to send some troops to Pilot Grove to police Corners Country. Joined by Maddox, Nance, and others, Lewis delivered the petition to Lieutenant H. E. Scott, who commanded the small post at Sherman. In part, the petition pointed out that the area's white Unionists and freedmen were afraid to work their fields for fear of outlaw or Klan raids. Some people had even started staying away from their homes at night. They hid and slept in the nearest woods. Peacock was among their number. Yet, he stayed close enough to his house to guard it, lest Lee and his men tried to harm Emaline or John Edgar.[27]

By the fall of 1868, Scott complied with Lewis's request by sending a small detachment commanded by Cpl. Frederick Herold to Pilot Grove. Area Unionists led by Peacock greeted the men when they arrived and briefed the corporal about all the doings in the Corners, especially the actions of the Lee guerrillas. Somewhat later, the criminal activities of Lee and other brigands became national news. On September 29, 1868, the *New York Tribune* attached a name to the roaming bands who loosely associated together, the *Tribune*'s editor calling them the "New Rebellion Gang." The *Tribune* reported that "for some time past the Eastern portion of the State [of Texas] has been infested by a number of bands of reckless outlaws whose principal occupation seems to be to kill defenseless and unoffending Union men and industrious [N]egroes." Led by men like Lee, Bickerstaff, and Baker, the gangs had "become a terror to law and order loving people" in East-Northeast Texas.[28]

Again, Lee—along with some of his relatives and some of his friends—was named as a prominent leader of Southern malefactors. Other sources also referred to the "Second Rebellion," naming the same group of young guns. Calling themselves the Ku Klux Klan, they roamed far and wide, committing more atrocities on freedmen and white Unionists. Some of the outlaws often worked as enforcers for the landed elite if they had trouble with their workforce. The *Tribune* said that at other times the raiders' actions appeared to be random, but close examination proved otherwise. They continued to exempt most die-hard Southerners from their violence and leave them in peace. A *Tribune* correspondent confirmed what a bureau agent had said earlier: The gang members would "kill a black for 75 cents." Yet, the brigands could not be apprehended because their white supporters always informed them of danger whenever soldiers or cooperating Texas Unionists were near: "Fed, secreted, and encouraged by a large number of people throughout the country," the desperadoes foiled the authorities "in every attempt at their capture." Northeast Texas was "in a terrible condition; the people evince a spirit of lawlessness and resistance to civil law, and only await [other opportunities to commit mayhem]. Law and order ceased to exist" and men like Lee were "cold blooded assassins" who "murdered men, women, and children."[29] Of course, Lewis Peacock already knew all that, and he did his best to keep military authorities abreast of the latest news from the Corners.

As if to prove that the *Tribune*'s assessment about the "Texas Troubles" was correct, one bureau agent trying to catch Baker simply gave up because the man had too much support and was most effective in controlling area blacks.[30] Observers often mentioned the outlaws and various terrorist groups in the same breath—and with good reason, for all of East Texas felt the sting of both groups whose memberships often overlapped.

The birth of the historic Ku Klux Klan took place in Pulaski County, Tennessee, in May or early June of 1866. Founded by Gen. Nathan Bedford Forrest, the Klan was originally a social club for the area's Southern military veterans, its meetings including elaborate initiation ceremonies, other rituals, and grand-sounding titles to make the members feel important. Copied by other counties in Tennessee, the different Klans evolved into terrorist groups that intended to control the new freedmen politically, economically, and socially. By July there were Klaverns all over Tennessee, their members persecuting white Unionists and blacks. Even the social club in Pulaski evolved into a terrorist society, despite General Forrest's effort to disband it because he could not tolerate the violence. Such groups swept the entire South between 1866 and 1867. There was, however, some confusion about identifying Klan groups, for not all went by the same name, and each group, usually organized at the county level, was autonomous.[31]

Actually, terrorist groups were organizing in Texas by mid- 1865, well before Forrest established his organization in Tennessee. That year, Col. George Custer's command included East-Northeast Texas, and he and his men confirmed that violent groups were springing up. The colonel told of a "Brotherhood" of whites in Freestone County that had coalesced. Its members collectively promised to drive all blacks out of their county. Despite the illogic of attacking their major labor force, the entire brotherhood swore not to allow ex-slaves to be employed in Freestone; to whip any blacks who tried to contract with whites; and to whip any whites who employed African Americans. Likewise, the *New Orleans Tribune* reported that in 1865 terrorists were already organizing in the Lone Star State well before the Klans in Tennessee.[32]

In Texas, terrorists groups variously named themselves the Ku Klux Rangers, the Knights of the White Camellia, the White Caps, Knights of the Red Hand, the Sons of Washington, the Knights of the Rising Son, the Teutonic Brotherhood, and so on. To further confuse the story of the expanding Klans, some observers—including newspaper editors and military men like Custer—at first labeled the terrorist groups the Knights of the Golden Circle (KGC), a secret antebellum pro-Southern organization that wanted to expand bondage into Central and South America and therefore to create an empire for slavery. The KGC also helped to spearhead the drive for secession and then to organize the first of the South's military units. Yet editors like those of the *New Orleans Tribune,* who reported that the KGC was re-arming in Texas and holding open meetings in most towns of the state, only erred about the name. The editors were correct about the new groups organizing and spreading chaos and death in their wake. Some contemporaries and later historians have credited Col. Roger Q. Mills, Confederate to the core, as the Klan leader who coordinated terrorist activity in Texas, but most of the groups operated at the county level and were autonomous. However, many such organizations cooperated with Klans in adjacent counties to spread more terror.[33]

Lee and the other brigands organized Klans in their region or joined when they learned of a Klan nearby. They also did Klan work in terrorizing the freedpeople to render them docile and to reinforce white supremacy. In his 1971 book on terrorism in the South, Allan Trelease counted Klans in some seventeen counties in Texas, but his report represented a monumental undercount. Later, researcher Barbara Clayton Barnhill found activity in almost eighty counties, including units in all the Corners counties and in most of the other counties in Northeast Texas as well. As early as 1866, a Klavern called McKinney, Collin County, home—a home that was dangerously close to the Corners. Its founder R. D. Allison, a veteran of both the Mexican War and the Civil War, visited Klaverns in the Volunteer State and secured a "model charter" from Pulaski. The Collin County Klavern soon attracted 200 members. By 1868 the three other counties that made up the Corners Country had Klans centered in Sherman, Greenville, and Bonham. Yet other nearby locales that had Klaverns included: Paris, Lamar County; Sulphur Springs, Hopkins County; Dallas, Dallas County; Kaufman, Kaufman County; Canton, Van Zandt County; Quitman, Wood County; Mount Pleasant, Titus County; Clarksville, Red River County; and Boston, Bowie County. Most renegades like Lee, Baker, Bickerstaff, and others were either leaders of Klansmen or cooperated closely with the terrorist groups. Baker probably joined the Klan in his area, while Bickerstaff was the head of the Klan in Hopkins County. Lee headed the Klansmen who lived in the Corners. Occasionally, he even marked his horse with a large "K" on both flanks. As late as 1868 sympathetic news sheets denied that terrorist groups existed. Instead the Loyal League was only playing political tricks.[34]

Men like Peacock knew different. Given his intelligence network among freed blacks, he learned early on about the Klan groups and understood just how dangerous they were. Yet, it was hard for Lewis to keep up with all the doings of violent men in Corners Country, for their crimes appeared to be legion. Lieutenant A. G. Malloy confirmed that many white supporters assisted Klansmen and outlaws like Baker, Bickerstaff, and Lee because they claimed they represented Dixie's Lost Cause. They were most useful in helping whites "control their freedmen and [do] not hesitate to shoot them on the slightest complaint made by their employers."[35] Another observer added that area whites cheated freedmen out of wages or their crop shares and mobbed them if they complained: "Civil law is a farce. . . . Freedmen have no chance for justice."[36] Yet another person reported that the blacks were not paid for their labor and that some were still held in semi-slavery. Some remained slaves as late as 1868, and murders of the freedmen were common while the perpetrators went unpunished.[37]

One historian listed the reported reasons why terrorists and outlaws killed blacks: "[F]reedman did not remove his hat when he passed him [a white man]; Negro would not allow himself to be whipped; freedman would not allow his wife to be whipped; he was carrying a letter to a Freedmen's Bureau official; kill Negroes to see them kick; wanted to thin out niggers a little; didn't hand over his money quick enough; wouldn't give up his whiskey flask."[38]

To make himself appear as a champion of the Lost Cause, Lee concocted an amazing story in 1868 which was published by the *Bonham News* of Fannin County on June 26. In it the captain related that in 1865, shortly after his heroic return from the war, Peacock and his men, wearing U.S. Army uniforms, arrested him in his home when he was sick and defenseless. Claiming that they were taking him to Sherman to stand trial for war crimes, they instead stopped in mid-route and went into the thicket in Choctaw Bottom. For thirty-six hours they detained him there. Finally one of the members of the posse explained to Lee that he could buy his way out of trouble. Lee then gave the posse his mule, saddle, and bridle along with a $20 gold piece in his pockets and signed a $2,000 note payable on demand. According to his account, upon being freed he went to Bonham and filed suit against his foes. However, a search of Fannin County courthouse records proved that Lee had lied about the entire incident.[39]

Many freedmen and white Unionists hoped that the army and the Freedmen's Bureau agents would protect them, but by 1868 federal forces in Texas had been reduced to 3,770 men who served at thirty-seven posts. The army stationed most of the men in West Texas on the Indian frontier. Only 1,291 of the men manned the nineteen interior garrisons which were east of the frontier. On the average, the interior garrisons did not even have company strength. Further, many garrisons were manned by infantrymen who were of little use because the more mobile Klansmen and outlaws usually had good mounts. Plus, as mentioned, the Freedmen's Bureau was so woefully undermanned and underfunded that it could not reach all areas of East and Northeast Texas. At the peak of its expansion in 1867, the bureau had only fifty-seven local posts and sixty-nine sub-assistant commissioners in the entire state. From ex-slaves and white Unionists, authorities continually received requests that more bureau stations be established—requests that could not be approved because of manpower and money shortages. Peacock repeatedly asked for a bureau station for Pilot Grove, but his wish went unfulfilled. He eventually understood that the loyalists in Corners Country would have to, in large part, depend on themselves for protection, a task made harder because of Lee's supporters.[40]

Other of the Corners' area Unionists, like Peacock, did what they could to recruit men to help their cause, to aid the Freedmen's Bureau, and to extend some assistance to area blacks. But Life in the Corners would soon explode into a nightmare for those Unionists.

Chapter 5

The Devil Stalks the Corners

At some point between 1865 and 1867, once he was on the run, Lee moved his gang's hideout to Wildcat Thicket, which was on Lee land in Fannin County near the Corners. He and some of his men burrowed into the bush, excavated part of it, and built a structure. For a roof they used an oilcloth which they had boiled in linseed oil to make the material water resistant. Then they piled bush, timber, and debris atop the shack to make it almost indistinguishable from Mother Nature. By day it was barely visible up close. By night the place was invisible. The thicket had an elliptical shape. It was approximately seven miles long and four miles wide at its widest part. Lee and his men did good construction work, for when the authorities placed a price on his head, no one—not bounty hunters, not Unionists, not the army—ever found his den. The place remained a secret even when soldiers scouted the area in winter when much of the thicket's foliage had disappeared. From 1865 until 1869 when he was killed, Lee and his daring guerrillas used the place as a headquarters and as a safe house as well. Some members of the gang always guarded the entrances. And whenever Bob wanted to go out during the day, he usually waited until one of his relatives or other supporters came near and told one of the guards that it was safe for Bob to surface publicly. By night, he and his men could slip in and out at will. Even after Congress tried to crack down on Southerners, no federals ever found the hideout.[1]

Because of chaos and Klan violence in the South, coupled with the whites' determination to subdue the new freed slaves with devices such as the Black Codes, in January of 1867, the Republican-dominated United States Congress took control of the Reconstruction process from President Andrew Johnson. The Reconstruction acts of 1867 dissolved civilian state government in all the states of the old Confederacy, Tennessee excepted. The acts created five military districts. Merged, Texas and Louisiana made up the Fifth Military District.

A major general in blue, commanding troops of occupation, controlled each district. Aside from bringing law and order, each general was charged with registering voters, the new electorate including black men as well as white men. Next, the commander supervised new elections to state constitutional conventions, afterward also monitoring elections to restore civilian government. At that point the general's tasks were finished, and the high command withdrew the troops of occupation from the South. Therein lay one great flaw in the Reconstruction process. Although reforming Republican governments came to power throughout most of the old Confederacy, those governments were put in immediate jeopardy, for there were but few troops to protect them and enforce reformist laws. When the troops withdrew, the War of Reconstruction escalated. Now, as never before, Southern loyalists viciously attacked blacks and their white Unionist allies.

A creek bottom in Wildcat Thicket near Bob Lee's home. Photo by David Carter. Courtesy Larry Peacock.

As Reconstruction stretched into months and years, Lee and his men, like Klansmen statewide and other notorious brigands, continued their violent campaign against area freedmen, and in the doing, the line between Unionists and unreconstructed Rebels became more pronounced. Lee and others like him attacked Freedmen's Bureau agents, assaulted black school children, burned African American school houses and churches, and intimidated and sometimes killed teachers and preachers. They also attacked black community buildings when meetings were underway and killed those whom they could.[2]

In February, 1867, violence once again flared in the Corners after Lee rode into Pilot Grove for a day of drinking and merriment at the local saloon. Unionist Jim Maddox, a Peacock supporter, came in. Although Maddox had fought for the Confederacy, he was a decent fellow who joined Peacock in the Unionist camp, in part because he accepted the results of the Civil War and in part because he could not support the extreme actions that Lee's raiders were taking. Soon, Lee and Maddox were arguing about the way Lee and other Rebels were treating the freedpeople and the area's white Unionists. Hostile words flew, and the two went into the street to settle with each other. A gun battle erupted. Maddox got the best of it, wounding Lee with a bullet that grazed the outlaw's skull just above the ear. Apparently, the bullet knocked Lee unconscious—a wound serious enough to require medical help. Taken to the house of W. H. Pierce, the local physician who sided with the Lee faction, Bob received treatment and then remained with the Pierce family for several days to convalesce.[3] However, there emerged different accounts of the Maddox-Lee clash.

Lay historians with Southern propensities who wrote in defense of Lee probably stretched the truth by claiming that in the street, Maddox lost heart, made an apology, and laughed off the argument. Lee, according to such accounts, relaxed and moved toward the saloon. Maddox drew a gun and fired while Lee's back was turned. Such action was unlikely because Maddox was a hard-bitten battle-scarred veteran of the gray just as Lee was. Maddox was no coward, especially not after surviving four years of brutal warfare.[4] The problem with such a tale is that no researchers who looked into the Lee-Peacock struggle ever cited historical documents to prove their assertions. No eye witnesses were quoted. No one later wrote a memoir attesting to the facts. No legal authority ever reported a crime.

Further, more than one hearsay rendition of the meeting in the street exists. According to one account, the men did not fight immediately. Rather, after some hard words, Maddox simply left Lee where he was—in the saloon drinking his fill. Later, Lee went outside to talk to a freedman about hiring him to work at the Lee farm. Supposedly, Jim saw Lee thus occupied, slipped up behind the captain, and shot him. But, this story, like the others, is not documented. In yet another retelling of the incident, Lee was in the blacksmith's shop probably attending to a matter involving his horse when Maddox shot him.[5] All that is known for certain is that there was a fight, and Maddox won it.

On February 24 Unionist Hugh Hudson went to the Pierce place, probably charged by Peacock with finding Lee. Peacock's authority for directing Hudson rested in his close relationship with the army and the Freedmen's Bureau in addition to his commanding presence among Unionists who looked to him for leadership. Hudson did not get to search the house. There was an altercation outside. After hard words were exchanged, Hudson shot Lee's man Pierce, who died three days later. Thereafter, the struggle between Lee's men and the Unionists escalated. As for Hudson: Lee later tracked him down and murdered him. Further, Dorinda Pierce—embittered by the loss of her brother—entered the conflict. She pretended to make friends with the wife of a Peacock follower and then began to spy for the Lees, gathering information about what the Peacock-Unionist faction was planning to do, where they were at certain intervals, and how they planned to react to Lee's moves at strategic times. She thus became a source who passed along valuable information to Lee and his bunch.[6]

Meanwhile, in February of 1867, Sherman's Freedmen's Bureau Agent Albert Evans informed his superiors of the dire state of affairs in the volatile region. Peacock was sending Evans regular information about the chaos. Referring to

Lee and others like him, Evans reported that "there is a controlling influence here against the Government in every respect, and an outspoken hatred of the North and all [people] that were . . . connected to putting down the late rebellion." He added that "there is violent opposition to the interest of the freedmen in every particular. I am now confirmed in my opinion that justice cannot . . . be rendered to freedmen by the civil courts in this section of the state."[7]

Evans went on to chronicle the deaths of several blacks who were murdered by men in disguise, probably by Klansmen or by the Lee raiders. Evans said, for example, that on February 16, three former slaves who lived in Grayson County's part of the Corners were sitting at home around their fire when brigands broke into the cabin and killed them. Six days later, another area freedmen was found dead in the northern part of the county. The bureau man added that he was virtually a prisoner, for he could not leave Sherman without military protection. The forlorn agent also commented that he could not do his job without being sustained by troops. "The professional men of the brush are numerous here," he complained. "The slaughtering of freedmen still goes on . . . the section [of the region] bordering the Red River is in a deplorable condition."[8]

In yet another incident, Dave Johnson—"Dave" might have been Dick Johnson of the Lee gang—murdered several blacks in northern Grayson and boasted of being a "nigger killer." Even if Dave was not a Lee man, he was doing terrorist work for Lee's guerrillas and the area's Klan groups. Evans also had information that killers had murdered many more area blacks, but he could not confirm such reports, for he had little possibility of investigating remote areas for fear of his life. As late as August of 1867, Bureau Agent Anthony Bryant, who had replaced Evans, lamented that of all the civil officers in Grayson County, only one, Solomon Bostick, would give freedpeople justice. Clearly, Lewis Peacock, who was trying to lead the Union men, was involved in dangerous business that was growing more deadly every day.[9]

Meanwhile, Simp Dixon of the Lee wild bunch had another run-in with the law. He accosted and severely beat the freedman West Parker while Parker's family looked on. Then, he forced the African American out of his own home while threatening to kill him. Parker's offense? According to Bureau Agent Evans, the freedman had been working hard, making some money, and improving his standard of living. Simp simply hated to see any blacks doing well, rising above their station. The county sheriff tried to arrest Simp, but Evans reported that the effort was not successful, saying that "it is constantly the case somehow that the officers are ever unfortunate in apprehending a certain class of offenders," implying that the county authorities would not arrest Lee men or other desperadoes who represented the Lost Cause.[10]

On February 14, new trouble developed in Pilot Grove. Bushwhackers accosted a physician in the town saloon. They shot and killed the man before making a quick, clean getaway. The murder prompted an outcry from Peacock who got in touch with Bureau Agent Evans. After hearing the news, Evans condemned the civil authorities. He noted that a grand jury had recently failed to render indictments in many cases where blacks were victims of crimes. He added that the district court had just finished a session, but many cases wherein freedpeople were the plaintiffs resulted in dismissals after defense attorneys made just one or two statements. Blacks had little chance for justice when they went before the area's courts.[11]

Meanwhile, on April 8, Lee and five of his raiders committed a bit of devilry at Farmersville in Collin County and murdered a Union man named Taber. Shortly, two of Tally's unidentified friends found Lee at home—why had he left his hideout?—and tried to kill him. Bob, his younger brother William, and four gang members pursued the assailants and caught them near Farmersville, where they killed one and wounded the other.[12]

New arrest warrants then went out on Lee. Yet, even as bureau and army authorities were trying to bring him in, Lee continued to terrorize freedmen, most of whom were sharecroppers who were living with soul-crushing poverty only to see their lives made harder by the doings of the renegades. In effect, the captain worked for their employers by driving the blacks away after harvest so the employers could claim the entire yield of crops. Then, farmers asserted that the black laborers had run away and had broken their contracts. In such cases landlords took the entire crop. In the Corners, Peacock tried to stop such abuses, but he did not have the kind of success that he wanted. As time passed, many freedmen stopped reporting the abuses, for fear of retaliation. Although Peacock continued to try to get information from the ex-slaves, at times they offered little help because of their fear that they would be sought out and killed.[13]

In mid-1867, Freedmen's Bureau Inspector Col. William H. Sinclair added his voice to Peacock's and others who continued to complain about injustices perpetrated by unreconstructed Rebels. Sinclair reported that the white Unionists and the free blacks in Northeast Texas were living in "pandemonium itself." In the Corners counties, a "deplorable" condition had developed. Landowners, Sinclair charged, had not paid blacks for the previous year's work. The freedmen continued to labor in a system that was "servitude worse then slavery." Gangs of cutthroats and Klansmen beat, shot, and killed some of their number daily, but local authorities protected such murderers. Helpless white Unionists and blacks watched known murderers freely enter the towns in Corners Country and "go [in and] out[,] against whom there are indictments for the worse crimes in the hands of the sheriff." According to Colonel Sinclair, "civil law is dead."[14]

Continuing his report, the inspector said that desperado Elisha Guest, who often rode with Lee, had killed at least eight to ten freedmen in Corners Country but remained at large, terrorizing area blacks at will. Among his other atrocities, Guest shot a black woman who was in a "family way[,] cut out her womb with its living contents [still inside,] and exhibited [the fetus to others] in his drunken glee."[15]

According to Galveston's *Flake's Semi-Weekly Bulletin,* Guest had been known to kill up to three freedmen a day. Wherever he rode—and he allied with Lee and often rode in the Corners counties—field hands who saw and recognized him became terrified, dropping their tools and running straight for the nearest woods. The *Bulletin* added that on one occasion four brave Unionists captured Guest and took him to the Clarksville jail, but a sympathetic jailor secured his cell lock with a common padlock only. After the jailor conveniently left the building there was no one to monitor Guest, who broke the lock and made an easy escape. Continuing, the *Bulletin* added that "there are dozens of such men [as Guest] in this region [Northeast Texas] who rank as heroes in the eyes of thousands, who gladly harbor and abet them."[16] Sinclair agreed with the *Bulletin* completely. Indeed, the *Bulletin*'s editor had not exaggerated. There were scores of such men, Sinclair howled. Compared to Northeast Texas, he asserted that the southern region of Texas was like a paradise, a statement that men like Peacock agreed with. Another Union man averred that outrages against the former slaves were so numerous that little note was made of them.[17]

Traveling through Northeast Texas shortly after Sinclair, another bureau man, C. S. Roberts, confirmed that both the *Bulletin* and the inspector had told the truth. Klansmen and outlaws savaged the area, said Roberts. But reliable information about their whereabouts was impossible to attain. "Efficiently organized," for the "express purpose of committing crime," the raiders robbed, whipped, and murdered. Yet, they had a network of "secret friends, spies" who warned them whenever authorities planned to arrest them. About Northeast Texas, Roberts exclaimed: "God knows that there is no other region in the United States so cursed with crime [or] so filled with lawless men, who have done their lawless acts so unblushingly as in this North-Eastern Texas."[18] Such was the climate that Unionists like Peacock had to contend with. It seemed that no matter how hard Peacock worked to help the bureau and the army, his efforts came up short because he faced powerful opposition. Consequently, more white Unionists and free blacks died. Although he could not have known it at the time, Peacock, himself, was facing impending doom. Indeed, many of the renegades marked him as an enemy to be stalked and killed.

Another man to come increasingly under attack was Peacock ally Hardin Hart, a former bureau agent who once manned a post in Greenville. By May,

1867, he had been appointed district judge, his district including all the Corners counties. He intended to bring crimes against freedmen and Unionists to an end and to bring desperadoes and Klansmen to heel. Given his views, he was always in close touch with Peacock and other Union men in the Corners. A staunch Unionist before, during, and after the war, Hardin Hart was born on August 23, 1814, in West Virginia. He was the oldest son of John F. Hart, who came to Texas by way of Indiana in 1833 and opened a store in Jonesborough (or Jonesboro) in present-day Red River County. During the Texas Revolution when Gen. Sam Houston and his tiny army was retreating before the massive forces of General Santa Anna, John Hart organized a military company called "Hart's Mounted Men." Planning to join Houston and perhaps save his army, Hart and his fighters arrived at San Jacinto too late to take part in the epic battle wherein Texas won its independence. Nevertheless, John Hart had shown a lot of sand. In 1837 Captain Hart moved with his family to Warren, then in Fannin County (now Grayson).[19]

Hardin Hart was the older brother of Martin Hart and both practiced law, moving to Greenville in the late 1840s. Both eventually served in the Texas legislature: Hardin, state senator, 1849–1854; Martin, state representative, 1857–1858. Both became and remained Houston loyalists and vigorously opposed secession, just as Houston did. Martin was one of the signers of the Unionist "Address to the People of Texas," the 1861 plea for Texans to remain with the Union. During the war, Martin achieved wide notice for being a counterpart to Quantrill. In 1862, he raised a company of men, about thirty-five or forty strong with most coming from Hunt and Fannin counties. He then led the group as it marched out of Texas under a Lone Star flag. Hart's irregulars headed northeastwardly, used a ruse to move through Confederate-held Springfield, Missouri, and wound up in St. Louis. There, the men proved that they were not traitors to the United States. They volunteered their services to the Union government, an offer the commander in St. Louis quickly accepted. Commissioned a captain, Hart took charge of the First Texas Cavalry Regiment (North).

Hart lobbied hard for an invasion of Texas via Indian Territory. Although his superiors did not approve that plan, Hart won lasting fame by leading his men to Arkansas to begin a campaign against Confederates there. He also fought in Missouri and Indian Territory. After Hart and his men had performed admirably for the Union, Rebels captured them on January 19, 1863, near Fort Smith. The Confederate authorities there hanged both the captain and his lieutenant on January 22 but not before Hart asked for leniency for the rest of his men. Ironically, Grayson County's T. C. Bass—ardent secessionist before the war, author of Sherman's "Flag Flap," and an old enemy of Hart—was the officer at Fort Smith who gave a firing squad the order to execute the Union stalwart.

Some of Hart's men managed to escape and made it safely back to Northeast Texas where a few hid in Jernigan's Thicket for a time. Authorities eventually captured six of Hart's followers, however, and hanged them after quick trials.[20]

That Martin fought for the Union made his immediate family much hated, many of whom were murdered during the War of Reconstruction, the victims including his son and one of his nephews. About Martin, most Confederates no doubt agreed with the editor of Marshall's *Texas Republican* who called Martin's Union service "open treason." After the war, Southern partisans in the Corners counties felt the same about the older brother Hardin: They believed Hardin Hart guilty of treason and felt that he dishonored Dixie. Then came Hardin Hart's service with the Freedmen's Bureau (he was the agent who forced Bob Lee to free his black laborers) before he became a district judge. Hardin Hart became a marked man whom the Lee gang threatened many times and tried to kill on several occasions. He was a proverbial thorn in the side of the malefactors, but he reported in May of 1867 that he had been harassed again, that he feared for his life, and that he could not effectively do his job. He said that he could not hold district court in any place other than Greenville, a town that now had a military garrison. He asked for troops to protect him whenever he needed to hold court in the other counties in his district, counties that included the ones that converged at the Corners. In response, military headquarters sent Hart six men, but events would prove that the detachment was too small to protect the hated Unionist judge effectively.[21]

By July of 1867, while Hart was still virtually under siege, Union men in Grayson, Hunt, Collin, and Fannin counties were losing heart because of the constant attacks by terrorist groups like the Klan and Lee's guerrillas. According to one observer, the Union men were strong in number, but they were still discouraged by violence all around them and by the failure of the civil courts to take appropriate action. Peacock and his supporters continued to fight the terrorists and feed information to Union authorities, but their task appeared hopeless. From Sherman, William Sinclair, a future state legislator, declared that the entire civil government of the state was nothing more than a "Grand Rebel Organization." He favored removing the entire government and turning control over to white Union men and freedmen.[22] One reason they were discouraged was that an influx of undesirables were streaming into the Corners' counties. Men who had once ridden with irregulars like Quantrill and Joe Shelby were infesting the region, and they were of the "worst character." One observer went so far as the claim that "they are the cause of most of the disorder . . . in this portion of the state."[23]

Further, Confederate loyalists abetted and harbored Lee and his men. J. Alfred Drye of Pilot Grove was one of them. From the summer of 1867 into 1868, he furnished supplies and information to the desperadoes. Drye always got word to Lee about troop movements and the activities of others in authority. Drye also tried to monitor Peacock's actions and reported his doings to the desperado. When necessary Drye hid Lee men in his home, feeding them and their horses and supplying them with all items they needed including ammunition.[24] Other favorite haunts where Lee and his gang had friends included White Rock, Hunt County; Kentucky-Town in Grayson; Farmersville in Collin; and Old Warren and Orangeville in Fannin. They also occasionally crossed the Red and got into the Choctaw Nation.[25]

For a time, the cocky Lee could come and go in Corners Country as he pleased. He and several members of his gang openly rode into Greenville in the summer of 1867 to attend a picnic. Just to make an empathic statement, Lee stopped outside town and used ripe poke berry juice to paint a large "K" on both flanks of his horse. Clearly, he flaunted his membership in the area Klan and dared any Unionists to say or do anything about it. Later, he attended a horse race near Greenville where he saw the Unionist Henry Boren. The two men had a tense confrontation, both with shotguns in hand pointed toward each other, but Henry's bravery apparently stood Lee down, for the unreconstructed Rebel decided not to truck with Boren. The captain did not want to participate in a double-homicide if he were to be one of the victims.[26]

In September, 1867, Robert Fitzhugh—another Lee sympathizer who frequently harbored the gang—came to the attention of Peacock and the Union authorities, as did some Fitzhugh relatives. Fitzhugh was a man of property, owning a farm and a steam-driven flour mill near McKinney. A die-hard Southern ruffian who often frequented the saloons of McKinney, he usually got roaring drunk and then went about looking for white Union men or blacks to torment. He did not fear for himself and was always accompanied by a retinue of body guards. According to Collin County's J. W. Thomas, a McKinney newspaper editor, Fitzhugh was a "drunken, hostile, bullying, despicable, and quarrelsome man" who always had it in for Unionists and freedmen. On one occasion, in drunken revelry, he assaulted a physician in McKinney for no other reason than that the man was willing to give medical attention to the area's former chattels. But authorities did not arrest Fitzhugh. Officials were either scared of him and his followers or were sympathetic with him because of their loyalty to the Lost Cause.[27]

On September 26, Fitzhugh came into McKinney just as a grand jury had adjourned for the day. He accosted John Scott, the foreman of the jury, in Newsome's Saloon. Trying to provoke a fight, Fitzhugh harangued the foreman, knowing that an indictment might soon be handed down against him. When Scott's response was simply to leave, Fitzhugh loudly cursed him, saying among other things that Scott belonged "to the Negro equality party."[28]

Next, Fitzhugh sauntered over to G. E. Ramey's general store where he found Unionist Judge Edward Bowlby, one of the county voter registrars. The drunken Fitzhugh started insulting the judge, at one point threatening to kill him. Like Scott in the saloon, Bowlby just decided to walk out. Then, the violent man turned to Unionist Ramey and began to berate him. Ramey ignored the insults. Fitzhugh—armed with a six-shooter, a derringer, and a Bowie knife—advanced on Ramey who was sitting down. Fitzhugh raised his arm, six-gun in hand, and attempted to crack Ramey's skull. But another customer intervened in time to grab the gun arm and prevent the blow. In his statement to the authorities, Ramey labeled Fitzhugh's action as attempted murder; yet, the Rebel was not brought to justice.[29]

Ramey filed charges on October 7, 1867, but Fitzhugh remained at large, ultimately fled Collin County, and took a trip to hide in another part of East Texas. Unionists questioned why the county authorities took no action. After mentioning that the principal sheriff of Collin County was absent and citing a busy schedule, Deputy Sheriff R. C. White claimed that he just did not have time to find Fitzhugh and arrest him. Since the miscreant was elsewhere as of November, there was nothing, White said, that he could do. To the charge that county officers would not do their duty and arrest Fitzhugh, deposed Governor James W. Thockmorton signed a petition saying that there had never been any difficulties in executing the laws of Texas in Collin County.[30]

Thus, did Fitzhugh, another Lee man, contribute to the instability of the Corners' counties; however, he was eventually brought to justice—at least temporarily. A Collin County grand jury handed down several more indictments against him, but even after the charges, he continued to assault area freedmen and white Unionists. Troopers finally found and arrested the malefactor and by order of General Reynolds shipped him off to Austin. Reynolds soon paroled him but ordered him to remain in the state capital. Thereafter, the general listened to Fitzhugh's continuing heartfelt requests to return home; moreover, his friends also lobbied Reynolds who finally relented and allowed the whining Fitzhugh to return to Collin County where he again started to cause trouble as the War of Reconstruction ran its course.[31]

The rest of 1867 continued to see more violence in the Corners and the larger region of Northeast Texas. The Freedmen's Bureau tried to help former slaves in the area by establishing sub-stations in both Sherman and Greenville and by giving both agents small detachments of Union soldiers to call on if more trouble developed. Knowing that the bureau was close, Peacock's morale improved as did the morale of his supporters, but if Lewis thought that better days were ahead, he was wrong. Lee and the raiders still had Peacock as a primary target. Northeast Texas remained out of control. Lee and his men enlarged their killing field by riding through all the northern counties and temporarily joining such gangs as those lead by Baker and Bickerstaff when it was time to attack again. From Mount Pleasant, for example, came new reports of beatings and murders. Additionally, Capt. Charles Rand, bureau man in Clarksville, was set upon by a mob who accosted him in the county courthouse. After taking a savage beating, Rand asked that a personal guard of at least four men be sent to him. But the damage had already been done; because of the mob's actions, area Unionists and blacks were cowed. Fearing for their lives, they refused to come forward and name criminals. According to Bvt. Col. S. H. Starr, "there is a gang of men robbing negroes all over the country—of clothing, bedding, money, arms, household goods, and even crockery and cooking utensils, stripping their cabins. . . . Yet, whites and blacks are so intimidated . . . that they dare not name the parties although they know them." Continuing, Starr added that "lawlessness and violence prevail all over the country" and that "affairs are very much worse in all North-Eastern Texas at the present time than they have ever been since my arrival here."[32]

In January of 1868, the Lee-Peacock struggle again intensified when death-dealing recommenced. Lee and some of his men tracked the Unionist Hugh Hudson to Hopkins County and found him near the stage stop at Saltillo, a regular way station for stagecoaches, wagon trains, solitary travelers, and Dixon Lines. When they found Hudson, Lee and his men murdered him, an act of revenge because Hudson had killed Pierce, the physician who had treated and harbored Lee after Maddox shot him. Since Hopkins was Ben Bickerstaff country, Ben and some of his gang may have been involved and may have assisted Lee and his bunch.[33]

According to one account, the Mississippi physician W. C. Holmes—who had moved to Pilot Grove to take over Pierce's practice—was at a campfire at Saltillo when the murder occurred. He was on the stage headed east, planning to return to Mississippi to claim his bride and bring her to the Lone Star State. After supper, a man came near and asked Holmes if he would walk a piece down the road, saying that Hugh Hudson had just died. Holmes had never seen Hudson but had heard others describe him. Holmes believed that the dead man generally fit the description of Hudson. But the doctor was puzzled about being asked to see the body. Later, he surmised that the Lee men had requested him to view the corpse so that when he returned to Pilot Grove, he could confirm the killing and thereby help spread the terror. The incident ended when Holmes turned back toward his campfire and began walking away just as the Lee men started digging a hole into which to pitch the newly departed.[34]

In the spring of 1868, another Unionist, Elijah "Lige" Clark, met the same fate as Hudson. Although the Dixon family was firmly in Lee's camp, Clark was sweet on Hester Anne, Irish Jack's oldest daughter. He went to the Dixon place to court his belle. Lige thought that he could safely do so because he had been a childhood friend of all the Dixon children. After Anne invited him into the house, he placed his handgun on a table in the hall to let all know his call was friendly. Lige asked Hester Anne to go to a party with him. The girl apparently spurned his advances; whereupon, Clark became angry. Just as he was storming out of the house, Anne's brother Billy rode up. Lige and Billy had hard words, leading to an altercation, the childhood friendship notwithstanding. Just sixteen years old, Billy shot and killed Lige.[35]

Because of such murders, civilian Unionists in the Corners finally had had enough. Led by Peacock, they met in Pilot Grove to discuss their plight. No doubt Lewis and the others recounted the violence, terror, and murder. Peacock and the others then planned a course. They again began a petition wherein they wrote of all the atrocities that had occurred in the Corners. Peacock and a few others took the petition to Lt. H. E. Scott at Sherman. The civilians begged Scott for a sufficient number of troops to protect them from "the depredations and outrages of outsiders."[36] When they spoke of outsiders, Peacock and the others may have meant that ruffians like Bickerstaff, Baker, and their men had joined the Lee raiders in their attempts to clean out all the Unionists in the area. Scott was sympathetic to the Unionists plight. For the second time Corporal Herold and a small force were detached, Scott ordering them to go to Pilot Grove.[37]

After reaching their new post, Herold's contingent joined the civilian Unionists in the Corners and planned a joint campaign to destroy the Lee renegades. With Peacock serving as a scout and guide, a federal patrol went looking for Lee, Simp, Billy Dixon, Billy Clements, and Fletch Everheart, as well as Lige Clark whose loyalty was questioned. (At the time, the Unionists did not know that Lige was dead.) The troopers did not achieve immediate results; they failed to locate any members of the Lee bunch. One negative result of increased patrols was that, henceforth, Peacock's life was in even greater danger because the raiders identified him as the leading Unionist in the Corners, the one who was willing to fight. Lee and others believed that if they could but eliminate Peacock, their war would be won.[38] Now, Peacock's life was not worth straw.

After Herold's unproductive sweep, events started moving quickly. More death-dealing was at hand. Jack Dixon started a freight wagon loaded with cotton down the Jefferson Road with Billy and his cousin Charlie serving as the teamsters. On the return trip, they planned to haul back household goods. Meanwhile, area Unionists apparently learned of Clark's death. Assisted by civilian Union League members, one of whom was Peacock who served as a scout, Union soldiers led by Herold formed a posse. They intended to find Billy and bring him back to answer a murder charge for killing Clark. Billy evidently resisted arrest. Posse members killed him for the effort. Because he had not been a party to the Clark murder, cousin Charlie was left to go his own way.[39] There was no question about Bob Lee and his men seeking revenge for Billy's death; the only question was—when?

Accurate details surrounding the story of Billy's demise may never be known, for different accounts give contradictory information. Bob Lee, in his dubious 1868 letter in *Bonham Texas News,* has Billy being attacked by a party of thirty Union men—some troopers, some civilians—about twenty miles from Hog-Eye down the Jefferson Road. When attacked, Billy supposedly took refugee in the old Terry Mill. After Billy held the posse off for a time, the posse threatened to burn the mill down. The Unionists struck a bargain, saying that they would guarantee his safety if he would surrender. According to Bob, when Billy came to the mill door and threw down his weapons, the Unionists opened up on him, riddling him with lead. Then, Bob wrote, they robbed Billy's pockets and even stole his spurs.[40] G. W. King, a contemporary of Lee and Peacock, accepted part of Lee's tale—with one reservation. King held that Billy came out of the mill firing his six-guns. The posse had little choice but to kill him.[41]

Shortly after Billy's death, a major incident occurred in Pilot Grove. Corporal Herold and a small squad had identified one man on whom there was an outstanding arrest warrant. When the soldiers tried to arrest the man, he ran. A chase was on with Herold and his men in hot pursuit while the would-be escapee desperately tried to outrun his foes. Some Unionists in town joined the foot race. They included Peacock, L. D. Nance, James Maddox, and others. J. Alfred Drye—a man who frequently harbored Bob Lee—stormed out of his store, stopped the pursuers, and had words with Herold. Drye heatedly exclaimed that "no damned Yankee should pursue, fire upon, or arrest anyone in Pilot Grove . . . as long as he [Drye] could stand on his feet, or had a load in his six shooter." Drye then drew two pistols and told Herold that he (Drye) could raise fifty men in fifteen minutes, "enough to clear out the whole lay out," referring to Herold, his squad, and the Unionists with them. Drye added that "God dam him if he did not do it." Brave or foolhardy, Drye then had the audacity to fire on Herold and Pvt. Thomas Halley. The inept civilian missed both shots, but one ball passed through Halley's cartridge box and thereby gave the private a tremendous surprise. Next, J. W. Clements—another Lee man who was wanted—joined in, cutting loose on the soldiers and the loyal civilians.[42]

From store fronts and alley ways, other men fired on the soldiers and their civilian volunteers. Peacock immediately began returning fire as did the others with him. Luckily Drye, Clements, and their allies all missed their marks as the federals ducked for cover. No one was hurt, but in all the confusion, the wanted man got away. Peacock helped Corporal Herold and his men capture five of the men who had fired on them. Accompanied by Peacock and a few other civilians, the corporal's squad took them to Sherman, where Lieutenant Scott released three without charges because no witnesses could identify them as being the shooters, while two others, Drye and J. W. Clements, posted bonds of $2,000 each. Observers who identified Drye and Clements as two of the gunmen included Peacock, Nance, Maddox, and other Unionists who had participated in the battle.[43]

Meanwhile, the Lee bunch planned their revenge for Billy Dixon's death. Regardless of the exact circumstances of the youngster's death, one fact was clear: The gang intended to extract their pound of flesh, and Peacock was still their main target. On a beautiful May day, Lee and his raiders rode for the Pilot Grove vicinity, apparently on their way to Peacock's farm. The lucky Unionist, however, was on the road himself about a mile east of his farm when he spotted the renegades. Later reporting the event, he said: "I went on business a mile east of my house and saw Bob Lee, Simp Dixon, Dick Johnson, [William] Beard, and John Marshall coming in the direction of Pilot Grove. They all had guns." Continuing, Peacock added that "this was after the troubles had commenced around here. I had not been attacked by Lee at this time but had got information that they intended to kill me." Lewis added that "I understand that they intended to either kill all of the Union men or make them leave the country. I and other Union men have been in fear of our lives from these men and some have left the country and given away almost everything they had."[44] Peacock left unsaid the obvious—that he knew to duck for cover and not let the renegades see him.

Shortly, the Lee faction had at least two opportunities to gain a measure of revenge, and, again, both times the major target was Peacock. If Lee deprived the Unionists of their strongest leader, the others might be easier to control. James H. Morrisson, William McCallom, M. L. Boling, and Charles Saunders, all from Fannin County and the Corners area, later testified that in April of 1868 about four miles from Pilot Grove, they saw the "Man Eater," Dick Johnson, Simp Dixon, John Marshal, William Beard (alias "Jones"), and one other man they did not know. According to Morrisson, "they were all heavily armed, and Lee intimated that they were after Peacock and Saunders and that they would like to catch them on the prairie" so they could "burn their shirts [kill them]."[45] Saunders added that "Lee, Dixon and William (or John) Marshal cursed Lewis and his men and predicted that they would [kill Peacock] in less than a week."[46]

Brazenly, Lee and his comrades increasingly came into Pilot Grove, hoping to find Peacock or other Unionists alone. Other than enjoying themselves in the saloon, their only activity was to search for Peacock on each trip, while also looking for Maddox, Saunders, and other Unionists, but the guerrillas never found them. According to resident D. L. Lewis, he often saw Lee, Beard, John Marshal, and others in the village and "they seemed to be well armed. They had shot guns and some of them had pistols. Lee had [both] a shot gun and pistols."[47]

Continuing through April and May of 1868, the area's woebegone Unionists continued their plea for more troop support. Peacock continued to complain that lives were in danger whenever Lee and his men came to Pilot Grove. Further, many Union men had to stay out of town and obviously could not conduct their business with the renegades around. Peacock told military authorities that a large force was needed at the Corners. One of the loyal men, Jesse A. Ashberry, president of the Board of Registrars for Dallas County, proclaimed that Collin, Hunt, Dallas, and Kaufman counties were completely out of control. Ashberry added that all over the region, Unionists were forced to go into hiding, having to abandon their farms and homes. Peacock was among their number, now usually sleeping in the woods more often than before. Entire families became destitute as a result, said Ashberry. He appealed to the army, saying that many more troops were needed in order to restore law and order in the region.[48] Meanwhile, the Lee bunch had other successes. By June of 1868, after run-ins with Lee men, several Peacock allies had fled the Corners simply because they wanted to stay alive. They knew that Lee and his group would not be satisfied until they had killed all the Union leaders.[49]

Yet another attempt was made on Peacock's life, this time apparently led by the Dixons who wanted to avenge for Billy Dixon's death. On May 15, 1868, the outlaws, led by Simp Dixon, caught Peacock plowing his field. When the raiders started firing, the Unionist returned lead for lead, himself being an expert shootist and now going everywhere armed after his life had been threatened. Although the Lee men wounded Peacock, they could not get close enough for a kill. He saved his life by holding them off, perhaps also saving the lives of his wife Emaline and his young son John. After the shootout, Emaline dressed Lewis's wounds.[50]

Lee men soon came at Peacock again, this time catching him in Pilot Grove with Unionist Saunders but with no other allies present. Peacock and Saunders were vulnerable, and the Rebels wasted no time taking advantage. Determined to send them directly to the afterworld, the Lee bunch rushed the two loyalists with guns blazing, but they failed in their purpose. Although the *Sherman Courier* erroneously reported their deaths, as did Galveston's *Flake's Semi-Weekly Bulletin,* the two gritty Unionists saved their own lives once again by returning fire, thus holding the outlaws at bay yet another time. Peacock was wounded again in the shootout but survived.[51]

Shortly, Lee and his gang accosted John D. Coffee, a Peacock supporter, whom they shot and wounded while the man had his child in his arms. Luckily,

Coffee shielded his child, and both survived. Observers knew that the Dixons, led by Simp, and the Lee raiders, were responsible for the incident.[52] Although the Dixons failed to dispatch Coffee, Simp soon targeted other Unionists, including F. P. Alexander who was ambushed close to Orangeville, near Bonham, when he and eight other traders were returning from Jefferson. The unfortunate Alexander was wounded, but he escaped with his life. Fannin County's C. M. Wilcox, the district court clerk who reported the attack on Coffee and Alexander to the governor, went on to say that Simp and Bob Lee were carrying out a civil war in the Pilot Grove area. Continuing, Wilcox mentioned that a federal patrol along with four civilian volunteers, one of whom was Peacock, had lately been in Bonham. Wilcox said that Lee and his renegades attacked the patrol and killed three of the Union volunteers. Although a lot of lead was thrown around during the fight, Lewis was not harmed. Next, Wilcox casually mentioned that Cullen Baker was also involved in the attack, a statement showing that the outlaw leaders and their gangs often assisted one another. It was hard to know where one outlaw bunch left off and where another took its place. The district clerk closed his letter by saying, "I am told that 214 men have been killed within a short time in the section above referred to [the Corners vicinity]."[53]

Soon Lee had another opportunity to kill Peacock. In mid-May, members of the Corners' Union League held an evening meeting at the Nance family farm, for Dow Nance was one of the leaders of the loyalists. The men assembled in Dow's big horse lot. The group included Peacock; brothers Dan and Clay Saunders; John Baldock who was a close friend of Dow; "Doc" Wilson; James Maddox; and several other men. Someone sympathetic with the Lee gang (perhaps Lee's spy Dorinda Pierce) learned of the meeting and sent word to the captain who was hiding in Wildcat Thicket. Lee refused to bide his time any longer; the situation was perfect for a lightning strike.[54]

Out of the thicket stormed the raiders, one of whom may have been the professional gunman Bowman. Like an avalanche, the Lee-led bandits roared forward toward the Nance farm. When they got there, they caught Peacock and the other Unionists by complete surprise. As the shootout began, it appeared that Lee and the raiders could finally deal a death blow to Unionism in Corners Country. As gunfire continued, chaos reigned. Peacock and the others recovered, however, and made a stand, firing round after round, hoping to hold their enemies at bay. They did, but two of the Union men paid the supreme price before the surviving victims could accurately return fire and drive the marauders away. As the Lee bunch stole away with their only casualty being Dick Johnson who had been slightly wounded, Dow Nance and James Baldock lay dead near the corral. Dan Saunders was critically wounded but survived. Along with some other men whose names are lost to history, Peacock was also wounded yet again but lived. One of the men temporarily patched Lewis's wound which allowed him to return home to Emaline who treated the wound properly.[55]

A secondary version of the raid gives different details. It has the Unionists mount up at Nance's corral and ride north for fear that Lee and his followers might well know of their meeting. They were looking for a safe, hidden place. Lee's band set up an "ambushcade," Bob ordering that Peacock was his—and only his—target. In the affray, Lee—an excellent marksman—shot Peacock, wounding him severely but not killing him. The Unionist had been saved by his horse. On rocky ground, the steed swerved just as Lee fired, else Lewis would have certainly died.[56]

Whatever the details, two more Union leaders were now dead. Peacock and the others took the bodies home to their families. The Nance and Gentry families took Dow's death particularly hard. He left behind his pregnant wife Mary Anne, Parson Gentry's daughter, who was expecting her child at any time. On May 25, Lee and Simp Dixon murdered yet another area loyalist, Ruben Hogue, with Fannin County being the site of the slaying. Although contemporaries left no specific details, Lee and his men also killed yet another Unionist, Bud Favors, while two other men—Doc Wilson and James Maddox, staunch Peacock supporters—headed for a healthier climate than the Corners. Maddox ended up settling anew at Hornsby's Bend, a small place near Austin where he farmed and lived peacefully until his death in the early 1920s.[57]

Meanwhile, Lee and his wild bunch continued their terroristic campaign. According to Peacock, his adversaries made yet another attempt on his life. On June 15, he was out cow hunting with three other men, one being Saunders, when Lee and his raiders ambushed the Unionists who were "fired on from the brush," as Peacock put it. Although surprised, the loyalists quickly ducked for cover and returned fire. Lee and his men killed two of the Unionists and wounded Saunders again, but Peacock was lucky this time. He came away unscathed. Soon, Unionist J. D. Ivey, whose place was in Fannin County near the Corners, had a harrowing experience which proved that it was Lee who made the attack on June 15. In the midst of their campaign against Peacock, Lee and William Beard, who was still using the name "Jones," stopped at Ivey's house in late June. "I [Ivey] asked him [Lee] if he was Bob Lee 'the man eater.' He said he was. He said he and his 'boys' did the [latest] shooting."[58]

A few weeks later, Ivey was at a religious meeting at an area parson's house when others arrived, the new arrivals including Lee, Simp Dixon, Dick Johnson, and John Marshal. They were all armed, said Ivey, adding that Lee was definitely the leader. The fearful Ivey was seeing the heart of the Lee gang. He was most happy when the meeting ended, and he could return home.[59]

Shortly after Ivey saw Lee for the second time, an area bureau man reported that Baker, Bickerstaff, Lee, Jack English, Dick Johnson, Simp Dixon and "several more desperadoes of that class are banded together" and that they had "recently murdered six or seven white men."[60] Lee was personally responsible for two of the murders. He killed Peacock supporter Dan Saunders and another man who may also have been close to the Unionist leader, but few details exist about the slaying of Saunders or the other man. It is known that Lee himself shot both men off their horses and approached Saunders before he died, Lee telling him that it was nothing personal, that Saunders just ran with the wrong crowd. Losing Saunders—one of the staunchest Unionists in Lewis's camp—was a major blow to Peacock. No one could take his place.[61]

Such successful operations by the Lee outlaws and by other renegades in Northeast Texas—led by the now familiar Bickerstaff, Baker, English, Guest, Duty, and others—convinced General Reynolds that he had to plan a crackdown in Corners' Country and in the wider region as well. In addition, he was already receiving criticism for not acting more forcefully to bring law and order to Eastern Texas. Although he was tardy with his decision, the general now intended to give the Klansmen and desperadoes all the trouble that they could handle.

While Reynolds was still planning a campaign, Paris Bureau Agent DeWitt C. Brown again reported that there was now a cabal of outlaws who existed in loose alliances and that they had recently murdered several white men and an untold number of freedmen. Yet, they had enough citizen support that they could ride through the towns in their area "with not a soul to molest them."[62] According to Brown, the list now included Baker, Bickerstaff, "Indian" Bill English, George English, Dick Harper, Lee Rames, Guest, Duty, and others. Corners' area notables who made Brown's list included Lee as well as his friends: Dick Johnson and Sam (Simp) Dixon.[63]

Brown was correct in making his list and correct again when mentioning all the civilians who aided the brigands. For example, Bernard Patterson and family, whose farm was in Lamar County, helped Southern ruffians at every opportunity. Bernard's son James later recalled that Bickerstaff, Simp Dixon and others always hid in Patterson's three-acre grape orchard whenever they were in the area and that his father always sent him out with food and water to give to the desperadoes. An officer in the local pre-war Secession Club of Lamar County, Patterson supported the men because they claimed to represent the Lost Cause and because all of them wanted to clean out bureau agents, free blacks, and white Unionists. As if to prove that charges of conspiracy were accurate, Baker and four other men invaded Lee territory. They rode to Bonham where they found and killed a Unionist whom they had been pursuing. Because Lee always had good information supplied by supporters, he and some of his men probably welcomed their accomplice and helped the Baker party when they tracked and murdered the Union man.[64]

Certainly, with the Klan flourishing everywhere, with Lee and his raiders continuing to hold down the Corners Country, with Baker holding his own to the east, with Bickerstaff controlling his territory to the southeast, ex-Confederates using the Lost Cause and malefactors of all stripes seemed to be winning the War of Reconstruction or the "New Rebellion," as Northern newspapermen continued to call it. Peacock agreed that a new kind of war was ongoing, and he knew he was one of the foremost targets. Agent Brown was now absolutely certain that the outlaws were banded together and committed lawless acts such as robbery and murder and that they controlled virtually all the counties in Northeast Texas including the four counties that converged to create the Corners. They committed murders in one place and then rushed to hide in another where they assumed a new alias and invented another personal history.[65]

The desperadoes, along with Klansmen, were most successful. By the fall of 1868, Texas authorities had issued approximately 5,000 murder indictments, but they had executed just one man, a freedman from Houston. Analysis revealed that there were more killings in Northeastern Texas than in the southern, middle, or western parts of the state. Furthermore, such violence was understated, for freedmen and white Unionists failed to report many crimes out of fear of retribution that might result in their deaths. Many of the freedmen also stopped participating in politics. They gave up their right to vote rather than contend with massive white retaliation, including attacks by the Klans of the area or the outlaw gangs that insisted on white supremacy. In Northeast Texas, race relations resembled slavery, for—according to Bureau Inspector Sinclair—area freedmen "dare not and do not presume to do anything contrary to the will of those who in times past have dictated . . . their line of conduct."[66]

An incident involving Lee's ally Bickerstaff illustrated the audacity of the renegades. Riding with a certain Bowman (perhaps Mace Bowman) and a Baptist preacher named Ellis, Bickerstaff popped up in Navarro County in June of 1868, where his party robbed a freedman. Some of Corsicana's townspeople, apparently tired of such events, managed to find and arrest the robbers who were caught in the Corsicana countryside. But that night in camp, the outlaws overpowered a lone guard and escaped. The escapade showed that Bickerstaff had a long reach, indeed.[67]

Next, Fannin County authorities finally tried to crack down on the criminals. A county grand jury indicted Lee and Simp Dixon for the murder of Ruben Hogue. Pursuant to the indictment, Judge Hart issued warrants for the arrest of the two malefactors. The constable tried to served the warrants, but claimed that he could not because Lee and Dixon were always in the company of ten to twelve men, all heavily armed, each having from two to four six-guns. Each one also sported at least one double-barreled shotgun. The constable noted that he could not recruit a posse large enough to challenge the Lee bunch.[68] It is not known if the constable was honest or if he was a Lee partisan looking for excuses for not apprehending the desperadoes.

Chapter 6

Chaffee's Guerrillas and the Federal Crackdown

In June of 1868, Maj. Gen. Joseph J. Reynolds, commander of the Fifth Military District, decided to use massive force to suppress the Klan and the outlaw gangs operating in Northeast Texas, a difficult task when one remembers that Texas still had an Indian frontier and a defense perimeter that covered approximately 1,300 miles. Contending with that boundary bled away troops that could otherwise have been spared to uphold law and order in East Texas. Yet, before Reynolds actually put his plans in motion, Baker, Bickerstaff, Lee, and others took actions that may have forced the general's hand earlier than he anticipated.

The notorious Ben Griffith rode openly into Clarksville just after sundown on July 20, 1868. In addition to a double-barreled shotgun resting cocked across his saddle, he had three sixguns. A crowd gathered to hear him hold forth about his recent escapades, including the robbing and burning of an army commissary wagon train and the killing of two soldiers and five freedmen. He bragged that he and his men planned to rob another wagon train. After announcing that Baker, Bickerstaff, Bob Lee, and English were waiting for him in the bush, he disappeared into a store and soon emerged with a bottle of whiskey.[1]

After jumping back atop his horse, he shouted "look out niggers!" as he rode away, while Rebel yells and the laughter of the white crowd followed him. But before he left the town limits, he accosted freedman Charles Dyer and stole the black man's gun. Dyer ran to tell local bureau man Capt. Charles Rand, who had earlier been assaulted and viciously beaten by local malefactors. Rand, the local sheriff, and a posse of three (only three men in the entire town would volunteer) quickly pursued Griffin. They found him about a mile out of town on the Boston Road where he had drawn a gun on a young freedman, intending to kill him. Seeing the posse, Griffin spurred his horse for a getaway, hoping to reach Lee, Bickerstaff, English and their men, but shots from the posse knocked him off his horse and killed him. After watching that scene, Lee, Bickerstaff and the other raiders disappeared. Rand had Griffith's body buried in Clarksville and paid for the burial with funds that the brigand had on his person when he went to meet the grim reaper. In a later report to a superior, Rand said that the other renegades including Lee, Bickerstaff, and Baker had threatened to kill him to gain revenge for Griffith's death. Rand lamented that he had no protection. He ended his report with a classic understatement: "To stay [in Clarksville] alone with not a soldier within 60 miles and every second man a sympathizer with the desperadoes is to say the least very unpleasant."[2]

After Griffin's death, Baker, Bickerstaff, Lee and others became even more determined to escalate their all-out war on federal forces and to drive them from Northeast Texas. The raiders may have numbered up to seventy-five or so men, while having several hundred more volunteers who occasionally rode with them. In one early action, Baker ambushed Paris's Bureau man DeWitt Brown as he crossed the Bois d' Arc River near town, shooting his horse out from under him. That was enough for Brown: He quit his job and fled the area. Meanwhile, Bickerstaff and some of his bunch—including George Branch, along with G. G. and William Bowman—attacked another train of army commissary wagons. After taking control of the wagons, the polite Bickerstaff gave the teamsters a receipt for the goods and for their wagons. He left them standing in the road afoot before bidding them adieu and hauling his booty away. Why he did not kill the teamsters remains a mystery. Next popping up in Clarksville, Bickerstaff found that townspeople had laid siege to Rand's office, with the bureau man trapped inside. The miscreant and his band gleefully joined the siege, no doubt planning to rid the world of yet another Freedmen's Bureau agent. However, the innovative Rand managed to escape at night, he and his small military guard disguised in civilian clothes.[3]

The Brown incident, coupled with Rand's travail and Bickerstaff's antics, might have prompted Reynolds to initiate his campaign to bring the Northeast Texas murderers to heel. As well, some newspapers were increasingly taking the military to task for not doing enough. The editor of Marshall's *Texas Republican* wondered in print about just how long the federal troops would allow men like Lee, Bickerstaff, and Baker to dominate the Northeast Texas region and to continue their habit of "levying tribute" from the military and civilians alike. Further, Union men like Peacock continued to feed the army and the bureau information about the murders and mayhem inflicted on them. Peacock was adamant. He and other loyalists needed help.[4]

Acting independently, Lt. Thomas Tolman tried to supply that help. Soon to be promoted to captain, Tolman led another of his several cavalry raids on the Lee farm in early August of 1868 after Lee and his men robbed an army commissary wagon train. The lieutenant hoped that the sudden appearance of the patrol might catch Lee off guard. But, likely warned by his partisans, neither the terrorist nor any of his bunch were there when the troopers arrived. But Tolman searched the house and found at least two more bags of United States mail, with locks broken open. The desperado had obviously stolen the bags from the wagon train, then rummaged through them, taking whatever he wanted.[5] Tolman's latest raid, however, foreshadowed the federal crackdown that Reynolds was planning.

Just after Tolman's action, Reynolds on August 11 ordered Lt. Charles A. Vernou to tour Northeastern Texas to investigate the various disturbances including those made by Lee and his guerrillas. As if to announce their presence to Vernou, on August 14, near Sulphur Springs, Bickerstaff and a party of his men that included the man named Branch and the two Bowmans ambushed and murdered two of Capt. Adna R. Chaffee's troopers. Influenced by news of such atrocities, on August 27, General Reynolds placed a $1,000 reward on the heads of Bob Lee, Ben Bickerstaff, and Cullen Montgomery Baker, dead or alive, asking bounty hunters to deliver them to post commanders either at Austin or Marshall. The reward was later extended to include most of the unholy triumvirate's top lieutenants, including Simp Dixon and Dick Johnson. By September of 1868, the general had developed a plan involving cavalry and infantry. He ordered an additional regiment of infantry to reinforce the small garrison at Marshall, to await further orders. Cavalry would have been preferable, for the gangs of Lee, Bickerstaff, and Baker "were all well-mounted and organized." Men afoot could not even hope to cope with mounted renegades like Lee and his fellows in crime.[6]

Even as authorities posted rewards and began new field operations, the bandits seemed to become more audacious. Bickerstaff and his men, still operating in and around Hopkins County, corralled a freedman and whipped him smartly before allowing him to escape close to the small garrison in Sulphur Springs. The former slave ran straight for town and complained to the commander of the federal detachment. Then came a small squad of cavalry—led by the freedman—who rode straight into an ambuscade where several of the men were wounded, and some may have been killed. The gang that attacked them suffered no casualties because they were well concealed in a thicket. As subsequent events proved, Bickerstaff practically controlled the area, and a majority of white men in Hopkins County may have belonged to the Klan, which amounted to a large support group. The outlaw still had a long reach, roaming far and wide to spread destruction and to kill freed slaves and white Unionists, women as well as men.[7]

Indeed, Bickerstaff's range was greater than that of some of the other gang leaders. He struck as far south as Navarro County, also raiding into Wood, Van Zandt, and Hunt counties, Hunt considered to be Lee's territory. Whenever the captain learned that Bickerstaff was near, he and some of his band always found the bushwhacker, cooperated in his schemes, and accompanied him back to Hopkins County when the deathdealing was done. On at least one occasion, Bickerstaff, Lee, and some of their men held a meeting, then gave public notice that they intended to kill all freedmen caught between the Red River and Sander's Creek. Bickerstaff even negotiated with Lee and Baker about a formal alliance, proposing that the men band together under the command of Baker as the captain and go to all-out war with the Yankees. Although a formal arrangement never materialized, it was clear that the desperadoes continued to remain in contact and intended to work together closely to defeat the Reconstruction process. Baker, Bickerstaff, Guest, English, Lee, and other outlaws—all remained active and violent, as did the region's Klans.[8]

By September of 1868, the state of anarchy in the Corners counties and larger Northeast Texas became so pronounced that Deputy United States Marshal D. W. Stedham, headquartered in Sherman, wrote General Reynolds, declaring that "the law cannot be enforced without military assistance. In my portion of the district[,] my life has been threatened and I cannot perform my official duties without protection." Stedham said that on August 19 the gun-toting Rebel W. W. Gunter and several other armed men had prevented Stedham from executing a process of the United States Circuit Court by force of arms. He added that "on the night of the twenty-fifth of August[,] I had to make my escape from Whitesburg, Grayson Co. to avoid being murdered by a mob led by M. S. Diamond." The deputy also said that "the loyal men of this portion of Texas are threatened daily and have not the liberty of speech." The marshal advised General Reynolds that "I do think that the government ought to give her loyal citizens protection or they will be compelled to leave their homes and flee the country . . . to save their lives."[9]

Peacock and other loyal citizens of Grayson County agreed with Stedham and wanted military action. One major problem was that District Judge Hardin Hart still had not been able to hold court in Sherman because of all the death threats that he faced. That the courts could not meet had a demoralizing effect, said one citizen. In Grayson County's small freedman community of Keytown, for example, former bondspeople were packing up and leaving after having been threatened by the Lee gang, members of which also posted notes in the county at various places telling all Unionist officials to resign or face death. Collin County had the same problems. The McKinney jail was apparently porous, for most felons incarcerated there managed, with the help of friends, to escape. Shelton L. Howard was one who got away. He had murdered a bureau man in the Dallas area. As Dallas had no jail, authorities there took him to the McKinney jail, from which he soon escaped with the help of others. Although the military had earlier been removed from Sherman, in early September a new squad of fifteen soldiers arrived in town, but their small numbers meant that they could control only the county seat, not the countryside. In rural areas, loyalists like Peacock were still left to fend for themselves, a fact that Peacock continued to protest. He knew that his own life was in danger as were those of other Unionists. Yet, they could not just pick up and leave. Many had friends and relatives in the Corners counties. Plus, many had too much money invested in their farms or their businesses to flee.[10]

The editor of the *Paris Vindicator* greatly respected the desperadoes' power. Indeed, he was at his wits end. He suggested "buying off Lee, Bickerstaff & Co., by paying them a liberal subsidy."[11] Clearly, the federal commanders in Texas had to take stronger action to bring all malefactors to justice. In August, soon after he had ordered a company of infantry to reinforce Marshall, Major General Reynolds implemented his unfolding plan for a more forceful crack down. The heart of the strategy was to keep at least one hundred cavalrymen in the field at all times to pursue, to hound, to arrest, to kill the lawbreakers, or to drive them out of the region.[12]

Accordingly, Reynolds ordered Brevet Major Chaffee and Captain Tolman, then stationed on the Indian frontier, to take their companies of the Sixth Cavalry Regiment to Sulphur Springs. Once there, they were soon reinforced by another one hundred men. Sulphur Springs was a target because it had lately been besieged by outlaws. Observers had seen the unholy triumvirate—Lee, Baker, and Bickerstaff, along with English—in the county. Further, their alliance was becoming stronger, the gangs acting more in concert than ever before. Altogether, they could now assemble at least two hundred men, maybe more.[13]

Reynolds next ordered Lt. Col. S. H. Starr, commander at Fort Richardson, to detach sixty or seventy more cavalrymen to head a wagon train that would reinforce Chaffee and Tolman while also bringing supplies to them. The general then told W. B. Pease of Company D of the Seventeenth U.S. Infantry to reinforce the garrison at Sulphur Springs. Once in the town, Pease soon reported that he was at a post that was in the most lawless area of Texas. In October, he wrote superiors, telling them that the federals would need at least six months to clean out the area completely. Meanwhile, the general commanded that the federal forces *not* target non-violent supporters of the gangs and *not* destroy the private property of civilians. Then, by name, the general listed the quarry of Chaffee and Tolman: Lee, both English boys, Bickerstaff, John "Pomp" Duty, Elisha Guest, Baker, and all their men. The command gave the officers a list of civilian Unionists who they could call on for help. Peacock's name was on the list, and he was most willing to help the authorities and perhaps save his own life. Subsequent events would prove that he was fighting a losing battle.[14]

New depredations encouraged the federals to get tougher. In October Baker and some of his men went to Bowie County where they ambushed and murdered Bureau Agent William S. Kirkman in the middle of the night while he was getting ready to leave his post the next morning. Then, crossing into

Arkansas, Baker and his minions murdered an army officer along with Porter Andrews, who was a federal tax collector, and Bureau Agent Hiram F. Willis. For good measure, they also killed the black driver who directed their coach.[15]

Later writing a history of the Sixth Cavalry, William H. Carter, a member of the unit during Reconstruction, remembered that "after the close of the Rebellion the country [East Texas] was overrun with desperadoes and outlaws who were even worse than the hostile Comanches . . . [the Sixth Cavalry had] to institute lawful proceedings where anarchy reigned."[16] Carter added that Bob Lee's gang was "one of the most notorious" in Northeast Texas.[17]

Before organizing for the new crack down, a few of Lee's men had been killed and that made the work of Chaffee and Tolman a little easier. Earlier, on March 7, 1868, Corporal Herold of Troop D of the Sixth Cavalry demonstrated the success the federals could have if circumstances were favorable. Herold left Sherman with a detachment of thirteen enlisted men and some civilian guides. Peacock joined them when they arrived in Pilot Grove. Then the hunt was on. With Peacock serving as guide and scout, the patrol's quarry was Lee and any of his raiders whom they could find. The search led to the Battle of Read Creek Swamp where the detachment killed two of Lee's men and captured another five. Peacock especially had his eyes looking for Lee, but the captain and most of his important lieutenants got away. Still, Herold's actions proved that a campaign of attrition stood a good chance of success.[18]

Once Chaffee and Tolman arrived in East Texas, Tolman and a small squad rode into Sulphur Springs where Bickerstaff had his unofficial headquarters. Knowing Lee's power, Chaffee and Tolman also sent a small detachment to Pilot Grove. Tolman then turned his attention to Bickerstaff while Chaffee took off on a scout. Since Bickerstaff controlled the county, events proved that Tolman faced a serious problem. Before reinforcements could arrive, his small force was soon besieged by the desperadoes. Meanwhile, Lee, Bickerstaff and their men continued to bushwhack soldiers and to steal army supplies. Bickerstaff often set up the federals by using clever ruses, mostly by taking advantage of area blacks. In August, for example, shortly after the first contingent of federals reached Sulphur Springs, he whipped a freedwoman smartly, then let her go.[19]

After the woman reported the assault, Tolman sent a seven-man patrol under Sgt. Edward Grey to investigate the charges. As the patrol returned to headquarters, Bickerstaff ambushed the Yankees, killing Gray, another trooper, and a freedman who was serving as a guide. Bickerstaff had an estimated twenty to thirty men—most having both pistols and shotguns—who simply overwhelmed the small squad of federals. The death of a Private Miller was particularly brutal. First, a brigand shot the young man off his horse and then approached him on foot. The boy begged for a drink of water just before the murderer shot him point-blank in the head.[20]

A courier reported to Tolman even as the battle was raging. The captain sent reinforcements, but the raiders had fled by the time the rescuers arrived. Next, Bickerstaff assembled about 150 ruffians who virtually surrounded Sulphur Springs and continued the siege of the rest of Tolman's small command. Bickerstaff audaciously sent word to the captain, saying that he could assemble 350 men if necessary to drive the Union men out. The outlaw told Tolman the truth. Within a short time, the scourge assembled even more, his army swelling to at least 500 men, some of whom were Lee men. Believing that he was in total control, Bickerstaff warned Tolman that if the troops did not leave, he would exterminate them, that he would kill each and every one of the Northerners. Meanwhile, Tolman reported to superiors that with the small force under his command—only twenty-five men, some of whom were sick and therefore unfit for duty—he could do practically nothing at all, especially because the Rebels continued to receive the help of local civilians who provisioned them and warned them of any approaching enemies. The outlaws did not fight military-style, Tolman added. Instead, the captain said, "the desperados . . . greatly outnumber us and fight from the bush."[21] Luckily, the garrison was a good one. Surrounded by a stockade ten-feet high with open ports to fire through, the camp encompassed an entire city block. That strong base allowed Tolman and his handful of men to withstand the ongoing siege.[22]

Earlier, Tolman suggested a good tactic for dealing with the raiders and Klansmen for implementing Reynolds's overall strategy. First, the captain wanted a large number of reinforcements, requesting at least 200 men, with the forces and supplies concentrated in two places: Pilot Grove (a move that showed grudging respect for Lee's nefarious abilities and also recognizing that civilian Unionists like Peacock would help the troopers) and Sulphur Springs (a move that showed even more grudging respect for Bickerstaff, the renegade with the longest reach). Tolman told superiors that in all of Northeast Texas many more soldiers were needed to "put down the desperate gangs of Bickerstaff, English, Baker, and Lee, all of which are connected together." Next, Tolman advocated a virtual war of attrition: "The best method to get rid of them would be to send a large force to move from Pilot Grove, near where Lee operates down through this part of the country[,] and to keep the force in the country till the desperadoes and outlaws are driven out [or killed]."[23] He planned to hound the outlaws, to chase them all over East Texas, and to pick them off one-by-one if necessary. Tolman was a hard man who had a lot of sand. Like Peacock, he hated the men who were spreading so much terror. He wanted to give the guerrillas an appropriate send-off while putting them on the road to hell.[24] His proposed strategy exactly matched that of Reynolds who became even more determined to take effective action.

The first problem, however, was to relieve the trapped troopers by sending reinforcements to break the siege. Desperadoes and Klansmen had now stopped all supply wagons from reaching Tolman. His command was isolated and needed outside help; the troopers were running out of food and water. To relieve the beleaguered officer and his men, Lt. J. H. Sands in Pilot Grove took up the march on September 3, 1868, with most of his thirty-five men. In his later report, Sands placed the number of Bickerstaff's men at near 500. Apparently, many of the otherwise sober citizens of Hopkins County had joined the siege and had continued to bawl about burning out the federals and killing them. As fortune would have it, Sands also had at his disposal Lieutenant Vernou's detachment from the Fourth Cavalry and a Lieutenant Larenburg's force from the Seventh Infantry, both units then being temporarily in Pilot Grove.[25]

With Vernou taking overall command, Sands also ordered a detail at Sherman to join his contingent. Sands's men covered twenty-three miles the first day, even though the forced march took the federals through the dense thickets that were the heart of Lee's stomping grounds. Peacock and at least one other local Unionist led the column, serving as scouts, while warning Sands that the Lee bunch could strike at any minute from out of the bush. After listening to Peacock, Sands decided to take precautions. He was a professional no-nonsense soldier like Tolman, and he decided to shift to a war footing. He sent out skirmishers to prevent a surprise ambuscade. The lieutenant's action kept the Lee gang entirely at bay. Sands also placed guards around Lieutenant Vernou's supply wagons. Peacock stayed close, continuing to advise Sands. That night Sands set out pickets. He was prepared to fight a pitched battle if necessary. In the second day's march, Sands's relief column, as if converging on a battle site, covered an unheard of fifty-six miles, a magnificent logistical feat that must have been hard on both man and beast. Peacock guided the detachment through the countryside, showing them the shortest route to Sulphur Springs.[26]

After making preparations to fight his way into Sulphur Springs, Sands marched in to relieve Tolman and found his command "under arms and ready to give us a volley." Bickerstaff and his followers had scattered, preferring not to truck with a large force of professional sodiers. But Vernou added that "Capt. Tolman and his command [were] in a desperate position," having been surrounded for a week by at least 200 men who "cut him off" from his communications. Tolman had acted bravely, holding the post with a small force that ultimately numbered just thirty-one men, some of them sick, against vastly superior forces. But, then, he was a disciplined military officer up against civilian riff-raff who hesitated to engage in a stand-up battle. Later, the federals received word that a local farmer who lived about three miles from town was purported to be one of the leaders of the desperadoes. Tolman dispatched Sands, Peacock, and a force of about fifty to go to the farm and investigate. They surprised about 150 raiders who had gathered there. A fight ensued wherein several horses became the only mortalities before the outlaw band lost heart and fled.[27]

The federals were successful in breaking the siege, in subduing and scattering the enemy, and in sending them scampering for the thick bush near the farm. The Union men captured several stolen horses and a number of small arms. Led by Peacock, they chased the fleeing malefactors, killing two of them and capturing a few more. That night Sands set out pickets to guard against a surprise attack. With no effect, the enemy forces fired on the pickets about midnight, but the guards responded in kind and quiet returned to the camp. The next day, near Sulphur Springs, a guerrilla force led by Bickerstaff attacked a commissary train led by a Lieutenant Robinson. When Sands learned of the development, he personally led a twenty-five man relief column to save Robinson and his men. With Peacock leading the way, Sands's force surprised some of Bickerstaff's men and chased them into nearby woods. Later praised by his superiors for swift action, Sands managed to win his battle; Bickerstaff broke off the engagement and fled rather than continue to truck with the Union forces.[28]

The next day, Sands took a column of about fifty men back to Pilot Grove. About ten miles out of Sulphur Springs, his skirmishers ran into another surprise attack but managed to drive their enemies into a dense thicket. Sands tried to pursue them but discovered that it was impossible because of the denseness of the bush. Sands's men moved on to Pilot Grove without further incident. Ater his Sulphur Springs campaign in the War of Reconstruction, Sands reported that "more troops are badly needed in this country and at this post [Pilot Grove] which I should not be surprised at any moment to have attacked." He also asked for more horses because many of his men had no mounts—and infantry could not chase the cavalry of Bob Lee and his raiders.[29] Once back on duty at Pilot Grove, Sands and his men, with Peacock serving as a scout, patrolled the area and arrested several criminals, a move that a Unionist observer said had a "good effect" in restoring the confidence of the "law and order portion of the people." Sands's work, the observer continued, had caused "many of the lawless [people] to leave that vicinity [Pilot Grove] and disorganize[d] them."[30]

Yet, the guerillas were far from cowed, according to the editor of the *Paris Vindicator,* the one who had earlier proposed that the people buy peace from "Lee, Bickerstaff & Co." by paying them to leave honest people alone. According to the editor, the violent men were doing the work of the Democratic party in bringing chaos to Northeast Texas. The editor was referring to the ongoing political struggle between the Democrats and the Republicans to control the state.[31]

Found near a freedmen's village in Lamar County, sticking on trees along Sander's Creek, was the following warning:

> Notice is hereby given to all it may concern that Biggerstaff [sic] & Co., and Bob Lee & Co., will visit this neighborhood on the 12th inst., and will continue from day to day until the Radical Party is exterminated or shows a perfect willingness to support the democratic party for any and every office whatever, this notice is principally intended for Charles Lee, and the other colored gentry living between the Red River and Sander's Creek. All that cannot comply with the order had better hunt holes in the earth at once. We hope that all those who belong to the Conservative Party will sustain us.
>
> Yours, Friends to the Constitution and enemies to Congress.[32]

The note proved that Lee and Bickerstaff understood the political situation in Texas and that they had good chances of survival if they continued to drape themselves in the Lost Cause and posture as Confederate heroes trying to save the Lone Star State for the old pro-slavery party. On the heels of the Sander's Creek announcement came a report from Sherman that Lee and other brigands had written all Republican office holders and other Union men, Peacock included, in Grayson County and ordered them to resign immediately and to leave the county. Further, Lee ordered all freedpeople in the area to leave the state altogether, the outlaw saying that disobedience would mean "immediate, instant death."[33]

After saying that the recent arrival of troops at Pilot Grove had to a degree restored area Unionists' confidence in law and order, Sherman Republican C. C. Binkley said that more needed to be done in Northeast Texas generally. With Grayson County Judge J. D. Gurge concurring, Binkley pin-pointed some of the causes of the upsurge of violent suppression. He asserted that "the lawless manifestations may be accounted for from various reasons." He explained that one of the principal objects to be attained by "the notice and threats to Union men, white and black[,] was to discourage them and render them powerless at the anticipated Election." He added that the outlaws tried "to compel the Unionists through fraud to leave the country, this having to a great extent been accomplished."[34]

In mentioning the anticipated election, Binkley referred to the 1869 statewide contests that would pit different wings of the Democratic party against the new Republican party headed by Civil War veteran Edmund J. Davis, who fought for the Union during the conflict before coming home and entering politics. It was expected that the election would be hotly contested, and many Democrats searched for any means, fair or foul, to discourage white Unionists and freedmen from voting. Lee was playing into the situation, hoping to be seen as a great defender of Texas; whereas, Peacock was talking to the freedmen, asking them to remember the party that had freed them and to remember all the death and destruction that the raiders had caused.[35]

One person to come under increasing attack by the desperadoes was the intrepid Hardin Hart, the one-time Civil War Unionist and Freedmen's Bureau agent who had become judge of the Seventh Judicial District of Texas, the district including all the Corners' counties along with Denton, Wise, Jack, Young, Clay, Montague, and Cooke. Threatened by Lee and other renegades, Hart rode to Pilot Grove to seek the protection of Lieutenant Sands and Peacock, from whence he contacted Governor Elisha Pease. Writing on September 17, 1868, Hart told Pease that "I have not been able to hold court at Grayson, Fannin and Hunt on account of a regular organized band who has overrun the country."[36] Continuing, he added that "I intend to hold court in Collin . . . [but] I do not think that I can hold court at any other place except that without a guard of soldiers." Further, he needed soldiers to enforce his orders; civilian officers would not. He went on to ask Pease for a squad of ten men, commanded by a commissioned officer whom he wanted to meet him in Denton.[37] Hart's plea prompted Governor Pease to contact General Reynolds. The governor recapitulated Hart's circumstances and averred that the judge was "a man who is not easily frightened and I am satisfied that such a guard is necessary."[38]

G. A. Evarts of Sherman echoed the concerns of Judge Hart and Governor Pease. Writing on September 1, he contended that "in the Northern portion of Texas We have had no District Courts this year since in April. . . . Our Judge, the Hon. Hardin Hart, as we learn, believes that he cannot hold the Courts only at the sacrifice of his life." Evarts said that "the very fact that no courts have been held has had a demoralizing effect." He added that a number of people charged with felonies were in the McKinney jail, awaiting trials that had been postponed because of general violence and threats against Judge Hart. Evarts wondered how long the prisoners could be securely kept in a porous jail where several men had already made successful escapes. Unknown persons, he continued, have told freedmen to leave the county or be killed. Of course, one of those unknown people was Bob Lee.[39] White Unionists, too, Everts held, would have to leave to stay alive. W. L. Taylor, Clerk of the District Court, and L. Bostick, Sherman justice of the peace, endorsed Evarts statement, all three men begging for help.[40]

Lieutenant Vernou, who played a key role in helping Sands relieve Tolman, added his voice to those of Evarts, Buckley, Governor Pease, Hardin Hart, and others. The lieutenant told superiors that "I cannot give you any idea of the state of affairs in this country. The whole Population of this country with few exceptions are in arms against the government."[41] Vernou went from Pilot Grove to visit the civil officers of Grayson County in Sherman. He learned in Sherman that before the small contingent of fifteen federals had returned to the county seat, brigands had been doing pretty much what they pleased. In a telling comment about the state of affairs in the Corners counties, Vernou recommended that to secure Pilot Grove, an entire company of cavalry would be necessary. That was exactly what Peacock and others had earlier asked to be done.[42]

Previously, Vernou had requested that a force of at least 200 men be sent to pacify all of Corners Country. After talking with Peacock, Vernou well understood the dangers involved in dealing with the Lee raiders.[43] Although Reynolds originally ignored much of the advice given by Vernou and civilians like Evarts and Peacock, he tried to do as requested. The general detailed the guard that Hart requested by ordering the command at Fort Richardson to send the men to protect the judge and, perhaps, keep him alive even though he was a primary target of the Lee men, second only to Peacock himself.[44]

Once Chaffee and Tolman implemented General Reynolds's larger plan, they continued to rely on Peacock as an advisor and as a scout. Helped by only a handful of civilian Unionists like Peacock, Chaffee and Tolman had to use harsh measures to get results, such harsh measures that the two officers and their men became known as "Chaffee's Guerrillas." Many civilians throughout the area who aided and abetted the murderers found themselves brutally treated by Chaffee's men, the punishment for some including being strung up by their thumbs. Many Unionist observers noted, however, that the bloody business of finding Rebel murderers forced harsh measures to bring the law breakers and their accomplices to heel. After all he had been through and all that his friends had suffered, Peacock well understood that the troopers were engaged in a new type of warfare.[45]

Although Tolman later faced a military tribunal that disapproved of his methods and reprimanded him for the brutal discipline that he imposed on his troopers and handed out to civilians as well, the tactics brought some success. Chaffee and Tolman chased Lee, Bickerstaff, and other raiders across all of East Texas. In a three-month campaign, the federals traveled a total of 1,000 miles, and troopers caught and killed several of Bickerstaff's gang who were brave enough to come into the Pilot Grove saloon. Peacock was in town, alerted the federals, and then helped them dispatch the desperadoes. Peacock had won another victory. Before they were killed, Bickerstaff's men might well have been searching for Bob Lee, hoping to put themselves under his protection so that they could enter Lee's hidden place in Wildcat Thicket.[46]

Even as the federals were tasting a little success, many Lee sympathizers continued aiding and abetting him and his wild bunch. Such supporters included John W. Marshal, Sr., and his family. In mid-September, a Sergeant Swift led a detachment of troopers to do some business in Hog-Eye, where the group camped for a night. The next day on the return trip to Pilot Grove, they passed close to Marshal's farmhouse. Within a mile of the place, some of the soldiers, including Cpl. William Edwards, saw two men jump atop their horses and gallop away, as if trying to escape. That caused the squad to veer toward the house. Marshal's wife came out, and Swift asked about the men who rode away. She claimed that one was her son, John, Jr., and that the other was one of his friends. Then, she pointed in the wrong direction, apparently hoping to confuse the troopers. Sergeant asked why they had run. The woman said they did not "run. They walked."[47]

After Swift said that "I have heard about some of your doings around here," the woman countered with "and I have heard of some of yours." Realizing that he would get no truthful information from the woman, Swift gave orders to fall in, and the squad rode away. "When we were about a hundred yards from the house," the sergeant later reported, "they commenced blowing a horn, and when we were about two hundred yards away . . . I looked back and saw a flag near the top of the house . . . sticking out a small hole . . . someone was waving it."[48] Yet, Sergeant Swift knew that to return would only lead to a new signal to tell the renegades to stay away and that the woman would only spin more falsehoods.[49] In addition to the Marshals, a Blankenship family who lived in the Corners area also harbored Lee and other members of his gang when necessary, providing food, water, and supplies, including ammunition.[50] Such was the nature of Corners Country during the War of Reconstruction. Such was the nature of things that men like Swift, Peacock, and other Unionists had to deal with.

John Marshal, Sr., however, was soon brought to justice when Major Chaffee personally led a detachment out of Sulphur Springs and returned to the Marshal place on November 8. The major arrested Marshal, charging him with bushwhacking, with being a member of the Lee raiders, and with harboring other members of the gang. Chaffee took Marshal to the guardhouse in Sulphur Springs and tossed him into it. Marshal had plenty of company. Chaffee's guerillas had arrested twelve more men. Charged with being members of Bickerstaff's gang were A. G. Vandiver, George Branch, G. G. Bowman, William Bowman, and the Reverend William Ellis—all languished in the guardhouse. Chaffee was also holding several others on various charges, including assaulting freedmen.[51]

Meanwhile, Lieutenant Vernou remained in the field, continuing to gain information for Reynolds and other superiors. After talking with locals in several towns, the lieutenant reported that Lee was one of the most popular men in all the counties that converged at the Corners. At one point, Vernou returned to Pilot Grove to inspect the area and to confer with Peacock and Lieutenant Sands, who had returned to Pilot Grove with a small detachment of men. Pilot Grove Unionist C. C. Binkley told Vernou that prior to the troops' arrival, there had been a total disregard for law and order and that Union men and the freedpeople were constantly in danger because of Lee, his gang, and other malefactors like Bickerstaff and Cullen Baker. Binkley went on to say that Sands and his men—given the serious problems they faced—were doing a good job. Speaking to Vernou, Peacock agreed with Binkley, adding that under no circumstances should the troopers leave Pilot Grove, for more lives would be forfeit.[52]

Making another report on October 19, 1868, Vernou told General Reynolds that Sands was indeed doing a good job even though he only had thirty-five men. He added that about fifteen civilian Union men were aiding Sands, performing the work of enlisted men for corn and rations. Peacock and some of his close associates were included in the civilian group, many of them knowing that they were fighting for their very lives. The "Man Eater" was after the loyal civilians, intending to kill them, Vernou said, adding that many of the white Unionists—like some area freedmen—continued hiding out in the woods at night to ensure that they would live to see sunrise. Peacock was one of those Unionists; fearing for his life, he began spending most of his nights sleeping in the brush near his house. He remained close enough to watch his place and to protect Emaline and John Edgar, if necessary. Lee's guerrilla war against the forces of the Union was definitely escalating and becoming more effective, even though the soldiers had occasional victories. Lieutenant Vernou added that Lee appeared to have the support of many civilians who "would not only give him all the aid in their power, but will even help him with force of arms if necessary." That judgement parallels the local lore of Corners Country, a tale about how many a farmer kept a full crib of corn for the Lee bunch's horses should the gang decide to come their way. Despite the long odds of catching Lee, Sands kept a non-commissioned officer and a detachment of several men lying in the brush near Wildcat Thicket, hoping to find Lee going in or coming out. Peacock occasionally joined them, for he did have a little knowledge about the area.[53]

Peacock's ally Judge Hart faced a tragedy at the same time. Sometime between August and the end of September, guerrillas found the judge's nephew, Capt. Martin Hart's son, in Hunt County without protection. They murdered the young man. His mother and widow signed a joint affidavit that implicated certain parties in the murder plot, but the new sheriff of Hunt County failed to take action. W. B. Pease, a former bureau agent, now commanding the post at Sulphur Springs, intervened and convinced the sheriff to go after the two alleged killers, one named Wings and the other named B. Harris, both of whom belonged to the Lee gang. An informant, a young man named Graham, who apparently joined the raiders but had second thoughts, told Pease that he had seen the crime and would testify in court. To assure that the sheriff and his posse did their work, Lt. William Van Horne and a five-man squad of troopers accompanied the posse. Pease then set out pickets on the roads leading to the homes of the murderers. Close to nightfall, just as the posse was reaching the house of one of the raiders, Van Horne, a former bureau agent, and others saw two parties of six to eight mounted men riding toward the house from opposite directions, but when the strangers saw the soldiers, both parties retreated and took to the woods for cover.[54]

On reaching the house, the posse noted that the place was forted-up, ready for battle. It was a dog-trot with chinks between some logs removed to make loopholes from which to fire rifles, shotguns, and six-guns. Although gunplay was a possibility, the sheriff convinced Wings and Harris to surrender peacefully after Lieutenant Van Horne promised that they would remain in the hands of the civilian authorities and would not be put in the hands of the United States Army. Inside the house were five men, some women, and several fretful children. Even after being arrested, one of the men bragged to Van Horne that if the posse had arrived a few minutes later, their friends would have arrived, and a "fierce resistance" would have been offered.[55]

Although it was twilight, after Wings and Harris agreed not to try to escape, the sheriff foolishly allowed them to ride their own horses to Greenville, nine or ten miles away. Of course, the twin terrors did not keep their pledges. Instead, when the riders reached a strip of woods near a ravine, Wings and Harris let out a yell, spurred their horses, raced them toward the woods, disappearing into the darkness. Their yells were likely a signal, for unseen parties in the woods answered with their own yells. Young Graham, who was still riding with the gang to gain more information, later told Van Horne that about fifty men, twenty-five on either side of the road, had been paralleling the route of the posse. The desperadoes were prepared to attack if necessary to liberate their fellows. Although at the time Van Horne did not know how numerous the enemy was, he wisely decided not to pursue with his small squad, especially not through a thick forest in the dead of night. On behalf of the Lee men Wings and Harris, ruffians soon threatened to kill the young murder victim's mother and wife, for the two women had named the killers.[56]

After Pease and his military contingent left Greenville, several men implicated in the murder gave up to civilian officials, but Wings was not among them. Further, those who surrendered were accompanied by at least fourteen other Lee men, all heavily armed, some of whom fired pistol shots into Judge Hart's tavern, where the two women were hiding. While shooting, at least one desperado shouted that the women "should leave the county, that they [the gang] would not allow them to live in it." About forty other raiders picketed all the roads leading to Greenville. They turned away anyone who might give evidence against their friends. Some members of the Lee bunch openly proclaimed that there would be a trial and that their friends would be declared innocent, for there would be no eye witnesses. The guerrillas also warned that no one who testified against the murderers would leave the town's public square alive. Local authorities had no choice but to postpone their examination of the crime.[57]

Straightaway, 150 men showed up for a meeting in the rural neighborhood where the murderers lived. Unanimously, they agreed to fight to stop the conviction of their friends, saying that they could raise another 125 allies and would have ample guns to drive the soldiers out of Hunt County. Pease later held that most of the men belonged to the Ku Klux Klan. Further, an informant said that many of the men had come from far and wide in groups. One contemporary account reported that Bickerstaff and Guest were there as were many others from all over Northeast Texas. They introduced themselves as "Bob Lee men," "Bickerstaff men," "Farrar men," and "Marshal men." Some of the renegades later learned the identity of Pease's informant, the young Graham. Whereupon, B. Harris, his son Thomas, James Babb, and Thomas Coker all vowed to kill the brave heart.[58]

Reporting to superiors, Pease gave a darker picture of affairs in Hunt County than ever before. The raiders were gathering forces and becoming bolder as their numbers swelled. Both Lee and Bickerstaff were involved while young Graham was still under a death threat. Amid false rumors that raiders had killed Judge Hart, the judge's life was not worth straw. Given the conditions, the rumors could become facts at any time. Anonymous parties sent one magistrate a written notice that he must "quit the country" to live. Just the night before, Pease reported that ruffians fired on a small military patrol on the outskirts of Greenville. He added that "no freedman is safe beyond the limits of a military post, and Union men are in constant danger."[59] Ending his report, Pease believed that the only way to restore order was to wait until Chaffee and Tolman returned to the Greenville area and then launch a massive campaign against the law breakers.[60] In sum, Pease's report left no doubt that the Second Civil War was still ongoing and that Bob Lee remained one of the former Confederates' most sought-out ringleaders.

Tolman agreed with Pease and continued to try to take the battle to the enemy. Leading a squad of troopers, he went after Wings, the killer of Hart's nephew, who was reported to be in Wood County, near his home deep in the forest of the countryside. Once Tolman arrived, he searched the house but found only Wings's wife. He surmised that the man was hiding and sleeping in the woods and that his wife was supplying him food and water. The captain also learned from an informant that Bickerstaff, along with his constant companions, one Porter and one of the Bowman boys, had been seen in the vicinity. Tolman picked up their trail but lost it when his quarry crossed the Sabine. Next, the captain made for Bickerstaff's place in Hill County—the desperado took the name "Wilson" there—a spread earlier visited by Chaffee. Tolman reached and searched the property, but Bickerstaff was nowhere to be found. The captain did find, however, a large cache of stolen property, including government commissary stores and a wagon that belonged to a freedman from Jefferson. Tolman continued to follow the trail until he reached Ellis County where he located and arrested Porter and Bowman, but, again, Bickerstaff escaped. Tolman then made for Sulphur Springs, carrying his two prisoners in tow.[61]

In October, Union authorities received word that Lee was again temporarily using John W. Marshal, Sr.'s house near the Corners as another hiding place. For months Marshal had been under suspicion of harboring Lee and members of his gang; yet, each time federals placed Marshal in jail, he managed to get out. Peacock piloted a squad of troopers to the Marshal place, hoping to find and arrest Lee and any of his men who might be around. In near silence, the soldiers surrounded the house at 4:00 a.m. on October 5. After they called to the house and received no response, pandemonium broke loose as Peacock and the federals stormed the place. Once inside, the government men saw that Lee was nowhere to be found, but the squad arrested John W. Marshal, Sr.—again. He was later charged with aiding and abetting the Lee gang—again. Three Lee men in the house managed to make a run for it, but Peacock and a few other men gave chase and caught them about 250 yards away. Both were well armed but surrendered. Peacock identified them as John Marshal, Jr., William Marshal, and William Beard, all of whom were charged with the same crime as Marshal, Sr. A search of the house turned up just three double-barreled shotguns, something not unusual.[62]

After being lodged in a Pilot Grove jail, two of the detainees, called "notorious desperadoes," escaped in November. Headquarters investigated and held Lt. H. P. Eakin responsible and sternly reprimanded him.[63] But, other terrorists remained incarcerated. Shortly after the arrest of the Marshals and Beard, Lee threatened to attack the post at Pilot Grove to secure the release of the remaining prisoners, most being members of his guerrilla band. Warned by Peacock, officers led by Eakin took rigorous action to fortify and to make the post battle-ready. Their preparations must have discouraged Lee who decided not to mount an attack.[64] Meanwhile, the two Lee partisans who broke out of jail were still on the loose. But the hunt was on for them and for all of the Lee raiders, including their nefarious leader, a hunt made all the more difficult because so many people still shielded Lee while continuing to hold Lewis Peacock responsible for the area troubles. They were correct in part. Lewis remained the most outspoken Unionist champion in Corners Country and was obviously a brave man who backed his words with action when necessary.[65]

Even as Peacock was doing all he could to help the authorities, the federals soon missed an excellent chance to bring Lee to justice. En route to Pilot Grove from Sulphur Springs in early November, Lt. L. A. Abbott conducted a scout looking for Lee. The patrol surprised the captain and one of his men—a member of the Dixon clan—riding down the road about three miles from Pilot Grove. Abbott ordered a charge from about 300 yards away from the terrible twosome; whereupon, the outlaws left the road and spurred their horses toward the bush in an attempt to escape. Lee's horse stumbled and went down, throwing the criminal to the ground. But he rolled up just as one of Abbott's men was reaching him. Lee knocked the federal off his horse and commandeered it. He and his comrade escaped, while the federals ended up in possession of Lee's horse (one he had stolen, of course), his saddle (also stolen), his spare ammunition, and his whiskey flask.[66]

Lee remained on the loose to commit more depredations. At one point either he or his men, possibly Simp or Dick, killed the brothers Dol and Tom Waters, both of whom were close to Peacock and Henry Boren. But federals continued to stalk Lee and his most important lieutenants. In mid-November, the new Pilot Grove commander Lt. F. Maytheny received intelligence that some area settlers were harboring Lee and several of his men, all of whom had been within two miles of the lieutenant's camp. They apparently watched the town and the troopers, Lee hoping for a chance to attack. Maytheny sent out a scouting party that was in the field for three days. The scout's leader received word from Peacock and other Unionists that Tip Cole of Collin County had also harbored and fed Lee and several of his men and that Lee would probably attend a circus at Farmersville on November 19. The sergeant commanding the scout ordered his men to Farmersville. The group arrived a few minutes before the show closed. But either Bob Lee was not present when the performance finished, or the troopers did not recognize him. The sergeant later discovered that Lee was indeed at the show when the squad arrived, but that Cole had learned of the troop movement in time to warn the felon who made a safe getaway.[67]

After placing Cole under arrest and having a guard take him to the Pilot Grove jail, the remaining troopers made camp. The night was rainy and dark. Four Lee men—with Lee possibly being among them—managed to sneak up on one of two sentries and over-power and disarm him. Then, the renegades shot and killed him before firing on the other sentry whom they wounded severely. Rudely awakened, the sergeant rallied his men and began firing on the intruders who did not want to face the soldiers in a stand up battle. Instead, the Lee men made a quick retreat. Subsequently, Lieutenant Maytheny requested reinforcements from Sherman because he wanted to send out more scouting parties to locate Lee—after telling superiors that many citizens of Farmersville were Lee supporters who relayed information to him, fed him, and gave him board.[68]

Clearly, even as the sweep of "Chaffee's Guerrillas" was underway, Lee and his fellows were still dangerous to all military men and to all white and black civilian Unionists alike.

Yet, the law-and-order element continued to pursue the fugitive. In December of 1868, Peacock led a squad of soldiers and civilian volunteers who tracked the captain to a spot near Farmersville in Collin County. Peacock must have rejoiced, thinking that finally Lee would be brought to justice. Once again Lee's intelligence system aided the outlaw greatly, however. He and his gang set up an ambush for the Union men. The fighting was fierce, and the gunshots were many. The desperadoes killed one of the soldiers and wounded another before getting away without suffering any casualties. Considering that Peacock was Lee's number one target, the Union man was lucky to come out of the trap alive. A short time later, Peacock and another posse of about thirty men went to Daniel Lee's place, hoping that by making such a surprise move, they could catch his wayward son. The action failed in its purpose. Bob Lee was nowhere to be found.[69]

Meanwhile, the situation remained desperate enough that the entire nation began hearing of the bloodbath in Northeastern Texas. The Northern press began following the "Texas Troubles" more closely than before. To counter such coverage, H. C. Mack in his *Texas: Information for Emigrants* tried to minimize the number of guerrilla gangs and the inordinate amount of violence in the Lone Star State. Mack believed that reports of such violence likely reduced emigration. He argued that the Northern press was exaggerating. Mack admitted that Texas had a "few famous characters" and mentioned Baker, Bickerstaff, and Bob Lee by name. Then, he defended them while blaming Reconstruction policies and the negative actions of the occupying federal soldiers and Unionists like Peacock for causing the bloodshed.[70]

As Mack was reporting and as the Union sweep was continuing, finally the forces of law and order delivered some of their few victories, thanks to Thomas Orr, a crippled man who once stole a woman away from Baker. For that offense, Baker tracked and found Orr and hanged him only to botch the job, thus leaving an enemy alive. With the help of a few other men, Orr killed Baker in the late morning of January 6, 1869, as the killer and one of his men were sleeping off a drunk. Two days later, Lee was indicted for another murder, and on January 28, another arrest warrant went out against the captain. On March 1, Lee and Simp Dixon were indicted for the attempted murder of Peacock and one of the Saunders brothers.[71]

But even as the Unionists of Northeast Texas were winning a few victories, the renegades still seemed to have the upper hand. For one thing, many area residents still abetted Lee and his men. On a sweep in early January of 1869, Major Chaffee and a few of his fighters left Sulphur Springs and rode into Hunt

County looking for Lee and any of his men. They went through Greenville and wound up camping at Harold's Chapel, about ten miles northwest of the county seat. For ten days, the major sent out scouts of from six to ten men, but the patrols turned up nothing. Questioning area civilians, the major got no useful information. On the third day, Chaffee learned that Lee had taken breakfast with a Mr. Drakes who lived near White Rock. Upon questioning, neither Drakes nor anyone else in the settlement would tell the bluecoat about what direction Lee took when he left.[72]

Disgusted, Chaffee reported that the residents of White Rock "shield[ed] him [Lee] from our grasp and do not scruple to lie and deceive to any extent. They consider him justified in his acts, and believe [that Lee was reacting] to a wrong perpetrated upon him by the Peacock party." "Consequently," Chaffee added, "nearly every house is a welcome home [for Lee] and every man is his friend."[73] The disappointed Yankee also explained that "so long as this state of things exist, it is utterly impossible to get near him with soldiers in uniform." Obviously distraught, the major asked that his command be "relieved from this duty" and that his men be returned to their respective posts on the frontier.[74]

Chapter 7

Continuing Warfare and the End of the "Man Eater"

As if to validate Chaffee's concerns and his negative assessment of the realistic chances to capture Bob Lee, in late January, 1869, two members of the Lee gang murdered freedman John Coward who lived in Collin County near McKinney. An observer from the county called the black Texan the "most intelligent, industrious, and orderly of our Colored population."[1] The culprits were Bill Penn and Dow Witt, both of whom were close to Lee personally. Perhaps they killed Coward because he was intelligent, industrious, and orderly. Perhaps they could not tolerate a freedman actually improving his impoverished condition and rising above caste. Earlier, on January 9, a black man turned up dead in Collin County, his body found on the Farmersville-Greenville Road that cut through the Corners. The man had four bullet holes in his forehead, which was virtually blown away.[2] Could his killers have been Penn and Witt? Both desperadoes had openly declared that they intended to stalk and to kill federals, civilian Union men, and freedmen. Shortly, on January 29, the two outcasts came into McKinney late one afternoon, heavily armed with six-guns and shotguns. Looking for trouble, they "sauntered about the public square generally, scrutinizing several of our citizens very closely, as if looking for someone."[3]

Next, one of the deadly duo entered one store after another, still looking, while his comrade guarded each door with shotgun at the ready. About sundown they saddled up but only went as far as "Mrs. Hurt's Hotel," where they ate, each with his shotgun across his lap. Then, the two hearties went to a saloon to drink their fill, to make merry, and to cause as much general mayhem as they could. Freedman Coward passed by at exactly the wrong time and came to the attention of the twin terrors, who forced him into the street. Both made sport of him and ordered him to dance. When Coward said that he could not dance, would not do so, got back on the walkway, and just tried to walk away, either Penn or Witt shot him in the back, a typical shot for the Lee renegades. After Coward fell through the saloon door but was still alive, one of the killers got over Coward and shot again at close range, finally killing him. Next, the hotspurs saddled up, fired several shots across the public square, and rode off, while "hurrahing for Bob Lee."[4]

The next day Penn and Witt were riding along on the Pilot Grove—

Kentucky-Town Road when they encountered a small squad of troopers who had been sent to find and to arrest them. After a brisk skirmish of several minutes, the gun battle resulted in a fighting retreat by the felons, who tried to make an escape while leading a trooper's horse in tow. The two raiders and the troopers staged a running fight for quite a distance before Penn and Witt reached a thicket and disappeared. The outlaws were familiar with that thicket, and the troopers were not. The federals broke off their pursuit. As was usual for members of the Lee gang, after the murder the two ruffians stayed in hiding for a time while awaiting their next chance to strike.[5]

The murder of Coward was just for sport, but as he told others, the McKinney Unionist G. E. Ramey believed that the rebels were in town looking to assassinate him. Further, Ramey charged that Bob Fitzhugh was behind the plot to kill him, Fitzhugh having just been paroled from Austin by Reynolds and allowed to return home. Ramey considered himself lucky, for although Witt was a relative of Fitzhugh, Witt had never met Ramey and did not know what he looked like. Witt only had an oral description that proved inadequate for identification. Certainly Fitzhugh was out for revenge. He blamed Ramey and two other men for his earlier arrest and exile in Austin. Like Peacock, Ramey bemoaned the fact that no military troops had ever been placed in McKinney or anywhere else in Collin County.[6]

Ramey believed that the renegades apparently concluded that the county was the "safest place for them in Northern Texas. Penn and Witt are both well known here and also their friends . . . [including] Bob Lee." Fitzhugh's hard core stance plus his money and his ability to hide and to supply the Lee men, Ramey charged, allowed Fitzhugh "to control this class of men." Ramey went on to ask that a small force of cavalry *"at once"* be sent to McKinney (he wanted from forty-five to fifty men) and that a reward be put out on Penn and Witt. Ramey said that he could not depend on civilians, not even Union men, for help because all knew that their lives would be forfeit and their property taken should they oppose the Lee guerrillas. They knew that these "demons in human shape" would destroy them.[7] Clearly, McKinney needed but did not have a loyalist leader like Peacock.

County Judge L. Bowlby echoed Ramey's concerns, telling Governor Elisha Pease that "the good people of our county [need protection] from the savages of the cut-throats and outlaws that now infest our vicinity." Continuing, he exclaimed that "there has been no time since the close of the Rebellion so *desperate* as *now*. . . . The loyal men are in a perfect state of consternation, feeling safe only when under arms."[8]

Shortly after Witt and Penn killed Coward, two killers murdered a man in the Corners area south of Sherman. The victim was a Missouri farmer or merchant who had sold a large load of apples in McKinney for $500. The culprits who caught and killed him on the road from McKinney to Sherman were John Thompson and William Blackmore. Their obvious motive was robbery. They stopped the man on the road, intending to have the money. When the victim resisted, they killed him. After claiming the money, the killers fled. Later, rumors held that they had ridden with Quantrill during the war and then joined the Lee gang once the captain returned to the Corners. It is possible that Thompson and Blackmore believed that their victim was once a member of the Unionist Missouri Redlegs, giving them an additional motive to kill him. A combined military-civilian posse, possibly led by Peacock, found the two murderers—both originally from Missouri—hiding in an area farm house. After they surrendered, the posse hauled them to Sherman in chains. When a jury found the men guilty, District Judge Hardin Hart sentenced them to hang, a sentence carried out on March 28, 1869. The turnout for the hangings was grand. With many families bringing picnic lunches, all who gathered for the event enjoyed themselves thoroughly. Many Unionist witnesses may have rejoiced, especially because two more desperadoes who had preyed on them were now permanent guests of the grim reaper.[9]

Even as Unionists claimed a small victory, from January through February, Lee issued more threats, saying that he was going to direct a "wholesale slaughter in this country" once spring came and foliage returned to further cover the thick bush in the region, brush and thickets that had always made such excellent hiding places as well as good spots in which to set up surprise attacks.[10]

Given the support of many area residents, in late January or early February of 1869, Lee and his men began implementing his plan. They appeared to become braver even as some of their number were falling. They hatched a plot aimed at disposing of the federals in Corners Country. Now riding with at least sixteen men, Lee murdered a freedman whose place was about six miles from Sherman. In the doing, he provoked the authorities to send out more scouts. Then, he and his men set up several traps on the road from Sherman to Kentucky-Town. Lee's plan was to have his men lay in the bush at various hidden places and wait for small parties of troopers to come by. Then, the desperadoes could easily murder their quarry, possibly picking them off one, two, or three at a time. Lee's designs also continued to call for attacking army commissary wagons that came out of Pilot Grove headed for Sherman to resupply the soldiers there.[11]

In January of 1869, the high command considered removing the soldiers from Pilot Grove, for they were most concerned by the negative report that Major Chaffee had presented earlier, especially his statement that uniformed troops could never catch Lee. Troop removal, however, was a possibility that Peacock and his supporters abhorred—their lives would be in even greater jeopardy. About thirty such dismayed Unionists went to see Lieutenant Maytheny, still commanding the post at Pilot Grove, and made personal appeals. Presenting a petition signed by more than thirty-five men, including themselves, they told the lieutenant that chaos would reign if commanders removed the troops, and that their lives would be forfeit. "Our town," they said, "is entirely at the mercy of bad men and desperadoes[,] and the sacrifice of human life is of frequent occurrence."[12]

The alarmed petitioners warned that "should the place be abandoned[,] most of the people who have been friendly with the U.S. Govt. will have to leave." After mentioning that cavalry represented the only hope they had, the loyalists explained that "the officers of this post are thoroughly acquainted with every man [in the Corners] . . . [and would] know exactly what steps to take to bring the offenders to justice immediately."[13] Maytheny agreed, warning his superiors against removing the troops. He held that the lives of area Union men would be endangered even more than usual because "the country is infested with lawless and desperate men[,] the capture of whom is almost impossible."[14] The lieutenant commanding the post thus agreed with the men loyal to the federal government: He asked the high command to leave his men in Pilot Grove, for if they were removed "the lives of all the Union men . . . would be in jeopardy."[15]

As if to prove that the petitioners were correct in their assessment of the mayhem in the Corners' counties, in early February of 1869, Lee men Penn and Witt accosted a freedman near Aston's Mill in Grayson. The outlaws took the man's pistol and shotgun and killed him. Then the Lee boys went to the dead man's home and searched it. Finding no other weapons, they left but not before warning other area blacks that they would kill any and all other area freedmen if they were caught possessing weapons.[16]

In the midst of their anti-Union campaign, some Lee men became involved in yet another bizarre incident in the early spring. A Missouri Unionist who was a fruit-grower brought a load of his products into Texas, intending to sell his fruit at various military posts. He met three other Missouri fruit-peddlers on the trail. He bought their products and then employed them to help him get all the goods into Northeast Texas. When the Missourians reached the Bonham area, the loyalist—whose name is lost—made camp for himself, his wife, and his daughter. Then he rode into Bonham with the other three men. Once there, the three other Missouri men let out a cheer for Bob Lee. They announced that they were Confederates to the core, that they were acquainted with Bob Lee and the "New Rebellion Gang," and that they intended to join up. Whereupon, the three thieves fell upon the unsuspecting Missouri Unionist who escaped by running into the courthouse where he hid until nightfall. On escaping in the darkness and returning surreptitiously to his family, the Union man learned that the others had been back to his camp and had threatened to kill his wife and daughter. The fearful fellow immediately broke camp, hitched his team, and raced through the darkness to Pilot Grove where he found military protection and safety for himself, his family, and his goods.[17]

Soon after the incident, several Lee men—including Indian Bill English who had joined them—went into a Bonham café for a meal. While dining, they loudly promised that they intended to ravish the first woman whom they saw once they finished their repast. Later in the day, English killed a black woman and her child in cold blood, apparently for sport. Yet, civilian authorities were afraid—or unwilling—to attempt an arrest, for they knew that they would face Lee's retribution. The numbers of the desperado's supporters were swelling as more renegades joined him, his gang now outnumbering the troops in the area.[18]

To add to the Unionists untenable situation, in February of 1869 another misfortune befell Peacock's ally, Judge Hardin Hart. Hardin, the former Freedmen's Bureau agent, had become the judge of the Seventh Judicial District of Texas. Although details are sketchy, Hunt County Sheriff John Mason accosted Hart's son Thomas, had words with him, and then cut him in half with a shotgun blast from close range—this occurring after the judge had already lost his nephew to another murderer. Trouble between the Unionists and Rebels in the county had already resulted in the resignations of county deputies and the county coroner, and the murder complicated matters much further, prompting Governor Pease to intervene again by asking General Reynolds to take more forceful action to restore order to Northeast Texas. Although the Confederate sheriff's motives were unknown, a Hunt County Grand Jury indicted him for murder. Likely, Mason attacked Thomas just because he was the son of a leading Unionist. The controversy was heightened when the commander at the Post of Greenville, Maj. George E. Head, arrested Mason but inexplicably allowed him his personal freedom while being watched by only one guard. Head should have lodged Mason in jail. Mason? He never came to trial. After escaping his guard, he disappeared for a time, returning to Hunt County after the Democrats had redeemed the state.[19]

While Mason was facing his travail for murdering Hart's son, there were more dastardly doings in the Corners. Reporting from Pilot Grove in February, 1869, Lt. H. P. Eakin said that two Lee men—Bill Penn and a man named Clark (the mysterious Hayes might have been misidentified as Clark)—had attacked a military courier. The trooper was riding from Sherman toward Pilot Grove carrying U.S. mail and assorted military dispatches. Within about one-half mile of Pilot Grove, the raiders tried to shoot from a thicket, opening up with shotguns, but the day was rainy, and their guns did not fire. Thereupon, they drew their revolvers and fired repeatedly. But the momentary respite from the shotguns gave the courier time to spur his steed, to escape, and to race into Pilot Grove unharmed. A scouting party of only a few troopers immediately went out to look for Penn and Clark. Two of its members found the trail and followed it to Wilton Marshal's house where Penn and Clark threw up breastworks of wooden rails and planned to make a stand. When they opened up with shotguns that fired this time, the two troopers decided not to contest the desperadoes. The federals withdrew and rode back to the relative safety of Pilot Grove.[20]

About the same time, the rest of the scouting party, led by Peacock, went into Kentucky-Town. When the two troopers who had been shot at reported to Lieutenant Eakin, he sent all the men "he dared" back to the Marshal house. Just as the troopers arrived, the two renegades fled, heading toward Kentucky-Town. The federals gave chase all the way to and through the streets of that place, firing volley after volley from horseback. Their quarry escaped.[21]

As if to underscore the failures to catch the Lee men, Lieutenant Sands, who once again commanded at Pilot Grove, was sounding sour notes. Yes, he captured a number of bandit-Klansmen and sent them on to Sherman, he said in a report to his superiors, but he complained that his small force of thirty-five men and assorted worn out horses were not sufficient for controlling Klan and outlaw violence. After referring to widespread terrorism in the Corners area, he complained that he would soon lose some of his tiny command because the terms of service of several men were about to expire. When that time came, the lieutenant ominously predicted that he "would not even have enough men to hold the camp in case of a strong attack."[22]

A commander forwarded Sands's report to Washington as an example of the woeful situation that faced the undermanned U.S. Army in East Texas. Gen. William T. Sherman, commanding officer of all U.S. Armies, took note of the "Texas Troubles" and scribbled his endorsement, saying that General Reynolds must solve the problems and reestablish law and order.[23] Of course, Reynolds was already trying to do just what Sherman demanded and was depending heavily on Chaffee, Tolman, and garrison commanders like Sands who in turn needed all the help they could get from men like Peacock and other Unionists.

Even as the military reacted to the chaos in Northeast Texas, more trouble was on the way. In Grayson County, near the Corners, Lee man Dick Johnson accosted and killed a Colonel Ervin; the Johnson party included Simp Dixon, Penn, and Witt along with men only known as Chase and Clark (or Hayes). Next, they robbed freedman Jeremiah Everhart while he was standing in his own front yard. They took his sixgun and a small amount of money. Then, they calmly murdered him as his family looked on. All six men—Johnson, Dixon, Penn, Witt, Chase, and Clark—had at Everhart's young daughter, raping her repeatedly until they were entirely spent and could no longer perform. They did so "in the most brutal manner[,] each and every one of them participating in this inhuman act."[24] The man who reported the murder and multiple rape was none other than A. M. Bryant of Grayson County, who had just returned from Austin where he had been a delegate to the Texas Constitutional Convention. According to Governor Pease who learned of the brutality, Bryant was "not an alarmist and not likely to give an exaggerated statement."[25]

Following the murder of Everhart and the savaging of his daughter, the renegades took a twenty-day shooting spree, killing at least six, maybe seven, more blacks. Again, according to Bryant, who had once been a Freedman's Bureau agent, it was "strange to say that notwithstanding the government put down the late rebellion [the Civil War] the rebel element in this section of the state have the power to drive loyal men away from their homes and run out of the state. Clay Sa[u]nders and his brother Clark of Fannin County has (sic) had to leave . . . Lewis Peacock has had to [leave] this county and is I suppose at Jacksbourgh (sic)."[26] Bryant added that Penn had threatened to kill both himself (Bryant) and one of his sons. Bryant's associate R. D. King, a physician, also feared that Penn would kill him as well, simply because he was Bryant's friend.[27]

Like so many other Unionists, Bryant also charged that the local judges of Fannin, Grayson, and Collin counties were not doing their jobs. Further, he mentioned that the troops at Pilot Grove were not as effective as they once were because Lieutenant Sands and most of his men had been transferred back to Sherman. Bryant confirmed that "Sands kept this county too hot for Rogues." But, since his departure, the outlaws were having their way with all loyal men. Lee and his guerrillas still intended to exterminate their enemies. Bryant ended his report by begging for more troops. In his reference to Peacock's trip to Jacksboro, Bryant might simply be in err, or it is possible that Lewis was traveling a political circuit, urging people to support the new Texas Constitution that had been fashioned by the Texas State Constitutional Convention.[28]

In late February, the Lee followers—those with no warrants out on them—continued to grow bolder. They may well have been reacting to the new Constitution that gave blacks many new rights, including the right to vote. Their habit now included coming in groups to Pilot Grove's saloon heavily armed for nights of drunk revelry. While in town they also gained information about troop movements. At the same time they did what they could to bedevil the Unionists in town. As Lt. H. P. Eakin put it: "The desperadoes with which this country is infested" caused mayhem everywhere they went. Sands and most of his men had been transferred away, despite the pleadings of Peacock and others. After the transfer, only a small provost guard was left in Pilot Grove. The tiny squad did what it could to limit abuses, to try to restore peace and quiet. On the night of February 6, as Eakin later reported, a man named "Sturdy" finally pushed the provost guard too far. Sturdy called a Corporal Fowler, commander of the guard, a "damned Yankee son-of-a-bitch." Whereupon, the corporal decided not to truck with such a foul man. With but slight hesitation, he used his rifle to shoot Sturdy dead, firing no doubt because he feared that the renegades, emboldened by Sturdy's words, would gun him down as a prelude to beginning a major shootout. Later, the corporal's superiors investigated the incident and held him blameless because of the provocation in a dangerous situation. Peacock, for one, believed that such incidents would not have occurred if the command had left an adequate number of men in Pilot Grove.[29]

With violence escalating into 1869, the military considered another action that appeared to violate logic: They again foolishly considered removing District Judge Hart's personal military guard. Hart immediately wrote Governor Pease, saying that his protection must continue, for he still feared for his life, as well he should have after Rebels murdered both his nephew and son. Pease endorsed the request and sent it on to Maj. Gen. E. R. S. Canby, now commanding the Fifth Military District. Subsequently, the general issued Special Orders No. 40 and No. 42, directing that Hart's protection be continued as long as deemed necessary by the commander of the post at Greenville. The general assigned ten men to guard Hart so that the judge could continue his work.[30] Then came more good news for Unionists. On March 22, General Reynolds placed a $1,000 reward on the head of *all* members of "the Bob Lee Gang."[31]

On March 28, 1869, Lieutenant Sands, still in Sherman, received information that at least three of Lee's men—Bill Penn, Dow Witt, and the mysterious Hayes—had been seen near William Fitzhugh's place, about five miles north of McKinney. As mentioned, Colonel Fitzhugh was loyal to the Lost Cause and an acknowledged Lee sympathizer. Authorities believed that he was harboring the three outlaws. Judge Hart ordered Sgt. William McGraw to take a detachment and arrest the felons. McGraw's squad of soldiers was accompanied by several civilian volunteers. The men rode from Sherman to Pilot Grove to pick up Peacock who served as a guide for the rest of the trip. Then, the force rode on to McKinney where they were joined by Collin County Sheriff George Wilson, several of his deputies including men named Short and Hall, and a posse of about twenty-five other men. As torrential rain burst from the sky, the authorities' manpower numbered about forty or forty-five guns when they reached a flooding creek that only the sheriff and seven of the men were able to ford. Sheriff Wilson yelled to dismiss the men unable to cross, one of whom was Peacock who returned to his place in the Corners. With his remaining men, Wilson continued his trek. The group reached the Fitzhugh place by approximately 10 p.m. A search convinced the posse that their quarry was not there. Nearby, however, was William Beard's place. The Union men knew that he, too, was sympathetic toward Lee and his gang and sometimes rode with them.[32]

After reaching the Beard place, the posse surrounded his house on the chance that their targets were inside. Calling aloud for the outlaws to surrender, the Unionists readied for combat. Suddenly, Witt, armed with a shotgun, burst out of a stand of trees near the house. While cursing loudly, he ran to his horse firing one barrel at the Union men, who returned fire with a dozen quick bursts. Although Sergeant McGraw shot and wounded Witt's horse, the badman galloped away, and the chase was on. Authorities pursued Witt for about four or five miles. Finally, Mother Nature foiled Witt's attempted escape. When he was about six miles north of McKinney, he came to East Fork Creek which was swollen because of the rain.[33]

Witt managed to ford the creek, but some of the pursuers arrived just as he was climbing the opposite bank. A Private Henry and a Corporal Payne fired effective rounds. They shot Witt's horse out from under him and wounded the outlaw multiple times. Game to the end, Witt reached a knoll, dived behind it for a little cover, and got off his last shotgun blast and several more rounds from his two handguns. But unknown to the raider, Sheriff Wilson and Sergeant McGraw had forded the creek downstream and doubled back. They surprised Witt from behind. They fired the last shots of the battle, after which the murderer lay dead. The authorities reduced Lee's guerrilla population by one, but while the posse had concentrated on Witt, in the confusion Beard, Penn, and Hayes made an easy escape.[34]

The editor of the *McKinney Weekly Enquirer* made interesting comments when reporting the death of Witt: "The desperado who has kept the people of Collin County in alarm for some time has at last been overtaken by violent death. He made a desperate resistance, using his weapons as long as he was able to do so, but at last was brought to the ground and killed."[35] The mention that Witt kept the people in "alarm" suggests that many civilians in Corners Country may well have supported Unionists like Peacock, that not all area residents supported Lee, as traditional historians would contend. Yet, many loyalists hesitated to take an active part in the ongoing Second Civil War because they feared for their families lives as well as their own. Some seemed to become braver as the terror mounted; the Unionists following Peacock and the troopers continued to gain more support—at least moral support if nothing else.

When one recalls the votes on secession that came from the Corners counties, it is not surprising that Peacock and other Unionists had some support, especially after outlaws and Klansmen stepped up their campaigns of robbery and murder. Perhaps their violent acts finally offended many decent people who were ready for the troubles to end. As McKinney resident Ramey held: "The good citizens of this county are thoroughly aroused and seem determined to rid the Country of all lawless characters."[36] Unfortunately for Unionists like Ramey, the new rebellion of which the Lee-Peacock fight was a part was destined to last much longer.

After Witt was slain, the posse retreated to McKinney for the rest of the night, but at morning light, a small band of soldiers and civilians were on the move again, searching for the other three desperadoes. On March 30, an unidentified informant spotted Penn and Hayes, along with Dick Johnson—Simp's step-brother and the Lee man who had earlier killed Colonel Erwin—about four miles from McKinney going in the direction of Solomon Fitzhugh's place. Hearing the news after dark, Sheriff Wilson sent a courier to Pilot Grove to find Peacock and to ask him to bring any volunteers whom he could find to enlarge the posse. Roused from bed late at night, Peacock rounded up a few men, the group then riding to the vicinity of McKinney. The courier directed them to Wilson's camp which they reached in the dead of night. Wilson and Peacock led the mixed group of seven troopers and several civilian volunteers in the direction of Fitzhugh's farm. Along the way, Wilson directed his men to an area where he believed that the felons might have spent the night. The authorities searched several houses and barns but found no trace of the brigands. They next went to the Fitzhugh place, getting there at daybreak after scouting throughout a miserable, rainy night. Once there, a trooper looked into the horse lot and recognized one of the horses as being stolen. It turned out to be a fine animal that the mysterious Hayes had stolen from a man in Marshall. Yet another member of the group also recognized Penn's stolen horse.[37]

Although Dick Johnson was not to be found at Fitzhugh's, the posse tried to surprise the remaining outlaw pair, Penn and Hayes, but the two heard the authorities as they approached. The desperadoes did not wait for their adversaries to begin the action. Instead, one man in the posse saw the well-armed outlaws bolt from the house. They ducked into a nearby thicket. While Peacock and several other men tried to surround the brush, Sheriff Wilson and his deputy, William C. Hall, were the first to pursue. After jumping off their mounts, they rushed into the thicket. Trooper James Johnson was into the bush just an instant later. From a spot unseen, Penn opened fire and pandemonium broke loose. Deputy Hall was hit four times and soon died, while Johnson was severely wounded but was destined to recover. Wilson was also wounded as was Pvt. James Johns. The barrage from the outlaws sent the sheriff, Johnson, and Johns diving for cover.[38]

The guerrillas fell upon the dying Hall and took his Spencer rifle and his revolver; both then moved through the thicket to emerge on the other side and to make their escape. They managed to avoid Peacock and the other volunteers. Afoot, they ran down Rockwall Road but doubled back and reached the posse's horses, stealing two, one that belonged to the sheriff and one that belonged to a trooper. They were last seen riding in the direction of Farmersville, a place where they had many sympathizers. After the heavy rain, Sister Grove Creek was not fordable, but the outlaws and their stolen horses swam it and continued their escape. Much to Peacock's disgust, the outlaws remained free for a little longer and continued to bedevil the area's white and black Unionists, thus helping Bob Lee spread the terror.[39]

As luck would have it, since Penn had ridden away on the sheriff's horse, Wilson took Penn's stolen horse, one called a "pearl of the prairie" by its real owner in faraway Marshall, the word faraway again attesting to the immense range of the Northeast Texas gangs.[40] Angered that the pair had gotten away, Sergeant McGraw added a postscript: "The woods are full of men [like Penn and Hayes, but] I shall do my utmost to capture his [Lee's] band if possible."[41]

Although Penn and Hayes escaped, in early April of 1869, some good news again came to the loyal men in Corners Country. The increased military presence in Hopkins County and the $1,000 reward on his head forced the notorious Bickerstaff to look for greener, safer pastures; he knew when it was time to run. He moved his operations to Navarro County where he had earlier had much success. Going by the name Thomas and most likely allying himself with the Hardin family, he established a base near Corsicana and began terrorizing area freedmen and white Unionists. Usually in the company of Josiah Thompson, one of his major supporters, he was always heavily armed, and according to an area newspaper, "thefts were committed, plantations were visited in the absence of the owners, [N]egroes were assaulted . . . and robbed."[42]

Knowing that army personnel would soon show up in Corsicana because of their depredations, Bickerstaff and friends next headed for Johnson County to hide after they had committed their Navarro County crimes. In their new killing field, they originally had supporters. Still going by the name Thomas, Bickerstaff told the people of the Johnson County countryside that he was but a poor Civil War refugee whom Yankee soldiers had abused mightily. But, citizens of Alvarado noticed that "Mr. Thomas" was always heavily armed, constantly had his hands on his pistols, and never mingled with other people, except for Thompson, whom they despised because he was a whiskey peddler who off-and-on ran a saloon in town and thereby violated a local ordinance banning liquor. Then, new depredations began. As they had done in Navarro, the thieves, who were drunk most of their waking hours, began visiting plantations and farms when white owners were away, taking whatever they wished. They also looted the homes of blacks, stealing food, clothing, arms, and anything else of value. They assaulted freedmen. They raped freedwomen. Soon, the blacks in the rural countryside "fled their homes in terror," hid in the woods, and became "entirely useless as laborers."[43]

By February of 1869, some whites in Johnson County learned that "Mr. Thomas" was really Bickerstaff and that he and his men were behind the trouble occurring in the countryside. Local county officials and rank-and-file civilians in Alvarado finally decided that something had to be done after Bickerstaff and Thompson picked up the habit of coming into town late at night to get drunk, to whore around, to celebrate, and "to institute a carnival of robbery and other crimes."[44]

The last straw came when the two guerrillas burst into the county courthouse one day and disrupted grand jury proceedings. Their strong threats and hostile behavior so alarmed the weak-kneed District Judge A. B. Norton that he immediately fled in terror and quickly went into hiding while Bickerstaff and Thompson quietly slipped back to the Corsicana area. Reacting to the problem the outlaws posed, folks in Navarro County managed to do something no one else had done. They finally caught Bickerstaff after he robbed another black family, but the vigilantes were undercut by a local justice of the peace who released the killer, saying that he only threatened "damned niggers." Before leaving the county, Bickerstaff, still teamed with Thompson, robbed five more black families and shot two black men near Spring Hill.[45]

After leaving Navarro County, the cutthroat and Thompson were reinforced by other members of their band before committing more deprivations in Wood and Van Zandt counties. They even bravely ventured into Hunt County, part of Lee's stomping ground, to collect more of Bickerstaff's gang and to cause yet more mayhem in the black community and among the white Unionists. Some Lee men and possibly Lee, himself, temporarily joined Bickerstaff, no doubt hoping for a little fun and a share of the loot. Yet, the end was near. Bickerstaff again knew when it was time to run, for Chaffee and his men were closing in. Bickerstaff temporarily moved his headquarters to a spot between Oquilla Creek and the Brazos River, near Peoria in Hill County, about twenty-seven miles from Johnson County's Alvarado where Bickerstaff and Thompson had already committed atrocities. Along the Brazos, the gang tried to hide from authorities. Periodically, they also raided into the countryside. But word leaked out about Bickerstaff's presence. Whereupon, the desperado forgot all thoughts of stealth. Now openly going into Alvarado, Bickerstaff and Thompson threatened to kill the town's officials and to burn the hamlet to the ground. Some nights, they or other malefactors watched the homes of the most influential locals, hoping to catch them outside, to ambush them, and to fill them with lead.[46]

Some concerned residents of Alvarado appeared before the dismayed Judge Norton, then holding court in Cleburne. Next, they appeared before a Johnson County grand jury. The Alvarado contingent soon learned, however, that all of Bickerstaff's deadly antics had intimidated both the judge and the jury. The only thing the cowardly judge was willing to do was inform the Johnson County bunch that there was a $1,000 reward for Bickerstaff—dead or alive. Because the terrified Norton could not or would not act, many residents of Johnson County not only feared for their lives and property, but they also believed that emigration into the county would cease, that local prosperity would thus be in peril, and that the county would languish. Their motives for ridding themselves of Bickerstaff were mounting.[47]

Given that he had many Rebel supporters, Bickerstaff quickly learned of the meeting in Cleburne and had even been provided with a list of the names of the Alvarado men appearing there. Consequently, "Mr. Thomas" dropped all pretense just as more members of his raiders reached the area. Leaving his men at an old schoolhouse just outside Alvarado, on April 5, 1869, Bickerstaff, accompanied by Thompson, roared into town near sundown. Bickerstaff apparently thought that he could destroy the place without the use of his men. However, earlier Chaffee, Tolman, and some of their men had followed the trail of the members of Bickerstaff's band when they rode to join their leader.[48]

Knowing that it was likely that the renegades would create chaos for Alvarado, Chaffee and Tolman warned the town's authorities and civic leaders that bloodshed was probably in the offing. After the troopers left town to scout for the scoundrels, Alvarado's leaders formed a vigilance committee and laid plans to trap the desperadoes. When they rode in to "tree" the place, all the main street store owners retreated into their establishments. Believing that they were all frightened, Bickerstaff and Thompson "gave vent to a lusty laugh" and raised their hats to "salute" the town. Then, after drawing pistols, they rode up to the store of Powell and Williams, apparently intending to catch and murder Powell, one of the citizens who had earlier talked to Judge Norton. But a group of gutsy civilians—led by A. J. Baines, Stephen Mills, Special Officer M. P. Hunnicutt (a future state policeman), Samuel Milliken, and John and David Myers—armed to the teeth, poured into the streets from their stores. Quickly, they began delivering lead in massive and deadly doses. In the general mayhem, they gunned down Bickerstaff, who fell from his horse after taking a shotgun blast full in the face fired at point blank range, this happening after he had already been wounded. He was mortally injured and died about two hours later. The vigilantes finished Thompson the same way. Gun blasts knocked him off his horse, and he was likely dead before his body hit the ground.[49]

Led by Baines and the Myers brothers, the vigilantes then stormed out to the schoolhouse and managed to arrest several members of the gang who were still there. Taken to Waco under heavy guard, the men were turned over to military authorities. Also delivered to Waco were Bickerstaff's severed head and thirteen affidavits attesting to the crimes of the raider and his men. The $1,000 reward for Bickerstaff? Alvarado's leaders gratefully accepted it—the town needed a new schoolhouse.[50]

A poet at heart, the editor of the *Waxahachie Argus Extra* waxed ecstatic (even if he did get some of the details wrong) when reporting the demise of Thompson and Bickerstaff. Mentioning that Thompson had been living near Alvarado for about two years, that he seemed respectable, but that he "was seduced into a vicious career . . . by Bickerstaff," the poet continued:

> The good citizens of the village prepared Themselves with shooting apparatus for the purpose of ridding their community of these [two men], the greatest pests they had ever known. . . . The men rode up to the horse rack and dismounted, and so soon as they had alighted, a shower of death-dealing leaden balls was directed at them. Thompson was killed instantly, and Bickerstaff was struck in three places. Notwithstanding his frightful and mortal wounds . . . he fired two well-aimed shots at his adversaries. . . . When he was prostate upon the ground and his adversaries were gathered round, he exclaimed, 'You have killed as brave a man as there is in the South.' He was disposed to be communicative, but he failed to get any interested or attentive auditors. Thus passed from earth a man who had, doubtless, steeped himself in crimes as heinous and foul as are known in the annals of this country.[51]

Now, only one of Northeast Texas's outlaw triumvirate remained alive: the Corners' own "Captain" Bob Lee. Continuing their campaign against the guerrillas, the authorities in Corners Country went about the business of picking off Lee's men. First they looked for Penn and Hayes. For a brief time, the two hid out in the Red River bottoms or at White Rock in Hunt County. Alternately, they may have been in Kentucky-Town in Grayson, in their favorite haunts in Fannin, or even north of the river in the Indian Nations. All of the places were principal resorts of the bad men.[52]

Penn soon slipped back into the Kentucky-Town vicinity to hide with friends or relatives. While on the road north of the town, passing over a bridge, moving from one safe haven to another, Penn encountered a young freedman, Jerry Everheart. The felon apparently cursed the black youngster, and Everheart may have responded in kind, the result being that Penn killed him, firing lead into his mouth and throat. As events proved, Penn had murdered one too many blacks: Jerry was the former slave and a current employee of the Everheart family, a family headed by United States Marshal Bill Everheart. Penn and the marshal had once been friends, but now Bill Everheart decided that the young gun had to be stopped to prevent other such murders. Reportedly, Bill soon packed supplies and munitions for an extended trip, loaded his guns, saddled-up, and told his family that "I won't be back 'till Bill Penn is dead."[53]

Within a short time, while the stalwart Everheart and two deputies were scouting for Penn, rumors swept the Corners that Penn and Hayes had been sighted near a shack in the river bottoms north of Bonham. On April 7, Benjamin Goode sprang into action to help Everheart. A Unionist, Goode had recently been appointed as an additional sheriff of Grayson County by military order because the real sheriff was a Confederate who stonewalled all efforts to deal with the murderers. The "additional" sheriff put together a posse of ten men for a scout, then found and joined Everheart and his deputies. The group struck the trail of Penn and Hayes north of Bonham and tracked them to Ladonia, a small Fannin County settlement. Continuing on the trail, the posse followed them to Honey Grove, thence to the mouth of the Boggy River in extreme northeast Lamar County.[54]

On the night of April 20, 1869, Goode's bunch surrounded an old shack and called for the two young hotspurs, who had been joined by William Beard, to surrender. Instead, the renegades made a stand with guns blazing. For a time, a battle raged wherein the guerrillas "fought with desperation." Then, at one point, Penn burst from the house, firing with Colt revolvers, one in each hand. Likely, he hoped to fight his way to his horse. No match for the ten-man posse, he was quickly gunned down. Later to become sheriff of Grayson County, Bill Everheart approached Penn, whom he remembered as once a close childhood friend. No doubt thinking of that, Everheart knelt close to Penn who was on the ground, almost dead but trying to talk. That was Everheart's mistake. The marshal did not notice that Penn still had a weapon in one hand. Still clinging to life, the young gun whispered to the kneeling Everheart: "You got me, Bill." Then, in a defiant act, the one that would be his last, the young murderous member of the Lee gang squeezed off a final round in an effort meant to blow Everheart's head off. But the youngster was in the throes of pain, and his aim was no good. His bullet only grazed Everheart's ear and blew his hat off. But Penn had occupied the attention of his pursuers long enough for Hayes and Beard to escape.[55]

Penn: dead at twenty-two. He finally paid the supreme price for his many crimes. The posse then pursued Hayes and Beard who had escaped into Indian Territory. About thirty miles north of Sherman, the authorities found Beard hiding in a territorial sheriff's house where he was arrested. With the notorious Beard in tow, they took Penn's body to Sherman where Penn's sister, called a good girl, became frantic in her grieving when she saw the dead body. Some posse members later delivered his body to his mother who still lived on the family place near Kentucky-Town. Hayes? In the chaos that developed while the posse closed on Beard, he managed to escape, a flight that one of the authorities described as "miraculous." Beard also managed to escape.[56]

Simultaneously with the killing of Penn, military authorities identified a man who split time between Fannin County and the Indian Territory and who probably associated with the Lee gang; or at a minimum, he did the same kind of work in terrorizing area blacks and white Union men. The renegade was S. D. Turner who had been recently arrested in Fannin County for assault with intent to murder one of the county's deputy sheriffs. Indeed, he had threatened at least a dozen area Unionists who lived in constant dread that he would kill them. They must have celebrated when Sheriff M. W. Bledsoe arrested Turner, but he quickly escaped and went into hiding in the Nations, where the Indians knew him as "Cursing Turner." Authorities chased the man all the way north to Fort Gibson and then east to Fort Smith, Arkansas. Still, Cursing Turner could not be caught and continued his outlaw career even as he disappeared from the pages of history.[57]

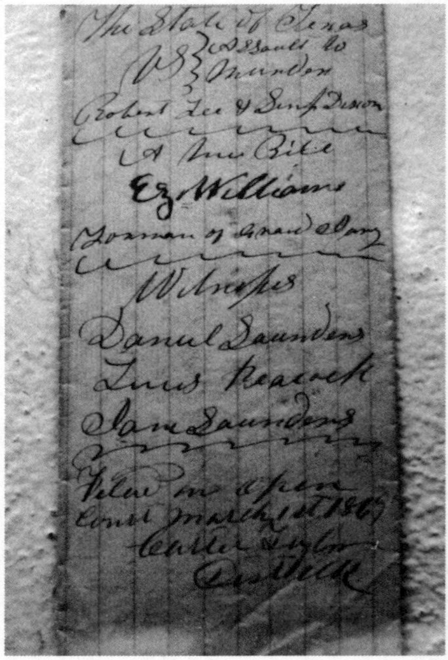

Grand Jury True Bill against Bob Lee and Simp Dixon, March 1, 1869, for assault and murder. Photo courtesy Larry Peacock.

Another known criminal who associated with the Lee gang was John Striklin, leader of a foul bunch that roamed mainly in Bosque, Hill, and Johnson counties. But April of 1869 found Striklin and some of his men in Hunt County where Lee men joined them. The raiders began stealing horses, at least one of which belonged to J. R. De Cordeva. Upon De Cordeva's complaint, Capt. A. C. Pettee, now commanding at Greenville, sent out a detachment that managed to find and arrest Striklin, who had to face justice. But the outlaw revealed nothing about the whereabouts of Bob Lee or any other raiders, including those in Lee's gang and those in his own.[58]

Soon, in early May, three unidentified bounty hunters showed up in Pilot Grove to play their part in the Lee-Peacock, loyalist-Confederate drama. They added their presence to what was becoming a carnival of sorts. The men were after the $1,000 reward on Lee's head, the same reward applying to any of Lee's men. The bounty hunters may have talked to Peacock and other Unionists who would have warned them about the dangerous Lee and also would have talked about the equally dangerous Wildcat Thicket. But if the bounty hunters were warned, they ignored the advice and that cost them their lives. Lee's system of intelligence was such that the desperado rapidly learned that three new guns were now after him. Even if they had not talked to Unionists who would have warned them, the three hunters next action appear idiotic in retrospect, for the decision that they made led directly to their demise. Leaving Pilot Grove at daybreak, they foolishly rode straight into Wildcat Thicket. Only Lee and a few of his men knew their way around in there. After the three became hopelessly lost even though they had not penetrated far, Lee or one of his men picked the bounty hunters off, one-by-one. At the nearby Lee home, Melinda Lee and Dorinda Pierce (the Lee spy) were in the kitchen having breakfast and talking about the day ahead (Dorinda was the teacher at the one-room Lee School and boarded with the Lees). The women heard one shot, then two, then three.[59] Melinda reportedly said softly, "I'm afraid they've got Bob."[60] Such proved not to be true. Worried and afraid, the brave women nevertheless ventured down the trail to the perimeter of the thicket. Going into it a short way, they stumbled upon three dead men, one-by-one, whom neither of the women knew. Later in the day, they returned with helpers, and as best they could, they buried the bodies.[61]

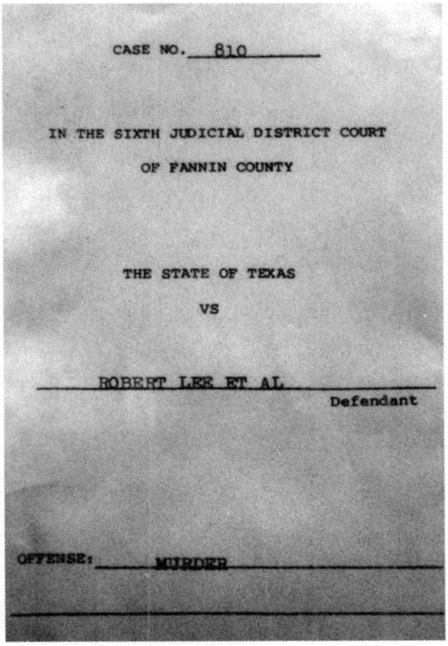

CASE NO. 810

IN THE SIXTH JUDICIAL DISTRICT COURT

OF FANNIN COUNTY

THE STATE OF TEXAS

VS

ROBERT LEE ET AL

Defendant

OFFENSE: MURDER

Murder indictment, Robert "Bob" Lee, et al., case 810, 1869, Fannin County Courthouse. Lee and his gang murdered Ruben Hogue. Photo courtesy Larry Peacock.

The new killings came to the attention of General Reynolds who confirmed the $1,000 reward for Lee and also reaffirmed the bounties of $1,000 for any of his men. The general still planned to hound the Lee gang until he had rid the world of them. But the real break for the federal authorities came when Peacock's friend Henry Boren, the wartime Unionist who had defied the Texas Confederates, became an informer. Much earlier, bad blood had developed between one of the Lee boys and Henry. The two fought it out in a bare-knuckle no-holds-barred contest. Henry won but incurred the wrath of Daniel. He sought Henry out and used his black snake whip to uphold the Lee family honor. Dan almost whipped Henry to death.[62]

Later, when the Civil War began, Henry became one of the leading Unionists in Corners Country, another fact that made him anathema to Lee and his raiders. Perhaps to gain revenge against the Lees but more likely because he was a sincere Unionist, Henry Boren eventually contacted Peacock and Union troopers. At the time Lt. Charles Campbell, now in command of the post at Pilot Grove, had small patrols in near constant motion, scouring the countryside looking for Lee and other lawless men. But Henry had expertise that all other loyal men lacked. He had spent time in all the area thickets when hiding from Confederate authorities during the war. That he knew his way around in Wildcat Thicket was most relevant to Campbell's way of thinking. Why Boren had not helped authorities earlier is a mystery, but on May 22, 1869, he came in to talk with Campbell. The lieutenant sent out a detachment of three sergeants and twelve more men, one of whom was Peacock—with Henry as their guide—to find Lee and arrest him. After Peacock picked up a trail, in a three-day campaign, the squad endured heavy thunderstorms, contended with swollen streams, slept in the open during downpours, and ate cold food. Then they made their way through heavy bottoms and dense underbrush. Still following the trail, they zig-zagged through Corners Country hoping to find Lee. The rains made the area almost impassable, but the men would not break off their search. Finally, the trail led them to Wildcat Thicket. Whereupon, Boren agreed to lead the troopers to the different entrances. With Peacock leading the authorities, the party left guards at every entrance to stop any escape attempts. Since Henry also knew the tiny trails through the thicket, he led the rest of the men in but a short way. The date was May 24, 1869, and a cold fate was closing in on Captain Bob Lee.[63]

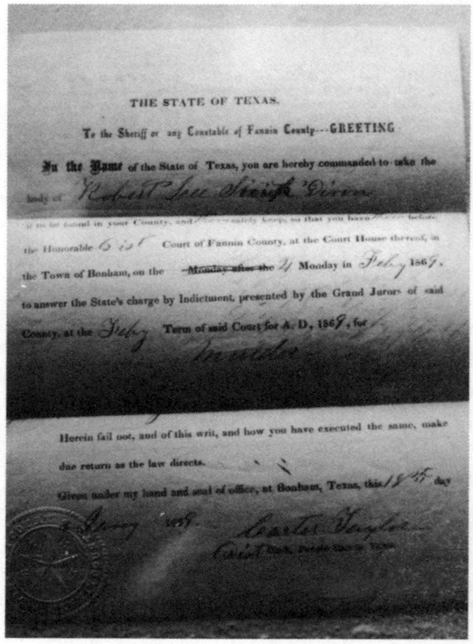

THE STATE OF TEXAS.

To the Sheriff or any Constable of Fannin County---GREETING

In the Name of the State of Texas, you are hereby commanded to take the body of Robert Lee

if to be found in your County, and ... safely keep, so that you have ... before the Honorable 6 ist Court of Fannin County, at the Court House thereof, in the Town of Bonham, on the ~~Monday after the~~ 4 Monday in Feby 1869, to answer the State's charge by Indictment, presented by the Grand Jurors of said County, at the Feby Term of said Court for A. D. 1869, for Murder

Herein fail not, and of this writ, and how you have executed the same, make due return as the law directs.

Given under my hand and seal of office, at Bonham, Texas, this 18th day ... 1869.

Carter Taylor

Murder warrant, February, 1869. Photo courtesy Larry Peacock.

The day before, some troopers assigned to watch the Lee home had spotted the outlaw in his yard playing with his three-year-old child. But the sergeant in charge of the detail refused to give the order to fire for fear of killing the little one. That very night, family members talked to Lee, urging him to flee, to go into hiding far away. Perhaps he could get to Mexico and stay there until die-hard Southerners redeemed the Lone Star State. Or he could go into hiding in the Indian Nations. Bob refused, saying that he feared his antagonists would kill his father or other relatives. He also believed that he had to stay to lead his partisans, who might all be hunted down should he leave. Despite his life of crime, Lee still had sand. He could not leave his family or his men. After having breakfast at home the next day, Lee mounted up, intending to return to the thicket and to take his men their breakfasts. He was almost in the thicket when he encountered the posse.[64]

Asked to surrender, Lee instead reached for one of his weapons, and the posse opened fire. Later, some sources said that Henry Boren—in a final act of revenge against Daniel for the whipping and against the Confederates who had hounded him during the war—fired the first shot. Then, all in the posse opened up. Hit at least eight times, Lee, saying not a word, without whimper or cry, slid from his saddle, dead by the time he hit the ground. His horse got away safely and loped home riderless. The empty saddle announced to wife Melinda and Dorinda that what they had earlier feared had now come true. The Confederate terror, the "Man Eater," Bob Lee was gone. Peacock's friend Stephen Marshall, a staunch Unionist, led the men who took the body to Lee Cemetery and buried it. Shortly before he died, Lee had boasted of killing forty-two men, mostly freedmen and their white Unionist allies.[65] Thus, many men had to pay the price in the bloody chain of events that finally put Lee in his grave: The last member of Northeast Texas's outlaw triumvirate was dead, but the Lee-Peacock affair was far from finished. Simp Dixon, Dick Johnson, and others were prepared to take Bob's place and continue their New Rebellion as the War of Reconstruction continued its violent course.

Bob Lee's Grave in Lee Cemetery near Leonard, Texas. Photo by David Carter. Courtesy Larry Peacock.

And continue it did. The bloody trail—one littered with scores of dead bodies that Lee and men like him had left behind—cowed most of the Union-

Lee Cemetery in Wildcat Thicket near Leonard, Texas. The sign was replaced with a state historical marker, which was then stolen. Photo courtesy Larry Peacock.

ists in Northeast-East Texas. The entire area remained chaotic. Bureau agents like James Curtis in Jefferson repeatedly complained that outlaws besieged the region. Reportedly, Dallas County, Titus County, and other East-Northeast Texas areas were still out of control. According to several sources, a state of near anarchy had existed in Palestine and Anderson County for about one year, about the same being true for Crockett and Houston counties. Plus, the situation in Corners Country remained volatile. The state of affairs became so intolerable to freedmen and Unionists that J. A. Wright, tax assessor and collector of Anderson County, closed his January 12, 1869, letter to Governor Pease with the words: "Do something for us for *God Sake.* 'Let us have Peace'."[66]

According to Unionists in Dallas, their town had been out of control since 1868 because their military garrison had been transferred. Parker of the Lee gang and other desperados had slipped into Dallas County and commenced to commit deviltry. The local Freedmen's Bureau agent, Capt. William Horton, fled after killers threatened his life. He said that he would return only if a bodyguard of troops protected him. In August, almost fifty prominent Dallasites signed a petition asking for government troops. The citizens begged for relief. By May, practically the entire population of Mount Pleasant in Titus County was in an open state of rebellion to hear Lt. C. G. Gordon tell it. With a detachment of men, he traveled from his post in Jefferson to Mount Pleasant, hoping to catch area outlaw Elijah Guest, a friend of Bob Lee, but found the town's residents, most of whom had harbored the renegade at one time or another, ready to take on the Yankees. Gordon did not find Guest, but he did arrest another Rebel, Jim Blake, along with Peter Denton, who was also a felon. Both were guilty of aiding Guest many times. Like other military officers, bureau men, and troopers, Lieutenant Gordon summed up the problem, alleging a mass conspiracy, saying that people in Northeast-East Texas were "in a state of sympathy with Guest and his Confederates." Gordon explained that "the only information that can be obtained [about] these desperados is through a few loyal citizens who have identified them-selves with the [Unionist] cause and who if immediate action is not taken . . . will pay the forfeit [with their lives].[67]

Only occasionally did loyalists have any victories, one of which occurred in July. Afraid for his life now that the federal crackdown had taken his leaders like Baker, Bickerstaff, and Lee, a Bowie County desperado, Alfred K. Ellett, turned himself in to the military post in Clarksville. He faced certain punishment, but he was fated to live. Guerrilla leader Henry Farrar, who usually ran with Bickerstaff and helped him with the siege of Sulphur Springs, was another matter. In September he was bedeviling the Corners counties, riding with Simp and Dick Johnson. The men were now operating mainly in Hunt and contributing to the general instability and mayhem of the area. Farrar intended to seize Lee's mantle, replace him, and commit more cold-blooded murders in the process. Military authorities could not arrest him because his informants always told him of troop movements and scouts made by civilian authorities. Often, the activities of Farrar and other raiders still prevented courts from sitting, just as in the past. In September, reports coming out of Sherman indicated that no district court had convened since April of 1868 when the last one opened in Denison. As he had complained of earlier, District Judge Hardin Hart believed that no courts in his district could be convened, saying that he would be sacrificing his life should he try. Hart knew of what he spoke. Earlier, in July of 1868, one of Lee's men had accosted Hart at home. The villain cursed and threatened the judge, who had the courage to engage in a shootout in his own front yard. Even though he knew that the Lee bunch would seek revenge, the judge killed the man in self defense.[68]

Despite Hart's fears for his own safety, he soon defied the desperadoes by trying to hold court in Greenville. Accompanied by a bodyguard of cavalrymen, commanded by Major John Kirk of Pennsylvania, Hart held his court in Bonham in September even as the Lee partisans were still active. Earlier, Kirk had protected him when he held court in McKinney and Bonham. So it was that the major, his detachment of one corporal and five privates, Hart, and District Attorney J. L. Gray saddled-up on September 3, 1869. On a newly cut road about twenty-five feet wide, the group headed toward Greenville where they would convene court once again. The new road cut through dense thickets in certain places. Simp Dixon, the mysterious Hayes, Farrar, and William Pettit were now leading Bob's gang. They and their men ambushed the judge's party en route when the group was about seven miles beyond Bonham. A witness identified the attackers as what was left of the Lee guerrillas and named the offenders.[69]

According to the *McKinney Messenger,* "six or seven fiends in human form, armed with shot guns, revolvers, and Spencer rifles" had picked a place where dense thickets bordered the road on both sides. The fiends had planned well. They had cut paths into their thickets and had even put up impressive breastworks of logs and brush. Farther down the road was another thicket similarly completed with paths and breastworks. Clearly, the desperadoes had split up, intending that if the first ambush failed, the second would have another chance to finish the judge. Later, the *Messenger* reported that both Hart and Gray were instantly killed. That proved to be an exaggerated rumor, but the truth was bad enough, as the *Messenger* corrected its later account of the incident.[70]

First, one of the gang shot Hart, hitting him in the right side of his chest near his heart. Another bullet also hit him on his right side. Yet more shots shattered one of his arms, breaking it in two places above his elbow. Later, that arm had to be amputated. Before going down, the judge recognized two of the murderers—Simp Dixon and Hayes. Others who attacked the judge and were recognized by the guards included William Pettit and Homer Clements. Also a victim of the gunplay, Gray was lucky. He only had his horse shot out from under him. The troopers? During the melee, four of them lost all heart. As fast as they could, they wheeled and spurred their steeds back toward Bonham, most willing to exchange the judge's life in return for their own. But Kirk and one brave trooper who refused to run fired round after round. They held off the killers long enough for Gray to drag Hart for about thirty yards into another thicket and hide.[71]

As the battle continued, Kirk tried to fight his way to Gray and Hart. He almost made it to them, but the assassins saw him and opened up. After they wounded him in the thigh, he gave up and made his retreat, accompanied by the lone trooper who had stayed with him to the end. Believing that they had killed Hart, the remnants of Lee's gang, not a one of whom had been hurt, then vanished; whereupon, the woebegone Gray went for help but got lost in a thicket and for a time wandered around in it lost, not being able to get out. Then, once he escaped the thicket, he could not find a house nearby. Meanwhile, the severely wounded judge gave up on Gray, got up, and crawled and staggered for about two miles before he found the nearest house, whose occupants cared for him.[72] Though grievously injured, Hart, minus one arm, survived, ultimately resumed his legal duties, and continued to play a role in the struggle as it ran its bloody course.

The *McKinney Messenger* reported that the day after the ambush, observers saw fifteen malefactors, two of whom were Hayes and Parker, all in one band on the Bonham-White Rock Road about four miles from White Rock. All the guerrillas were well armed. With guns drawn, they stopped a courier from Bonham who had been to Greenville to tell Hart's family of the disaster but to also assure them that the judge was still alive. After questioning the courier, the Rebels were chagrined to learn that they had not finished the judge, but they allowed the courier to go on his way unmolested.[73]

Immediately after the attempted assassination, some area loyalists wrote Governor Pease, saying that, even after the tragedy, court needed to be held to bring felons to justice. Such was the view of McKinney's Unionist politician James W. Thomas. Important civil and criminal cases were at hand, said Thomas. He wanted a special military court or a proper civilian court, suggesting that District Attorney Gray temporarily serve as judge in Hart's place.[74]

Thomas was also the editor of the *McKinney Messenger.* He finally realized something important, the recognition of which escaped many observers, including some people in authority. Thomas realized that the New Rebellion was real, that former Confederate Texans were fighting a Second Civil War, and that they intended to win this time. Thomas offered the following:

> This cowardly, vindictive and fiendish attack on Judge Hart demands . . . a prompt and vigorous effort . . . to bring the guilty parties to justice. A military force, sufficiently strong to scour the country in every direction, capture or exterminate the banded villains wherever found and bring them, their aiders and abetters to a justice which shall be both swift and sure should at once be sent here . . . it now being manifest that the only alternative left good citizens is to conquer a peace, the war to that end should be short, sharp, and decisive.[75]

Unfortunately, Thomas's desire to "conquer a peace" was not to be. As late as March of 1870, Judge Hart, minus one arm, was still not traveling his circuit. He was unable to hold his court anywhere but in Bonham where he had some protection. What was left of the Lee gang and other desperadoes still controlled most of the Corners' counties, and Hart believed that his life would only be "sacrificed" should he travel beyond the limits of safety, for "very bitter personal enemies" of his abounded. The Lee men still intended to kill Hart if they could.[76]

Clearly, Bob Lee's death had not ended the Lee-Peacock, loyalists *vs.*

Confederate struggle nor had it made living in Northeastern Texas much easier or safer. Much more mayhem developed before the rugged Lee-Peacock chapter of the Second Civil War ran its course. Writing from Greenville in July of 1869, Lt. William Hoffman may have given the best analysis of the turmoil, an analysis that is still thought provoking for those who study the Reconstruction era today. Speaking of the Corners counties and the larger East-Northeast Texas region, Hoffman said that the Southern Rebels' hatred for the white loyalists and for the freedmen was such that it could never be overcome. The freedmen's situation was deplorable, he said, as he echoed the sentiments of all those who had seen blacks robbed or beaten, raped or murdered. White Union civilians were similarly persecuted, with some of their number also being killed. Even worse, Lieutenant Hoffman surmised that the hatred would be passed from one generation to the next: "The coming generation, children and children's children[,] are zealously reared to the one great tenet: implacable hatred to the [Union] government."[77] The subsequent history of the South suggests that young Hoffman knew of what he spoke.

Chapter 8

The Lee-Peacock Struggle Plays Out

The morning after the troopers and their civilian volunteers rid the Corners counties of Bob Lee, Bill Boren—a Lee man who earlier may have been a Quantrill raider—rode out to his Uncle Henry Boren's place. Bill called out for his uncle who had just finished breakfast. Henry—the man who probably fired the first shot in the volley that killed Lee—came out into his front yard to see what his nephew wanted, but he came out hostile and armed. He knew that his nephew was a Rebel to the core and was a renegade who had ridden with Lee before joining the young murderer John Wesley Hardin. Henry verbally threatened his nephew, demanding that he leave immediately. Without any hesitation, Bill drew a revolver and shot his uncle to death, an act of revenge for Henry's part in the killing of Lee. Yet, Bill claimed self-defense. Some time later, after Peacock was killed, Bill—hiding out in Montague County in the company of young Hardin—wrote his Uncle Dick Boren, Henry's brother. In his missive, Bill tried to explain why he had killed his uncle Henry.[1] Upon reading the letter, one can easily grasp the extent of the extreme hatred that die-hard Southerners had for the Union and its supporters. Writing to his Uncle Dick, he declared:

> I know that you are aware that my feelings were entirely against the Union . . . and Henry was with us at first as you know and just as you were. I felt no anxiousness when Henry joined the Unionist cause as we had never seen eye to eye on [some] matters. . . . Oh, that godforsaken day when Henry stained the proud Texas name of Boren with the blood of cousin Bob Lee. . . .
>
> Now, you might still reflect that I am wayward in my actions because I joined the raiders and for this you no doubt condemn my shooting Henry but I say to you that under any circumstances and even if Henry had not been [a] relation I should have had to do the same [thing]. . . .
>
> That morning is burned in my mind like none other[.] I came to Henry's home and Enoch was chopping wood. I said 'Enoch is your father home?' And no sooner said than Henry came to his door and was armed and said 'god damn you, Bill get off my property.' . . .

> Of course, we argued and cousin Bob Lee was not yet in his grave and I profaned somewhat I admit and Henry pulled down on me with every intent to shoot me but I . . . was quicker. I felt no anxiousness over saving myself from certain destruction even though much has been put to [said] about Henry's gun being unfired and my being a raider shooting him in cold blood. . . .[2]

It is interesting that Bill Boren mentioned that he joined the raiders. He thereby admitted that he was in Lee's gang that persecuted freedmen, white Unionists, and U.S. troopers in Texas. Bill went on to lament that

> Much has been laid at my door since and god knows should I have known then what I have since learned I would not have joined the raiders then or run off later to be with friend Wes Hardin knowing him[,] as I have since learned of it and his ways—yet he has been a good friend and stood by me through it all. We have come back from the [Indian] territory together, and he says he will not come back to the four corners unless it is to dig up cousin Bob's gold but that being a small chance *he is going instead to search for the bastards who killed his own cousins* [authors' italics] if you will recall Wes having cause to mourn from the same faction [Unionists] that causes the Borens now to mourn.[3]

The statement places Hardin in the region when Peacock met his cruel fate and exposed the outlaw's motives for seeking and trying to kill Peacock and other area Unionists like him. Bill Boren? He was "baited" back to the Corners some years later. Henry's son Enoch killed him to avenge his father. In large part, just as the "Texas Troubles" sent Dixon men and boys to their graves, so, too, was the Boren family decimated, along with the Lee and Peacock families.[4]

With Bob Lee dead, his gang eventually disintegrated, and various of the malefactors scattered, some to parts unknown, while others continued to operate independently in Corners Country. Simp Dixon and Dick Johnson disappeared as did the mystery man known only as Hayes. Mace Bowman also vanished. One day he would turn up in New Mexico as a lawman. Dick rode for West Texas where he hid for a time while Simp headed south to lose himself in Navarro County where he had relatives, the Hardin bunch. For a time, he stayed with them and spent much of his time running with his cousin Johnny, only a sixteen-year-old who had already had brushes with the law and had killed at least one freedman. The two rode together hunting for wild game, going cow-hunting to capture a few strays, or just heading to town for a day of merriment in the saloon, where they celebrated their misspent lives.[5]

In May of 1869, they were out cow-hunting when a squad of six or seven Union troopers spotted them. The squad turned to ride toward the two cousins. Simp and Johnny had no intention of being questioned by the troopers; the boys jointly decided not to truck with them. Simp still had a price on his head, and one or more of the men in the squad might recognize him or Wes. The two young brave hearts decided that their best chance to escape was to attack the soldiers and perhaps take them by surprise. Firing lead as they charged, Simp and Wes killed two Union men. The other members of the squad became so frightened that they turned their horses, spurring them for a fast retreat. Even so, Simp knew that his visit to Navarro County was finished—lawmen or more troopers would soon close on him. He decided to go farther south to Limestone County where he had other Dixon relatives in the Springfield-Cotton Gin area. At dawn the next day, he rode away, his saddle bags full of food and ammunition for the pistols in his belt and for the shotgun hanging from his saddle horn. After Simp had gone a distance, young Hardin gave Simp a last wave and then added the best complement that one brigand could give another. Wes turned to two boys about his age and reported proudly: "There goes undoubtedly the most dangerous man in Texas."[6]

More gun play visited Corners Country. Quoting the *Waxahachie Argus,* the *Dallas Herald* proclaimed that "two [of the] citizens who assisted the Federal cavalry in the killing of Bob Lee some three months since, were both killed last week in Fannin County. One fell by the hand of Bob Lee's son, twelve years of age, and the other by one of Lee's friends, we learn from a private letter from Bonham."[7] However, first generation Lee descendants disputed the claim that Bob's son killed anyone.[8]

Later, on September 25, the *Dallas Herald* headline read: "SUICIDE OF NOTED DESPERADO," a statement meaning that another Lee man had exited this world. In his story, the *Herald*'s editor said that the mysterious Hayes, who had belonged to the Lee guerrillas, died by his own hand.[9] The newspaper man concluded that "one by one these outlaws are being removed, and we hope ere too long to be free of their presence."[10] Actually, the last days of Hayes—who had once joined Quantrill and later rode with Bloody Bill Anderson—were more complicated. After Lee fell, Hayes joined the desperado William Pettit, who terrorized both Collin and Dallas counties after having become a member of the Lee gang. In mid-1869, the duo murdered at least eight to ten freedmen and robbed many blacks who lived in northern Dallas County and probably those in southern Collin County as well. Yet, they safely hid in Dallas County which was virtually out of control. Dallas County Judge A. Bledsoe lamented that Pettit, Hayes, and men like them were fleeing other area counties and were collecting in his region where they thought they were safe. Plus, the local Klansmen continued running amok, beating, robbing, and killing blacks, including women. Dallas still did not have a secure jail, so the sheriff had been sending his prisoners to McKinney, but now Bledsoe said that McKinney's jail was overflowing. Consequently, the Dallas sheriff was doing his best to guard prisoners, but he could not depend on his deputies, for dependable guards were hard to find. Guards with Southern sympathies allowed prisoners to escape at a rate of about three a week. Meanwhile, Pettit had even threatened the life of the federal district judge. The outlaw also publically dared any authority to arrest him.[11]

Nevertheless, leaders in Dallas apparently stiffened their resolve. Pettit and Hayes were forced to slip back into Collin County to avoid arrest. Called a "noted robber, murderer, and assassin" by the editor of the *McKinney Messenger* (who got the names Parker and Hayes confused) Hayes, accompanied by Pettit, went into hiding in the home of the "widow" Fields. Her place was about ten miles northwest of McKinney. Calling themselves cattle drovers, they convinced Fields to let them stay the night after they told her that Hayes was suffering from a "rheumatic affection" (possibly true) and was "helpless." Hayes and Pettit had been in the party that tried to slay Judge Hardin Hart but apparently had not heard whether the attempt was successful. They asked Fields if she knew anything about the assassination. They wanted to know what area newspapers had said about it. No doubt they wanted to know if they were implicated in the cowardly attack, and if it had been successful in dispatching the judge.[12]

The next morning, a Saturday, Pettit abandoned his friend after riding to a physician Dulany's place and asking him to attend to Hayes, after which Pettit requested directions to Plano. When Hayes saw Dulany, his first reaction was to inquire about Pettit. Upon learning that he had been abandoned, Hayes cussed and became restless and uneasy. Then, on Sunday, a number of friends visited the Fields's household, most of them looking in on Hayes and offering encouragement, but their presence troubled him, for he feared being identified as the scoundrel whom he was, since he had committed so many heinous crimes. Under the headline "Another Desperado Gone," according to James Thomas of the *McKinney Messenger:*

> A guilty conscience needs no accuser. Imagining that he was, or would be, recognized, and seeing no chance of escape, he . . . [called] to his bedside a [N]egro boy who had been left in his room to wait on him, he told him to bring his saddle bags . . . he then instructed the boy to get out one of his pistols . . . he [Hayes] grasped [it] . . .

and deliberately [raised] it to his forehead and [shot himself in] the brain."[13]

The editor continued, saying that Hayes had ridden with Lee and had helped Lee and Dick Johnson murder Colonel Erwin of Grayson County, a soldier named Robinson, and "old man" Loving of Dallas County. "How many have fallen by his [Hayes] hands no man can tell," wrote the editor. Thomas also credited Hayes as being one of the leaders of the raiders who killed a man named Grey and tried to assassinate Judge Hart, mentioning that, on examination of Hayes dead body, Hayes had in his possession the judge's hat and other wearing apparel. Plus, Hayes had a pair of Colt revolvers, with ivory handles that once belonged to a federal "E. H." of "Co. D." A fount of knowledge, Thomas added that the horse Pettit rode on and the saddle upon which he sat belonged to District Attorney J. L. Gray, for the brand on the sorrel and the markings on the saddle proved as much.[14]

Despite the *Messenger*'s report about desperadoes continuing to fall, tragedies still abounded in the days ahead. After he left Navarro County and the Hardin family, Simp Dixon slipped into Limestone County where his relatives harbored him. He took the alias "Jones" and also may have used the name "Thompson." He became close to his cousins, the brothers Tom and Bud Dixon who later delivered their own brand of terrorism to the people in East Texas. He also developed a close relationship with Joe Hardin, John Wesley Hardin's brother. Simp usually stayed out of sight, but now there was something of a raider in him, something of a guerrilla fighter who was out of control. He could not live peacefully. He recruited a new gang, their number including some of his Limestone County relatives. He continued his campaign of terror by robbing and murdering more blacks. Some were shot, others were hanged. For example, Simp, probably accompanied by some of his new comrades, caught Seymour Abrams and Norville Rhodes on the old Springfield-Groesbeck Road and hanged them from a tree beside the trail. Soon, area freedmen were talking in hushed tones about "Dixie," a "nigger killer."[15]

Primary documents and secondary sources corroborate each other and confirm that, indeed, "Dixie" was Simp Dixon. Many freedmen began hiding and sleeping in the woods at night trembling with fear that he might be near and might come their way. Others forted-up in their cabins simply hoping that Dixie, like a living plague, would pass them by.[16] The hotspur also rode in adjacent Freestone County where he continued his murderous ways. The immediate vicinity of Cotton Gin, which was close to the northeastern Limestone County line, was the scene of the greatest terror, a place where Freedmen's Bureau Agent Charles Culver had already been murdered because he dared help the area's freedmen. Simp may also have continued to operate, off-and-on, in Navarro County in conjunction with cousin Wes Hardin.[17]

In Navarro County, authorities brought at least one member of the gang to justice, the circumstances being somewhat bizarre. On January 19, 1870, a group of seven white men accosted and whipped two blacks, John and Mary Riggs, both of whom soon filed complaints with the federal post commander in Corsicana. All the perpetrators fled except two: Bud Martin and John Stricklin who—as local intelligence had it—was a Lee man when in the Corners. Actually, authorities near the Corners had earlier arrested Stricklin, but he managed an escape. Corsicana Post Commander Lieutenant W. A. Borthwick captured both men who were heavily armed at the time. The authorities thus removed Martin and Stricklin as threats.[18]

Meanwhile, authorities were still after Simp. In February of 1871, the new state representative from Limestone County, the freedman David Medlock, informed Republican Governor E. J. Davis about the doings of Simp. In late January, Dixon went to Medlock's father's house. Impersonating a soldier, the uniformed Simp told Medlock's father that he had orders to confiscate all arms in the house, but the black Texan—surrounded by friends—refused to deal with Simp. Instead, he told the outlaw to get out. Dixon left but soon threatened the lives of freedmen Ralph Long and Merritt Trammel, who was a member of the Texas State Police, a new organization created by the new Republican state government, the agency charged with enforcing law and order in Texas. A few days later, intending to carry out his threat against Long and Trammel, Simp went to the small black community where the two men lived. Dixie had "two six shooters buckled around him and one in a holster on the horn of his saddle," according to Medlock.[19]

But a group of about ten freedmen saw Dixie's approach and rallied around to defend their two friends. Simp then rode away, but a new altercation followed on the next Sunday. Reverend Phillip Fields preached in the community's Baptist Church, staying afterward to do personal chores. Returning home about dusk, Fields was attacked and killed by a party of men most likely led by Simp. Of course, he was shot in the back, the usual method of attack for Lee men. Apparently, the killers allowed Fields one last prayer, for later examination of the shot's trajectory revealed that the victim was in a kneeling position when murdered.[20]

When the area's citizens could take no more, one of their number, Policeman Trammel, slipped away, rode to Waco, and summoned help. The help turned out to be an army detachment, commanded by Sgt. Adam Desch. Coming out of their post in Waco, with Trammell serving as a guide, the troopers finally tracked the outlaw. In late January or early February of 1870, the detachment found Dixie hiding in a house within three miles of Springfield, Limestone

County. When first spotted, Simp was in the front yard heading for the house just after turning his horse out. The soldiers demanded surrender, but Simp drew two revolvers and began firing.[21]

Realizing that he could not make it to his horse, Simp continued to fire while he retreated into nearby woods. As the skirmish continued, inexplicably a wagon driver with a four-horse team passed by on the road near the woods. Simp ran for the wagon and threatened to kill the man if he did not cut a horse loose. Instead of obeying, the frightened driver jumped from the wagon and fled in terror. Simp then cut a horse loose, but before he could mount it, a soldier rushed forward and shot the steed. Then Pvt. James Jackson rushed Dixon but stumbled and fell just before reaching his target.[22]

Dixon fell upon Jackson and tried to shoot him in the head, but the soldier caught the pistol just as Simp pulled the trigger. In grabbing the gun, Jackson managed to get one of his fingers between the hammer and firing pin. Then, he wrenched it from Simp and clubbed the outlaw in the forehead. By that time, Sergeant Desch had closed on Dixon. The intrepid Desch fired his carbine but once. Simp, the East Texas terror, now called Dixie, collapsed backwards, dying instantly. Later, Desch had words of praise for the four privates in the detachment, who had fought valiantly, adding that he and his squad left Simp's body by the roadside near farmer Dick Oliver's house. Newspaper men had a field day giving their accounts of the battle, but most embellished their stories; yet they were correct in reporting the outcome of the fight. According to the *Waco Register,* the "deceased is said to have been a confederate of Bob Lee and Bickerstaff and was charged with a number of murders in Eastern Texas. He is said to have been part of a band of professional murderers and cut-throats who infest the country."[23]

Some sources err by saying that Desch's men buried Dixon, without honors, in the Lewisville Cemetery, which was later known as the Fort Parker Memorial Cemetery. Instead, other men—their names forever lost to history—buried the body after the federals left. They dug his grave at a diagonal in relation to others, saying that they buried him crossways because he was always crossways with the world. Crossways indeed he was, for some latter day sources credit Simp with the deaths of thirty Yankees and white loyalists in addition to an untold number of freedmen, whose deaths were not always reported to the authorities. Indeed, as Wes Hardin had said earlier, Simp Dixon had been among the most dangerous men in Texas. Meanwhile, Desch and his men searched for but found no trace of Simp's cousin John Wesley Hardin who was rumored to be in the area. But rumor also had it that when he learned of Simp's death, Wes headed south on a fast horse and for a time vanished. What of Policeman Trammell who first summoned then led the patrol that killed Dixie? After Democrats "redeemed"

Texas in 1874, some of their number targeted Trammell for death. A strong man who fought back in self-defense, Trammell killed several whites. Whereupon, Democrat authorities branded him a desperado and hunted him as an outlaw. Governor Richard Coke put a $300 reward on the former policeman's head. Eventually, he had to use a cave in a bank of the Navasota River for a safe house. Later, he died at the hands of a criminal vaguely known only as "Old Hargrave" or "Old M. D. L. Harcrow" shortly after the killer had been released from the Springfield jail in May of 1875. Harcrow killed Trammell for the $300 reward, but area black woman Mollie Kirkland believed the plot was thicker. She accused the local authorities of orchestrating Trammell's murder. They offered to let Harcrow go free, she charged, if he would promise to kill the black man. Could Harcrow have been a member of the old Lee gang? Was he seeking revenge for the killing of Simp? Earlier, a man named "Hargrave" in Corners Country had ridden with Lee. Could Trammell's killer have been the same man? Later, the Trammell family had more grief. Area authorities arrested Wade Trammel, Merritt's brother, on dubious charges. Found guilty of murder by a kangaroo court, Wade was then hanged. His biggest crime likely consisted of being a black Unionist and the brother of a state policeman who had been a thorn in the side of the ex-Confederates.[24]

The atrocities committed in the Second Civil War stirred the freedmen's community. Whites who hated blacks still roamed Limestone and adjacent counties after Simp's death. Freedmen still lived with "continual dread." Representative Medlock begged Republican Governor Davis for relief. Medlock asked for "some means of safety from our enemies." The new representative said that "they consider their lives unsafe, especially in going abroad at night . . . [to attend] religious meetings. Not only in Limestone but in Falls, McLennan[,] and the adjacent counties the same condition of things exist."[25] Clearly, like Bob Lee, Baker, and Bickerstaff, Simp cast a long shadow, a long bloody one that lived on long after his death.

After Simp Dixon's demise, Bud and Tom Dixon, along with Joseph "Joe" Gibson Hardin, continued their nefarious activities, aiding John Wesley in his exploits. And Joe had angered many citizens in Limestone and Comanche counties through fraudulent and devious land schemes in addition to being branded as a cattle rustler. After John Wesley returned to the area and killed Brown County Deputy Sheriff Charles M. Webb, he wisely left the vicinity, but many family members remained. Shortly, local authorities arrested and jailed Joe and the two Dixons. About midnight on June 5, 1874, enraged inhabitants of Brown County stormed the courthouse, dragged the three prisoners some distance from Comanche and lynched them. Altogether, vigilantes or lawmen killed eight men, all either family members or friends of the Hardins. The authorities were slowly eliminating those who continued to defy the law.[26]

As authorities were active, the grim reaper returned to Corners Country. Shortly after Simp's death, Unionists in the area located Charlie Dixon, who had joined the raiders, and Dick Johnson, who had just returned from West Texas. Both men were in Black Jack Grove (a thicket near today's Cumby) in Hunt County where they had gone to pick up a load of lumber or to hide, depending upon which source one believes. Peacock, his civilian Unionists supporters, and a squad of troopers found their way through the thicket and discovered the men's hideout. The authorities immediately attacked, killing Charlie and wounding Dick who got away and headed back to West Texas once more, where he again hid for a time. At some point, the Peacock-led Unionists also killed Bob Dixon, another Lee partisan. Having lost too many people in his own family, old Irish Jack soon died of grief.[27]

After the killings, when news of Simp's death reached the Corners, Lee partisans twisted the facts once again. According to local lore, some of Peacock's loyal men from the Corners had tracked Simp down near Springfield and murdered him while he was, naturally, unarmed and defenseless. Most biased local accounts also had it that some area freedmen of the Corners might have been involved. Such stories, then, continued the myth that Peacock was a devil and that Lee, his gang, and his sympathizers were blameless victims. In fact no one from the Corners was involved in Simp's death. Only Trammell and the squad of men coming out of Waco took part in the attack that killed Simp. Another bit of folklore related that after Lee's death, Peacock quickly left Texas, after which the troubles in the Corners ended. While that tale is false, it is a fact that the Lee-Peacock struggle did indeed end soon. After they learned of Simp's death, the surviving Lees and Dixons sent word to Dick in West Texas that Simp was dead and thus continued building the chain of events that led to Peacock's murder.[28]

Lewis knew that he was still a marked man. Even after the killing of many Lee followers, Peacock's living enemies were still legion. At some point after Lee's death, Lewis packed up his family in 1869 and temporarily moved to Milam County near Davilla where he found work in a sawmill. He also did more work for the Republican party, campaigning for E. J. Davis and other candidates. During the elections that put Davis in the governor's chair and put the Republicans in charge of Texas, there was allegedly much fraud, a development that Peacock found himself caught up in. In Milam County federal authorities closed the polls on the second day of balloting after a major disturbance. An unkown assailant shot and wounded a military officer who was escorting about one hundred freedmen to Cameron, the county seat, where they would cast their ballots.

When the freedmen reached Cameron, a mob of some 150 to 175 Democrats from Port Sullivan collected at the county seat and refused to allow the blacks to vote, after which authorities closed the polls and confiscated the voting boxes. Peacock was most likely among the area loyalists who sought to no avail to have the votes counted that had been filed prior to the incident involving the riotous mob. The Milam returns were never counted, but the returns did later turn up at the National Archives in Washington as did all the ballots for the 1869 election. The ballots confirmed that Davis, indeed, won the race. Shortly after the election, Lewis soon made a costly mistake. Apparently believing that he and his family would be safe in the Corners because Republicans were supposedly now in control, Lewis escorted his wife and son back to their place in the Corners.[29]

When he received word of Simp's death, Dick Johnson took the news hard. He loved his stepbrother, and he vowed vengeance. After some time had passed and the heat was off him, Dick gathered his personal belongings, saddled up, and once again rode for the Corners. In the early summer of 1871, he quietly slipped back to the area and hid, probably in Wildcat Thicket. Joe Parker joined him there as did another unidentified man. Then on the night of June 13, they hid near Peacock's backyard and fell upon him as the new day dawned. As mentioned, Parson Gentry buried the body before the day was out and counseled Emaline to leave before any new trouble developed. Gentry also told her to contact John Edgar, who was working in another location, and to tell him not to return to the Corners, for Lee partisans would murder him just as they murdered his father. Thinking of her son first, the distraught widow agreed that either she or her son would indeed be killed in another act of revenge by Lee's followers. After throwing together a few belongings, she left the Corners for good. The two of them simply disappeared. As far as anyone in the Corners area knew, they just vanished, forever lost to history. In fact, Emaline went to her daughter Cathy's place, and John Edgar joined her there to hide for a time before later settling permanently west of Fort Worth. John Edgar became a successful farmer, eventually acquiring several tracts of land. He developed more than enough wealth to provide for his mother and for his own family as it came along. Lewis Peacock's survivors endured tragedy and heartache, they were uprooted, but they lived on, and their progeny exists to this day.[30]

Even as the killing of Lewis Peacock virtually ended the fighting in the Corners Country, there were still loose ends, including questions about Dick Johnson, Joe Parker, and the third unidentified man who combined forces to murder Peacock. Johnson's subsequent actions are known. After talking with relatives and listening to their advice, he jumped on a fast horse and headed north, not stopping until he reached a safe haven in Missouri. Apparently starting a new life, he resided there to a ripe old age. Alternately, folk sources report that he may have returned permanently to the Corners in the 1920s. While that is probably not true, it is known that near the end of his life, in the early 1920s, Dick indeed returned to the Corners at least once to visit relatives and old friends, but authorities were apparently not interested in resurrecting old charges. He never had to pay for Peacock's murder. What of Parker? There was money on his head, but he shifted the scene of his action and continued his depredations. Roaming through Dallas and Kaufman counties, he established an alliance with new cohort Billy Graves, and the two in turn forged relations with another band of renegades, including some Lee partisans, who terrorized the sober sorts of the two counties. The new gang apparently stole a number of horses for resale and committed several robberies before leaders in the two besieged counties took firm action—action designed to get rid of the guerrillas.[31]

Because of the misdeeds of Parker, Graves, and their new followers, military authorities sent a Lieutenant Cramen and a detachment of men to ferret out the outlaws. Additionally, settlers in Scyene, Dallas County, and its vicinity became determined to do all that was possible to help the military identify the raiders and their supporters. The sober citizens held a public meeting in Scyene wherein all present deplored the activities of a "band of desperadoes" and condemned all who harbored and gave aid to them. The group agreed to unite as one body to oppose all who disturbed the area and to report any renegades (and those who aided them) to the authorities. Further, the resolutions of the meeting were sent to the newspapers in Dallas, Collin, and Kaufman counties. Once manhandled by Bickerstaff and temporarily forced into hiding, the timid Judge A. B. Norton of the Fifth Judicial District congratulated the citizens for waking up and for realizing that they must help authorities if the region were to be saved from "robberies, horse stealing, murders, etc."[32] However, the judge did not mention his earlier cowardly behavior in running away from the likes of Bickerstaff and going into hiding.

Yet, for all their efforts, the actions of the military and the support citizens gave the soldiers only succeeded in driving Parker and Graves out of the area. The two malefactors moved northeast and slipped into Titus County. There, a few miles south of Mount Pleasant, in September, authorities trapped Parker and Graves inside a stable on the Jefferson Road, three miles south of the town. Both outlaws had hidden and slept in the woods but had stabled their horses. The authorities camped out nearby to await morn when Graves and Parker came for their mounts. After sunrise, they came for their horses, saddled-up, and got atop their steeds, but Graves and Parker were still in the horse lot when they heard a voice demanding their surrender. In the subsequent shootout, lawmen killed

Graves who was hit in the back by a pistol shot. They also grievously, but not mortally, wounded Parker, who was hit by both a pistol shot and the rounds of a double-barreled shotgun, the last of which knocked him off his horse.[33]

Lying on his back in the horse lot and thinking that he was dying, Parker gasped, "boys[,] you have killed the bravest man in Texas." Speaking in near whispers, he went on to tell the posse that he had murdered nine men and identified Lewis Peacock as being among their number. He also graciously confessed that he was a spectacular horse thief of great note. Little is known about the amazing Parker after the shootout except that he survived it and likely spent time incarcerated. But at some point, he became a free man again, perhaps by breaking out of jail, after which he rediscovered an old friend, Hunt County's Jim Roberts, another Lee man. Roberts replaced Graves, and the desperadoes continued their errant ways. The lucky Parker even survived a later newspaper death. In late 1871, *Flake's Daily Bulletin* of Galveston reported that he had been killed in Titus County by a man named Townsend. Yet, Parker lived for three more years. Finally, in 1874, James "Jim" Jones and a posse of officers and civilians tracked Parker down and found him in Collin County in a house northeast of Farmersville, near old Floyd. After the authorities surrounded the house, a voice called for the raider to surrender. He came out shooting instead; whereupon, Jones ended Parker's days with a head-shot that almost severed the outlaw's skull from his body. Jones? He received a $400 reward.[34]

In June of 1876, Parker's new partner in crime, the Lee man Roberts—who, like Parker, was a horse thief of note and a fugitive with several indictments against him in Hunt County—died from wounds inflicted by the Sherman city marshal after a shootout occurred in the street when Roberts resisted arrest. Yet another Lee man thus went to his final reward.[35] But, even after Parker's death and that of a new sidekick, on the matter of Peacock's assassination, the third man was never found, never identified. Was he Mace Bowman? Was he John Wesley Hardin? Or was he some other obscure ruffian? Today, the answer apparently matters not, for the Lee-Peacock fight and all its participants have passed from the pages of history into the mists of legend.[36]

Meanwhile, several major state newspapers carried stories about Peacock's murder. According to a Pilot Grove dispatch dated June 14, 1871, likely sent by Lee partisans, to *Flake's Daily Bulletin:*

> Last evening a squad of men, three in number, arrived with doubled-barreled shotguns, revolvers, et cetera, rode leisurely into our burg. . . . After staying a few minutes, they mounted their horses and rode off in an easterly direction. Since their departure, we are creditably informed that the famous Lewis Peacock, formerly chief-

> in-command of the Peacock Party, was shot to atoms this morning at sunrise in his yard. Political issues were not at all connected with this case.
>
> You have heard of the foul murder of Billy Dixon at Hog-Eye three years ago, and also the brutal killing of Elijah Clark. These are the cardinal points that prompted the destruction of Lewis Peacock. . . .
>
> Since writing the above, it is all confirmed. He [Peacock] is literally torn to pieces.[37]

The *Bulletin*'s account was muddled, for it was Billy of the Lee faction who killed Lige Clark. Additionally, the newspaper erred when saying that politics was not involved. If Lewis had not been a crusading Unionist who led the forces that tried to stand up to the ex-Confederate guerrillas, including the three who murdered him, he would have had a longer life. Newspapers in the Corners counties also carried word about Peacock's murder. For instance, the staunchly pro-Southern editor of the *Bonham Texas News* averred that "Lewis Peacock who is widely known in Texas as the former leader of a band of desperadoes and outlaws, was killed last Wednesday morning by a party of three men."[38]

Relative to varied accounts, both contemporary and after-the-fact, it is clear that the partisan Lee supporters' version of the killing is the story reported by most people and passed down to others over time. Only in that way could a Sam Houston Unionist be tarred once again, his reputation damned both in life and after death. And in the doing, myths replaced facts about the deadly goings-on in Corners Country. Just as the former Confederates' mythical views about the Civil War, the Lost Cause, and the subsequent War of Reconstruction were accepted around the state, so, too, were the mythical memories perpetuated in Corners Country, once a most vicious place where four county lines converge.

Epilogue

Various people have read bits and pieces about ex-Confederate Bob Lee's attempt to kill white loyalists and freedmen and about Lewis Peacock's efforts to stop him. Some researchers and readers have attempted to give the final body count of the imbroglio. One contemporary of the fight set the number at 214 as of mid-1868. Writing in 1981, Lea Lawlis of Northeast Texas agreed when she pegged the number at more than 200. Challenging Lawlis's figures, Larry Peacock conservatively put the number at nineteen, a count that he has revised upward mightily as he has done more research. Bob Lee, himself, claimed to have slain forty-two men just before he died, and he was not counting the killings by other members of his gang. For example, Simp Dixon killed at least thirty men and probably scores more for there was never any report about many of the blacks he murdered. Various members of his bunch also divulged how many murders they committed, with the count running anywhere from nine to thirty for select individuals. In *Mace Bowman: Texas Feudist, Western Lawman,* James Stephen Peters mentioned counts of from fifty to one hundred but personally believed the number was more like thirty before adding that "eighteen are known for certain."[1] In a magazine article that examined the struggle in the Corners, the lay historian Nick Jones dismissed Peters numbers out-of-hand and moved the figure back to "200-odd."[2] Of course, all the numbers are conjecture, for history will never give a final answer. When one remembers that collectively outlaws and Klan terrorists in Northeast Texas killed hundreds if not thousands of people, to set the count of the Lee gang's murders at 200 does not seem extreme, especially since Lee alone accounted for about twenty percent of the total and Simp Dixon alone added another fifteen percent. After all, as the Lee-Peacock struggle was ongoing, on June 4, 1868, C. M. Wilcox set the count at 214. Moreover, the deaths of many freedmen, one of the groups targeted for disaster, were never recorded or investigated by any authority. Certainly, Northeast Texas became a dark and bloody ground by 1862 and remained one until the former Confederates had won the Second Civil War.

In 1981, H. M. Gentry of Whitewright, grandson of Parson Martin Gentry, decided that Lewis Peacock's remains, lying in an unmarked grave, deserved a headstone. Parson Gentry had buried Peacock's body in a secret plot marked only by a Bois d' Arc stake for fear that vandals would desecrate the grave, as the ex-

Confederates no doubt would have, given their hatred for Peacock. Earlier, H. M. Gentry's friend Gus Holmes of Trenton took Gentry to the old cemetery and showed him the grave. Shortly, Holmes died, and Gentry realized that he was now the last person alive who knew the location of the grave. Being a good Samaritan, Gentry bought a headstone and had it engraved by the Love Monument Company. The stone now marks the spot, reading simply: "Lewis Peacock, April 23, 1829, June 14, 1871." Later, in the 1990s, Lewis's descendants, including Larry Peacock, placed a marble slab on the grave. It has the following information:

Lewis Peacock
1824–1871
HOMESTEADED NEAR HERE 1858
BORN IN NORTH CAROLINA
MARRIED EMALINE BENSON IN
WASHINGTON COUNTY GEORGIA 1846
TWO CHILDREN BORN OF THIS MARRIAGE
MALINDA CATHERINE AND JOHN EDGAR
AGENT AND GUNMAN FOR THE
FREEDMEN'S BUREAU
DURING TEXAS RECONSTRUCTION
SHOT AND KILLED AT HIS HOME
3 MILES SOUTHEAST OF HERE
AS A RESULT OF PARTICIPATION
IN TEXAS RECONSTRUCTION
BURIED HERE BY
THE REVEREND MARTIN GENTRY[3]

Although Lewis was never an official Freedmen's Bureau agent and although he probably did not think of himself as a gunman, the slab's message is essentially correct. Lewis was an unofficial agent who helped the federals all he could, and he certainly had to use his guns in self defense most often as the struggle in the Corners ran its bloody course and as he was almost constantly hounded by Lee and his raiders.

In the early 1980s, journalist Bob St. John of the *Dallas Morning News* bought into what was still called the Lee-Peacock Feud. He went to the Corners where he talked with Carl and Betty Stripling, owners of the Boot Hill Store at Pilot Grove. St. John talked to other area locals as well. He found that the history of the so-called feud was still contested ground: "If you say the wrong thing [about] any of the parties involved to the wrong person, you still will get an angry response or a dirty look."[4] St. John also commented that "although it has been about 110 years since it ended, the feud still is talked about locally as though it occurred just yesterday."[5] As Betty Stripling said, "everybody who grows up around here knows about Bob Lee and Lewis Peacock and their followers. It's a story that'll always be retold to kids and hashed over by adults."[6] She could have added that "everybody" disagrees about the exact facts of the case. Both St. John and Stripling accepted the traditional Southern interpretation of what was much more than a personal conflict.[7] More correctly, the story was part of a much larger chapter in Texas' Second Civil War that involved the struggle Unionists had to face in dealing with ex-Confederates, a struggle that men like Peacock ultimately lost.

George Lewis Peacock, grandson of Lewis Peacock, with child. George Peacock was co-author Larry Peacock's grandfather. Photo courtesy Larry Peacock.

In 1986 Kent Biffle, another reporter for the *Dallas Morning News,* became interested in the "murders at the Corners." He sought out Tom Hymer of Leonard, a small town near old Pilot Grove, Leonard having a population of about 1,500. Hymer complied when Biffle asked him to take him to see Bob Lee's grave. While they were driving to the old Lee Cemetery, Biffle asked if the locals talked much about the Lee-Peacock struggle. "Not much," said Hymer, who then admitted that he once got into big trouble when mentioning it. While Hymer and his friends had their daily coffee hour at the Leonard Pharmacy, talk turned to Bob Lee and Lewis Peacock. Hymer jumped in, saying that Lewis probably got what he deserved. "Man, they were all over me," Hymer exclaimed. The widow Johnnie Rogers and Alwyn Golden, retired postmaster of Leonard, "jumped me pretty good. I wasn't thinking, I guess. Mrs. Rogers name was Nance [before she married]." Her ancestors on the Nance side were Peacock supporters and loyal Unionists, and she would not allow Lewis's name to be tarred.[8]

Now, the Corners Country has entered a new millennium, and the story of the Lee-Peacock tangle in the telling and retelling will probably last until the next one. Perhaps lost in the telling and retelling is some of the truth. There was never a real feud, even though some participants were related, for the word feud suggests that only personal animosities existed between the two men—Lee and Peacock. Instead, a more accurate interpretation of events demonstrates that outlaws and Klansmen became determined to win the War of Reconstruction—to win the Second Civil War. They were willing to use any means necessary to achieve their victory. They persecuted, attacked, and killed federal soldiers, white civilian Unionists, and former slaves, especially those blacks who showed their new freedom by behaving like independent people. Lewis Peacock? He was only a Sam Houston Unionist before, during, and after the war. He was one of the loyal men sacrificed along the way while the former Confederates were winning the Texas War of Reconstruction.

Lewis Peacock's tombstone (top) *laid by his descendants. Lower tombstone laid by Homer Gentry, grandson of Parson Martin Gentry, 1981. Photo courtesy Larry Peacock.*

As David Pickering and Judy Falls point out in *Brush Men and Vigilantes: Civil War Dissent in Texas,* often victims like Peacock and his followers were later branded as desperadoes, deserters, and terrorists which is exactly what their persecutors really were. In turn, the real renegades, deserters, terrorists, and traitors were transformed into heroes whose murders came to be viewed as justified executions. The history of history is indeed strange, especially after partisans finish mangling it.[9] In the end, the Unionists of Corners Country engaged in a struggle to uphold the United States Constitution, to support the federal government, and to give the newly freed blacks a modicum of rights. Against overwhelming odds, they lost and were then remanded to the dust bin of history where faulty memories, twisted facts, and bizarre interpretations replaced the truth.

Historians Edgar Sneed and Barry A. Crouch are two of the many scholars who have studied the "history of history" during the Reconstruction era. In 1969, Sneed noted that almost all accounts of the early post-Civil War era in Texas had been written by Texans sympathetic with their ancestors' views, and they allowed their sympathies to color their analyses and final judgments.[10] Those Texans created a "traditional history, in which folk myth stands equal to historical analysis," not to mention the hard facts.[11] Sneed added that most historians had accepted the word of Southern Rebels without question; whereas, in fact the former Confederates, in a life-and-death struggle with Unionists, ignored "reality . . . [as] they vigorously denounced every real and imagined sin they could attribute to their enemies: Negroes, [N]ortherners, and Unionists."[12] In 1990, Crouch updated Sneed's analysis. Crouch noted that revisionists have made much progress in correcting the various myths of Reconstruction era, but he also revealed that the "readings available to the general public still convey the old story of military dominance and Radical misrule," facts that never were.[13]

Thus, Reconstruction myths and old hatreds die hard if they die at all. The foregoing point was illustrated when coauthors Peacock, Smallwood, and Crouch appeared on a Fort Worth television program. The coauthors advanced a revisionist view of Reconstruction by focusing on the Lee-Peacock reality rather than the old myths. Because Smallwood and Crouch lived safely out-of-state, the only coauthor who could be attacked was Peacock who lives in Burleson, just south of Fort Worth. And attacked he was. The man got hate mail via both regular post and e-mail. Some of the haters demanded proof that the revisionist view was correct. This book provides the truth by divulging the sources from which the revisionist view was drawn. Much of the material in this volume comes from primary sources—including those in the National Archives, the Texas State Library, and other library archives in the Lone Star State.

Certainly, the events of the Lee-Peacock struggle and the interpretations of it by traditional historians prove that myth indeed replaces history at times. Although a handful of present-day researchers are trying to set the record straight by reexamining the Reconstruction era and by moving beyond myth toward truth, their work has not been excepted by those white Southerners who think that the Civil War is still raging and that the South still has a chance to win.

Certainly more scholarly research on Reconstruction in the Lone Star State is needed, particularly on the violence of terrorist groups like the Klan and on the violence of the guerrillas, many of whom were also Klansmen. Both groups were most responsible for Texas' Second Civil War. They were most responsible for the ultimate victory by the Democratic redeemers, many of whom denied that there was in fact massive violence and that the violence was most responsible for their victory over the Republicans. The vicious history of Corners Country where four county lines converge proves otherwise. The pattern in the Corners was similar to the larger patterns of violence throughout all of East and Northeast Texas, especially in the countryside where chaos was the rule not the exception. Delving into the doings of Lee and all the other raiders mentioned in the book at least suggests that the larger pattern is fact and that this truth applies to Texas and the larger South as well.

Notes

Abbreviations Used

AGO	Adjutant General's Office
ARIS/TSL	Archives and Information Servies/Texas State Library
BRFAL	Bureau of Refugees, Freedmen, and Abandoned Lands
CFAH/UTA	Center for American History, University of Texas Library
DT	Department of Texas
5MD	Fifth Military District
GP	Governor's Papers (Texas State Library)
LR	Letters Received
LS	Letters Sent
NA	National Archives
NHT	New Handbook of Texas
RG	Record Group (in National Archives)
SWHQ	*Southwestern Historical Quarterly*
TAMC	Texas A&M–Commerce
VF	Vertical File

Introduction. Prelude to a Nightmare

1. The following sources are examples of informative expositions on how myth, memory, and propaganda have distorted the interpretations of the Civil War and Reconstruction eras: David W. Blight, *Race and Reunion: The Civil War in American Memory* (Cambridge: Harvard University Press, 2001); Gary W. Gallagher and Alan T. Nolan, eds., *The Myth of the Lost Cause and Civil War History* (Bloomington: Indiana University Press, 2001); and James M. McPherson, "Southern Comfort," *New York Times Review of Books* 48 (April 12, 2001), 28, 30–31. For Lee's sobriquet of "Man Easter," see Deposition, J. D. Ivey, October 10, 1868, in *United States vs. J. W. Marshal, et al.*, copy in H. Sands to Charles Morse, AAAG, October 15, 1868, LR, Box 5, DT, 5MD, RG 393, NA.
2. For the traditional treatment of the Lee-Peacock struggle see, for example, Gladys Ray, *Murder at the Corners* (San Antonio: Naylor, 1957); Graham Landrum and Allan Smith, *Grayson County: An Illustrated History of Grayson County, Texas* (2d ed.; Fort Worth: Historical Publishers, 1967), 72–74; Nick Jones, "The Lee-Peacock Feud," *Real West* (January 1979): 12–14, 52–53. For the traditional national overview of the Reconstruction myth see William A. Dunning's *Reconstruction, Political and Economic, 1865–1877* (New York: Harper Brothers, 1907) and Dunning's *Essays on Civil War and Reconstruction* (New York: Macmillan, 1904). On the myth, also see Dunning's pupil Walter L. Fleming, *Civil War and Reconstruction in Alabama* (New York: Columbia University Press, 1905). From the 1960s to the 1980s, some Texas historians still preached the Dunning myth. See, for example, W. C. Nunn's *Texas Under the Carpetbaggers* (Austin: University of Texas Press, 1962) and Nunn's *Escape from Reconstruction* (Fort Worth: Texas Christian University Press, 1962); for the traditional view also see Earnest Wallace's *Texas in Turmoil* (Austin: Steck-Vaughn, 1965) and his *The Howling of the Coyotes: Reconstruction Efforts to Divide Texas* (College Station: Texas A&M University Press, 1979).
3. Leading revisionists on Reconstruction Texas include Barry A. Crouch, Donaly Brice, Randolph B. Campbell, Carl Moneyhon, Dale Baum, James M. Smallwood, and various others. For the citations of the many secondary works on Reconstruction, see Bruce A. Glasrud and Laurie Champion, eds., *Exploring the Afro-Texas Experience: A Bibliography of Secondary Sources About Black Texans* (Alpine: Center for Big Bend Studies, 2000), 32–40. For violence across the wider South, see George C. Rable, *But There Was No Peace: The Rise of Violence in the Politics of Reconstruction* (Athens: University of Georgia Press, 1984) and Allen Trelease, *White Terror: The Ku Klux Klan Conspiracy and Southern Reconstruction* (New York: Harper and Row, 1971).

Chapter 1. Texas and the Second Civil War

1. *Flake's Daily Bulletin* (Galveston), June 28, 1871; Gladys B. Ray, *Murder at the Corners* (San Antonio: Naylor Press, 1957), 25, 95–96; J. Lee Stambaugh and Lillian J. Stambaugh, *A History of Collin County* [Texas] (Austin: Texas State Historical Association, 1958), 73; C. L. Sonnichsen, *I'll Die Before I'll Run: The Story of the Great Feuds of Texas* (New York: Harper & Brothers, 1951), 17–18; James Stephen Peters, *Mace Bowman: Texan Feudist, Western Lawman* (n.p.: Privately published, 1996), 41–49; Lillian Womack, "Leonard Man Recalls Story of Ancestors, Deadly Feud," n.d., newspaper clipping, Peacock-Crouch-Smallwood Collection, Archives, TAMC Library; G. W. King, interviewed by L. L. Bowman, July 22, 1931, in "Bob Lee," VF, L. L. Bowman Papers, Archives, TAMC Library;

Fannin County Plus, March 29, 1992. Shortly before his death, Lee claimed to have killed more than forty men.

2. G. W. King, interviewed by L. L. Bowman, July 22, 1931, in "Bob Lee," VF, L. L. Bowman Papers, Archives, TAMC Library; *Flake's Daily Bulletin,* June 28, 1871; *Fannin County Plus,* March 29, 1992; Ray, *Murder at the Corners,* 95–96; Sonnichson, *I'll Die Before I'll Run,* 17–18.

3. G. W. King, interviewed by L. L. Bowman, July 22, 1931, in "Bob Lee," VF, L. L. Bowman Papers, Archives, TAMC Library; *Fannin County Plus,* March 29, 1992; Dick Johnson, conversation with J. C. "Red" Smith, 1920s, Cleste, Texas, notes, copy in Peacock-Crouch-Smallwood Collection, Archives, TAMC Libary.

4. Dick Johnson, conversation with J. C. "Red" Smith, 1920s, Cleste, Texas, notes, copy in Peacock-Crouch-Smallwood Collection; *Fannin County Plus,* March 29, 1992; and see G. W. King, interviewed by L. L. Bowman, John Gentry, interviewed by L. L. Bowman, July 22, 1931, in "Bob Lee," VF, L. L. Bowman Papers, Archives, TAMC Library. King, a Kentuckian, settled in the Corners in 1859 and never left. He knew most of the principals in the local ex-Confederate-Unionist struggle. And see, *Flake's Daily Bulletin,* June 28, 1871; Ray, *Murder at the Corners,* 25, 95–96; Stambaugh and Stambaugh, *A History of Collin County,* 73; Sonnichsen, *I'll Die Before I'll Run,* 17–18.

5. Ray, *Murder at the Corners,* 25, 95–96; G. W. King, interviewed by L. L. Bowman, July 22, 1931, in "Bob Lee," VF, L. L. Bowman Papers, Archives, TAMC Library; Parson Martin Gentry, quoted in Ray, *Murder at the Corners,* 96. The killers quoted in Peters, *Mace Bowman,* 47, and in Ray, *Murder at the Corners,* 96. John Gentry was at home when the murderers came by and remembered that there were three men. See John Gentry, interviewed by L. L. Bowman, July 22, 1931, in "Bob Lee," VF, L. L. Bowman Papers, Archives, TAMC Library.

6. *Flake's Daily Bulletin,* June 28, 1871; L. Peacock, "notes on Lewis Peacock," in Peacock-Crouch-Smallwooid Collection, Archives, TAMC Library.

7. *Flake's Daily Bulletin,* June 28, 1871.

8. Stambaugh and Stambaugh, *History of Collin County,* 71.

9. For more on violence in the region see Andrew J. Hamilton to Andrew Johnson, March 1, 1866, Andrew Johnson Papers, Archives, Manuscript Division, Library of Congress; C. S. Robert to AAG, August 12, November 12, 1867, AC, Texas, LR, BRFAL, RG 105, S. H. Starr to Charles E. Morse, AAG, February 9, 1868, Texas, LR, DT, 5MD, RG 393, NA; James M. Smallwood, "When the Klan Rode: White Terror in Reconstruction Texas," *Journal of the West* 25 (October 1986): 4–13; also see James M. Smallwood, *Time of Hope, Time of Despair: Black Texans During Reconstruction* (New York: Kennikat Press, 1981); Barry A. Crouch, *The Freedmen's Bureau and Black Texans* (Austin: University of Texas Press, 1992); Barry A. Crouch and Donaly E. Brice, *Cullen Montgomery Baker: Reconstruction Desperado* (Baton Rouge: Louisiana State University Press, 1997); William L. Richter, *The Army in Texas During Reconstruction, 1865–1870* (College Station: Texas A&M University Press, 1987); William L. Richter, *Overreached On All Sides: The Freedmen's Bureau Administrators in Texas, 1865–1868* (College Station: Texas A&M University Press, 1991); Charles V. Kenner, "Racial Turmoil in Texas, 1865–1871" (M. A. thesis, North Texas State University, 1971); Rebecca A. Kosary, "Regression to Barbarism in Reconstruction Texas: An Analysis of White Violence against African-Americans from the Texas Freedmen's Bureau Records, 1865–1868" (M. A. thesis, Southwest Texas State University, 1999). For the "New Rebellion," see *New York Times,* July 17, 1865, and *New York Tribune,* September 29, 1868.

10. *Houston Tri-Weekly Telegraph,* June 7, 1865; *New York Times,* July 17, 1865; L. Robarts to Ashbel Smith, July 15, 1865, Ashbel Smith Papers, CAH, UTA Library; Smallwood, *Time of Hope, Time of Despair,* 25; Ernest Wallace, *Texas in Turmoil* (Austin: Steck-Vaughn Company, 1965), 139–46; James M. Smallwood, *Born in Dixie: The History of Smith County, Texas* (2 vols.; Austin: Eakin Press, 1999), 1: 236–38.

11. *Houston Tri-Weekly Telegraph,* June 7, 1865; *New York Times,* July 17, 1865; Roberts to Smith, June 15, 1865, A. Smith Papers, CAH, UTA Library; Smallwood, *Time of Hope, Time of Despair,* 25; Smallwood, *Born in Dixie,* 1: 237–38.

12. Kate Stone, *Brokenburn-The Journal of Kate Stone, 1861–1868,* John Q. Anderson, ed. (Baton Rouge: Louisiana State University Press, 1955), 226–27; and see Smallwood, *Born in Dixie,* 1: 237–38.

13. Smallwood, *Time of Hope, Time of Despair,* 25; and see *Flake's Daily Bulletin,* June 28, 1865; James E. Sefton, *The United States Army and Reconstruction, 1865–1877* (Baton Rouge: Louisiana State University Press, 1967), 261–62; Larry Peacock, "Reconstruction in Texas," 1, unpublished paper, Peacock-Crouch-Smallwood Collection, Archives, TAMC Library; Carl Moneyhon, "Reconstruction," *NHT* (6 vols.; Austin: Texas State Historical Association, 1998), 6: 474–81.

14. Smallwood, *Time of Hope, Time of Despair,* 25; Wallace, *Texas in Turmoil,* 165; L. Peacock, "Reconstruction in Texas," 1–2, unpublished paper, Peacock-Crouch-Smallwood Collection, Archives, TAMC Library.

15. Grayson County, manuscript census returns, 1850, 1860 (NA houses the returns); Donna J. Kumler, "Grayson County," *NHT,* 3: 298–99; Brian Hart, "Sherman, Texas," *NHT,* 5: 1021–23; Frank W. Johnson, et al., *A History of Texas and Texans* (4 vols.; Chicago: The American Historical Society, 1914), 2: 848–50. For more on Grayson County, see Graham Landrum and Allan Smith, *An Illustrated History of Grayson County, Texas* (2d ed.; Fort Worth: Historical Publishers, 1967), Mattie Davis Lucas and Mita Holsapple Hall, *A History of Grayson County, Texas* (Sherman: Scruggs Printing Company, 1936), and Members of the Grayson County Frontier Village, *The History of Grayson County, Texas* (Winston-Salem: Hunter Publishing Company, 1979).

16. Collin County, manuscript census returns, 1850, 1860; David Minor, "Collin County," *NHT,* 2: 214; David Minor, "McKinney, Texas," *NHT,* 4: 421; Johnson, *History of Texas,* 2: 862–63. For more on Collin County, see Stambaugh and Stambaugh, *History of Collin County.*

17. Fannin County, manuscript census returns, 1850, 1860; Kelly Pigott, "Fannin County," *NHT,* 2: 945–46; Diana J. Kleiner, "Bonham, Texas," *NHT,* 1: 633–34; Johnson, *History of Texas,* 2: 865–68. For more on Fannin County, see Floy Crandall Hodge, *A History of Fannin County: Featuring Pioneer Families* (Herford, Texas: Pioneer Publishers, 1966).

18. Hunt County, manuscript census returns, 1850, 1860; Cecil Harper, Jr., "Hunt County," *NHT,* 3: 784–86; Hart, "Greenville, Texas," *NHT,* 3: 321–22; Johnson, *History of Texas,* 2: 873–74. Also see Harper, "Slavery Without Cotton: Hunt County, Texas, 1846–1864," *SWHQ* 88 (April 1985): 387–405. For more on Hunt County, see W. Walworth Harrison, *History of Greenville and Hunt County, Texas* (Waco: Texian Press, 1976) and Francis Terry Ingmire, *Archives and Pioneers of Hunt County* (Creve Coeur, Mo.: Privately printed, 1975).

19. Grayson County, manuscript census returns, 1850, 1860; Collin County, manuscript census returns, 1850, 1860; Hunt County, manuscript census returns, 1850, 1860; Fannin County, manuscript census returns, 1850, 1860; Kumler, "Grayson County," *NHT,* 3: 298–99; Minor, "Collin County," *NHT,* 2: 214; Pigott, "Fannin County," 2: 945–46;

Harper, "Hunt County," *NHT,* 3: 784–86; Johnson, *History of Texas,* 2: 848–50, 862–63, 865–68, 873–74; Randolph Campbell, *An Empire for Slavery: The Peculiar Institution in Texas, 1821–1865* (Baton Rouge: Louisiana State University Press, 1989), 275.

20. See Smallwood, *Time of Hope, Time of Despair,* and Crouch, *The Freedmen's Bureau and Black Texans.*

21. For more on the Confederate bias in the interpretation of Reconstruction in Texas, see Crouch and Brice, *Cullen Montgomery Baker,* 1–9.

22. Crouch, *The Freedmen's Bureau and Black Texans,* 6, 14–21; Smallwood, *Time of Hope, Time of Despair,* 39–41.

23. *Flake's Daily Bulletin,* April 19, 1866; *Galveston Daily News,* March 6, 7, 1866; Crouch, *The Freedmen's Bureau and Black Texans,* 21–40; Smallwood, *Time of Hope, Time of Despair,* 40–41; Richter, "The Army and the Negro during Texas Reconstruction, 1865–1870," *East Texas Historical Journal* 10 (Spring 1972): 7–13; Roster of Texas's Bureau Agents, 1867, BFRAL, RG 105, NA. And see Richter's: *Overreached On All Sides* and *The Army in Texas During Reconstruction, 1865–1870;* L. Peacock, "Reconstruction in Texas," 2–3, unpublished paper, Peacock-Crouch-Smallwood Collection, Archives, TAMC Library.

24. L. Peacock, "Reconstruction in Texas," 3–4, unpublished paper, Peacock-Crouch-Smallwood Collection, Archives, TAMC Library; Moneyhon, "Reconstruction," *NHT,* 6: 474–81; for Throckmorton's career including his governorship, see Claude Elliott, *Leathercoat: The Life History of a Texas Patriot* (San Antonio: Standard Printing Company, 1938); Texas Secretary of State, election returns of 1866, ARIS/TSL; James Marten, ed., "The Lamentations of a Whig: James Throctmorton Writes a Letter," *Civil War History* 31 (June 1985): 163–70. And see Nora Estelle Owens, "Presidential Reconstruction in Texas: A Case Study" (Ph.D. diss., Auburn University, 1983).

25. U.S. Senate, *Senate Executive Documents,* 39th Cong., 2d sess., 1867 (serial 1276), Doc. No. 6, 221, 224–26; H. P. Gammel, Comp., *The Laws of Texas* (10 vols; Austin: Gammel Book Company, 1898), 4: 979–81, 5: 994–97, 1037–38, 1110–13, 1120–22. For a brief overview of the codes, see Smallwood, *Time of Hope, Time of Despair,* 54–59, 64, 123–24, 130–31. For more detail, see Crouch, "'All the Vile Passions': The Texas Black Code of 1866," *SWHQ* 97 (July 1993): 13–34.

Chapter 2. Pandemonium's New Home

1. *Cincinnati Commercial* quoted in the *Alabama State Journal* (Montgomery), January 30, 1869.

2. For yet more on the violence see Robert W. Shook, "Federal Occupation and Administration of Texas, 1865–1870" (Ph.D. diss., North Texas State University, 1970); Allen Trelease, *White Terror: The Ku Klux Klan Conspiracy and Southern Reconstruction* (New York: Harper and Row, 1971). Trelease maintains that there was a massive conspiracy among whites in Texas and the larger South to support terrorism to rid themselves of Republican rule. James M. Smallwood's research and the research of others supports Trelease's conclusion. See, James M. Smallwood, "When the Klan Rode: White Terror in Reconstruction Texas," *Journal of the West* 25 (October 1986): 4–13; Crouch, "A Spirit of Lawlessness: White Violence; Texas Blacks, 1865–1868," *Journal of Social History* 18 (1984): 217–32; Crouch, "Black Dreams and White Justice [Texas, 1865–1868], *Prologue* 6 (1974): 255–

65. And see Barbera Leah Clayton Barnhill, "The Lone Star Conspiracy: Racial Violence and the Ku Klux Klan Terror in Post-Civil War Texas, 1865–1877" (M.A. thesis, Oklahoma State University, 1979), 27. The sources on violence in Texas are legion. The primary records of both the Freedmen's Bureau (RG 105, NA) and the army post records for Texas (DT, 5MD, RG 393, NA) are replete with references to the chaos. It is clear that postwar violence was the key factor for the failure of Reconstruction.

3. Leonard Public Library, *A History of Leonard, Texas, 1880–1980* (Leonard, Texas: Privately published, n.d.), 17.

4. Grayson County, manuscript census returns, 1860, 1870. Pilot Grove was quite small. The censuses of 1860 and 1870 did not even list the place as a "town." Other nearby communities not listed as "towns" in the national count were Coffee's Trading Post, Dog-Town, Hog-Eye, and Kentucky-Town. See Graham Landrum and Allan Smith, *An Illustrated History of Grayson County, Texas* (2d ed.; Fort Worth: Historical Publishers, 1967), 34; Members of the Grayson County Frontier Village, *The History of Grayson County, Texas* (Winston-Salem, N.C.: Hunter Publishing, 1979), 75; Gladys B. Ray, *Murder at the Corners* (San Antonio: Naylor Press, 1957), vi–vii.

5. Grayson Frontier Village, *Grayson County,* 75; Ray, *Murder at the Corners,* vi–vii; Frank W. Johnson, et al., *A History of Texas and Texans* (4 vols.; Chicago: The American Historical Society, 1914), 2: 850.

6. Bureau of the Census, *Compendium of the Ninth Census of the United States* (Washington, D.C.: Government Printing Office, 1873), 92–95, 341–43.

7. John Carrier, "A Political History of Texas During Reconstruction, 1865–1874" (Ph.D. diss., Vanderbilt University, 1971), 206–07. Carrier called the Unionist-ex-Confederate struggle during Reconstruction a "race war." Also see Crouch, "Self-Determination and Local Black Leaders in Texas," *Phyon* 39 (1978): 344–55.

8. C. L. Sonnichsen, *I'll Die Before I'll Run: The Story of the Great Feuds of Texas* (New York: Harper & Brothers, 1951), 21–22; Floy Crandall Hodge, *A History of Fannin County Featuring Pioneer Families* (Hereford, Tx.: Pioneer Publishers, 1966), 79, 104; Ray, *Murder at the Corners,* vii; James Stephen Peters, *Mace Bowman: Texas Feudist, Western Lawman* (N.p.: Privately printed, 1996), 44; T. U. Taylor, "The Lee-Peacock Feud," *Frontier Times* 3 (May 1926): 1–2, copy in Peacock-Crouch-Smallwood Collection, Archives, TAMC Library; Leonard Library, "History of Leonard," 14; for Howell's comments see Alfred Howell to Morton Howell, May 14, 1854, Morton Boyte Howell Collection, Archives, TAMC Library; David Pickering and Judy Falls, *Brush Men and Vigilantes: Civil War Dissent in Texas* (College Station: Texas A&M University Press, 2000), 3–5, 18–20.

9. L. L. Bowman, "Jernigan's Thicket," unpublished manuscript, VF, L. L. Bowman Papers, Archives, TAMC Library; Janice Jernigan Kiker, "William Jernigan, Founder of Commerce [Texas], *Commerce Journal,* October 31, 1982; "Backward glances: Thicket was Outlaws' Refuge," newspaper clipping, in "Bob Lee," VF, Pickering-Falls Collection, Archives, TAMC Library; Pickering and Falls, *Brush Men and Vigilantes,* 5, 87.

10. A. Ray Stephens and William M. Holmes, *Historical Atlas of Texas* (Norman: University of Oklahoma Press, 1989), 38–39; David Minor, "Collin County," *NHT* (6 vols.; Austin: Texas State Historical Association, 1998), 2: 214; Donna J. Kumler, "Grayson County," *NHT,* 3: 299; Kelly Pigott, "Fannin County," *NHT,* 2: 945; Cecil Harper, Jr., "Hunt County," *NHT,* 3: 785; Nick Jones, "The Lee-Peacock Feud," *Real West: True Tales of the American Frontier* (January 1979): 12; Pickering and Falls, *Brush Men and Vigilantes,* 40; Dale Baum, *The*

Shattering of Texas Unionism: Politics in the Lone Star State During the Civil War Era (Baton Rouge: Louisiana State Univeristy Press, 1998), 73–74.

11. Stephens and Holmes, *Historical Atlas of Texas,* 38–39; Minor, "Collin County," *NHT,* 2: 214; Kumler, "Grayson County," *NHT,* 3: 299; Pigott, "Fannin County," *NHT,* 2: 945; Harper, "Hunt County," *NHT,* 3: 785; Jones, "Lee-Peacock Feud," 12; Pickering and Falls, *Brush Men and Vigilantes,* 40. Pigott makes a blunder in the article on "Fannin County" in the *NHT* by asserting that "Fannin County went with the Confederacy." The very opposite is true; the majority voted to remain with the Union.

12. For Houston's views see, for example, Edward R. Maher, "Sam Houston and Secession," *SWHQ* 55 (April, 1952): 452–53; James M. Smallwood, *Born in Dixie, The History of Smith County, Texas* (2 vols.; Austin: Eakin Press, 1999), 1: 161–62, 167. And see Landrum and Smith, *Grayson County,* 62–63.

13. Stephens and Holmes, *Historical Atlas of Texas,* 38–39; Landrum and Smith, *Grayson County,* 62–63; Jones, "The Lee-Peacock Feud," 12.

14. John Black and H. P. Allen, "Civil War Experiences Reflect Life of Hardship," *Honey Grove Signal-Citizen,* July 2, 1976; W. Gambill, Jr., to General Charles Griffin, May 14, 1867, copy in Pickering-Falls Collection, Archives, TAMC Library; Pickering and Falls, *Brush Men and Vigilantes,* 14, 149.

15. Terry G. Jordan, "The Imprint of the Upper and Lower South on Mid-Nineteenth-Century Texas," *Annals of the Association of American Geographers* 57 (December 1967): 688; Terry G. Jordan, "A Century and a Half of Ethnic Change in Texas, 1836–1986," *SWHQ* 89 (April 1986): 400–01; Pickering and Falls, *Brush Men and Vigilantes,* 6–8. For demographics also see Barnes F. Lathrop, "Migration into East Texas, 1836–1860," *SWHQ* 52 (July 1948): 1–31; Walter L. Buenger also discusses demographics: see his "Secession Revisited: The Texas Experience," *Civil War History* 30 (December 1984): 293–305 and his *Secession and the Union in Texas* (Austin: University of Texas Press, 1984); Baum, *Shattering Texas Unionism,* 73.

16. Buenger, *Secession and the Union in Texas,* 75; for the panic of 1860, see William W. White, "The Texas Slave Insurrection of 1860," *SWHQ* 52 (January 1949): 259–85; Paul D. Lack, "Slavery and Vigilantism in Austin, Texas, 1840–1860," *SWHQ* 85 (July 1981): 1–20; James M. Smallwood, *Born in Dixie: The History of Smith County, Texas* (2 vols.; Austin: Eakin Press, 1999), 1: 151–55.

17. Jordan, "Imprint of Upper and Lower South," 686. See also Buenger, *Secession and the Union in Texas.*

18. *New York Times,* March 25, 1866; Barnhill, "The Lone Star Conspiracy: Racial Violence and Ku Klux Klan Terror," 27; Stephens and Holmes, *Historical Atlas of Texas,* 38–39; James M. Smallwood, "Disaffection in Confederate Texas: The Great Hanging at Gainesville," *Civil War History* 22 (December 1976): 349–60; Richard B. McCaslin, *Tainted Breeze: The Great Hanging at Gainesville, Texas, 1862* (Baton Rouge: Louisiana State University Press, 1994); on Unionism also see Claude Elliott, "Union Sentiment in Texas, 1861–1865," *SWHQ* 50 (1947): 449–77; and see Frank Smyrl, "Unionism in Texas, 1856–1860, *SWHQ* 68 (October, 1864): 172–95; Smyrl, "Texans in the Union Army," *SWHQ* 65 (October, 1961): 234–50; Smyrl, "Unionism, Abolitionism, and Vigilantism in Texas, 1856–1865" (M.A. thesis, University of Texas, 1961); James Marten, *Texas Divided: Loyalty and Dissent in the Lone Star State, 1856–1874* (Lexington: University of Kentucky Press, 1990). For more on the Civil War chaos in Northeast Texas see Pickering and Falls, *Brush Men and*

Vigilantes and David Paul Smith, *Frontier Defense in the Civil War; Texas' Rangers and Rebels* (College Station: Texas A&M University Press, 1992); Baum, *Shattering Texas Unionism.*

19. Pickering and Falls, *Brush Men and Vigilantes,* 23.

20. Harrison, *History of Greenville and Hunt County,* 126–27; Pickering and Falls, *Brush Men and Vigilantes,* 15.

21. Crouch, "A 'Fiend in Human Shape'? William Clarke Quantrill and His Biographers," *Kansas History* 22 (Summer 1999): 143–49. The two best biographies of the man are Albert Castel's *William Clarke Quantrill: His Life and Times* (New York: Frederick Fell, 1962); and Edward L. Leslie's *The Devil Knows How to Ride: The True Story of William Clarke Quantrill and His Confederate Raiders* (New York: Random House, 1996).

22. Crouch, "A 'Fiend in Human Shape'?," 148–53; LeRoy Fischer and Larry C. Ramp, "Quantrill's Civil War Operations in Indian Territory," *Chronicles of Oklahoma* 46 (Summer 1968): 155–81; Ramp, "William C. Quantrill's Civil War Activities in Texas, 1861–1863," *Texas Military History* 8 (1970): 221–31.

23. Crouch, "A 'Fiend in Human Shape'?," 152–53.

24. Ibid, 154.

25. G. A. Dickerman, B. W. Bradly, et al., to Pendleton Murrah, November 9, 1864, GP, ARIS/TSL; Landrum and Smith, *Grayson County,* 68–69; for Quantrill in Sherman, also see Smith, *Texas' Rangers and Rebels,* 78–79; Pickering and Falls, *Brush Men and Vigilantes,* 21–22.

26. G. A. Dickerman, B. W. Bradley, et al., to Pendleton Murrah, November 9, 1864, GP, ARIS/TSL; Crouch, "A 'Fiend in Human Shape'?" 154–56; Landrum and Smith, *Grayson County,* 68–69; Joseph G. Rosa, *Age of the Gunfighter: Men and Weapons on the frontier, 1840–1900* (Norman: University of Oklahoma Press, 1993), 15, 37. For more on "Bloody Bill," see, Albert Castel and Thomas Goodrich, *Bloody Bill Anderson: The Short, Savage Life of a Civil War Guerrilla* (Mechanicsburg, Pennsylvania: Stackpole Books, 1998). Quantrill and Anderson came to detest each other.

27. James Hood, H. S. Bright, et al., to Murrah, n.d., GP, ARIS/TSL.

28. C. N. Breedlove to Murrah, November 19, 1864, GP, ARIS/TSL.

29. James W. Throckmorton to Murrah, December 9, 1864, GP, ARIS/TSL.

30. Ibid.

31. Henry McCulloch to John Bankhead Magruder, October 21, 1863, *The War of the Rebellion: A Compilation of the Official Records of the Union and Confederate Armies* (128 vols; Washington, D.C.: Government Printing Office, 1880–1901): 26, pt. 2: 344–45; Pickering and Falls, *Brush Men and Vigilantes,* 18; G. W. King, interviewed by L. L. Bowman, July 22, 1931, in "Bob Lee," VF, L. L. Bowman Papers, Archives, TAMC Library.

32. McCulloch to Henry Boren, October 24, 2863, *War of the Rebellion:* 26, pt. 2: 352; and see Taylor, "The Lee-Peacock Feud," 19; G. W. King, interviewed by L. L. Bowman, July 22, 1931, in "Bob Lee," VF, L. L. Bowman Papers, Archives, TAMC Library; Kerry Ross Boren to Chuck Parsons, November 27, 1975, copy in Peacock-Crouch-Smallwood Collection, Archives, TAMC Library.

33. G. W. King, interviewed by L. L. Bowman, July 22, 1931, in "Bob Lee," VF, L. L. Bowman Papers, Archives; *Clarksville Standard,* March 26, 1864.

34. Throckmorton to Murrah, December 9, 1864, GP, Archives, ARIS/TSL.

35. Ibid.

Chapter 3. Murder and Mayhem

1. *Texas Republican* (Marshall), August 4, 1865; *Clarksville Northern Standard,* July 8, August 5, 1865; David Pickering and Judy Falls, *Brush Men and Vigilantes: Civil War Dissent in Texas* (College Station: Texas A&M University Press, 2000), 105, 181; Norman C. Russell, "The History of Titus County Since 1860" (M.A. thesis, East Texas State Teachers College, 1937), 32–33; W. Walworth Harrison, "Martin Hart," VF, W. Walworth Harrison Collection, Archives, Greenville Public Library, Greenville, Texas.

2. Larry Reacock, "Genealogy Records of the Peacock Family," Peacock-Crouch-Smallwood Collection, Archives, TAMC Library; Washington County, Georgia, manuscript census returns, 1850.

3. Washington County, Georgia, manuscript census returns, 1850, Grayson County, Texas, manuscript census returns, 1860; L. Peacock, "Genealogy Records of the Peacock Family," James M. Smallwood, "The Lee-Peacock Feud," paper presented to the Fort Worth meeting of the "Peacock Family Association of the South," July 25, 1998, 1–5, Lewis Peacock to Lewis Benson, August 23, 1859, Peacock-Crouch-Smallwood Collection, Archives, TAMC Library; T. U. Taylor, "Lee-Peacock Feud," *Frontier Times* 3 (May 1926): 2–3, copy in Peacock-Crouch-Smallwood Collection, Archives, TAMC Library; C. L. Sonnichsen, *I'll Die Before I'll Run: The Story of the Great Feuds of Texas* (New York: Harper and Brothers, 1951), 22; the census figures are also reported by James Stephen Peters, *Mace Bowman: Texas Feudist, Western Lawman* (N.p.: Privately printed, 1996), 182; Leonard Public Library, *A History of Leonard, Texas, 1880–1980* (Lenard, Texas: Privately published, n.d.), 14; Graham Landrum and Allan Smith, *An Illustrated History of Grayson County, Texas* (2d ed.; Fort Worth: Historical Publishers, 1967), 72.

4. Deposition, Lewis Peacock, October 9, 1868, in *United States vs. J. W. Marshal, et al.,* copy in J. H. Sands to C. E. Morse, AAAG, October 15, 1868, LR, Box 12, DT, 5MD, RG 393, NA. Lewis Peacock's Deposition involved the trial of John Marshal, William Baird, and others for harboring the fugitive Bob Lee; Lewis Peacock to Lewis Benson, August 23, 1859, L. Peacock, "Lee-Peacock Feud," 1–7, unpublished paper, Peacock-Crouch-Smallwood Collection, Archives, TAMC Library; W. Walworth Harrison, *History of Greenville and Hunt County, Texas* (Waco: Texian Press, 1976), 132; J. Lee Stambaugh and Lillian J. Stambaugh, *A History of Collin County* [Texas] (Austin: Texas State Historical Association, 1958), 71; Sonnichsen, *I'll Die Before I'll Run,* 10; Gladys B. Ray, *Murder at the Corners* (San Antonio: Naylor Press, 1957), 23; Taylor, "Lee-Peacock Feud," 2–3; Peters, *Mace Bowman,* 42; Kent Biffle, "Bitter North Texas Feud Dogged Rebel to his Grave," *Dallas Morning News,* August 17, 1986; Nick Jones, "The Lee-Peacock Feud," *Real West: True Tales of the American Frontier* (January 1979): 13; Landrum and Smith, *Grayson County,* 72.

5. Deposition, Lewis Peacock, October 9, 1868, in *United States vs. J. W. Marshal, et al.,* copy in J. H. Sands to C. E. Morse, AAAG, October 15, 1868, LR, Box 12, DT, 5MD, RG 393, NA; L. Peacock, "Lee Peacock Feud," 1–7, unpublished paper; Lewis Peacock to Lewis Benson, August 23, 1859, Peacock-Crouch-Smallwood Collection, John Gentry, interviewed by L. L. Bowman, July 22, 1867, in "Bob Lee," VF, L. L. Bowman Papers, Archives, TAMC Library; Landrum and Smith, *Grayson County,* 72; Harrison, *History of Greenville and Hunt*

County, 132; Ray, *Murder at the Corners,* 23; Taylor, "Lee-Peacock Feud," 2–3; Stambaugh and Stambaugh, *History of Collin County,* 71; Sonnichsen, *I'll Die Before I'll Run,* 10.

6. Deposition, Lewis Peacock, October 9, 1868, in *United States vs. J. W. Marshal, et al.,* copy in J. H. Sands to C. E. Morse, AAAG, October 15, 1868, LR, Box 12, DT, 5MD, RG 393, NA; Harrison, *History of Greenville and Hunt County,* 132; Stambaugh and Stambaugh, *History of Collin County,* 71; Sonnichsen, *I'll Die Before I'll Run,* 10; Ray, *Murder at the Corners,* 23; Taylor, "Lee-Peacock Feud," 2–3; L. Peacock, "Lee-Peacock Feud," 1–7, Lewis Peacock to Lewis Benson, August 23, 1859, Peacock-Crouch-Smallwood Collection, Archives, TAMC Library; Peters, *Mace Bowman,* 42; Biffle, "Bitter North Texas Feud Dogged Rebel to his Grave," *Dallas Morning News,* August 17, 1986; Jones, "Lee-Peacock Feud," 13; Landrum and Smith, *Grayson County,* 72.

7. L. Peacock, "Lee-Peacock Feud," 1–7, Peacock-Crouch-Smallwood Collection, Archives, TAMC Library; Jones, "Lee-Peacock Feud," 13; Parker County, Texas, manuscript census returns, 1880. Peacock had many Union supporters in Corners Country, but less is known about them than their leader. Perhaps the dearth of records stem from the fact that the Unionists lost the War of Reconstruction in the Corners area just as they did in all of Texas; indeed, many of them were either killed or driven from the the region. No one preserved their personal histories, no one passed their stories down to later generations whose ancestors took part in the local Rebel-Unionist struggle. Peacock's wife Emaline could have provided many details from the Unionist point of view, but, after Lewis was killed in 1871, she and her teenage son John Edgar immediately fled and went into hiding. Following Parson Gentry's advice, Emaline may have gone to Springfield in Limestone County where her married twenty-two-year-old daughter Cathy had settled with her husband Austin. Later, Emaline and John moved to Parker County where the youngster eventually acquired several farms and became a prosperous man. Emaline never lost the fear of being found and killed, however, and she never got over her concern that the same thing might happen to her children and to her young son-in-law Austin. Because of those fears, she left her account of the Lee-Peacock affair unspoken; she took it with her to her grave.

8. "Charges and Specifications against J. Alfred Drye, Citizen of Pilot Grove, Grayson County, Texas," March [n.d.], 1868, in H. E. Scott, Post of Sherman, to AAAG C. E. Morse, March 12, 1868, LR, Box 5, DT, 5MD, RG 393; T. U. Taylor, "More About Bob Lee," *Frontier Times* 5 (March 1928): 252–53.

9. Deposition, Lewis Peacock, October 9, Deposition, J. D. Ivey, October 10, Deposition, John Sinclair, October 10, Deposition, H. C. Saunders, October 10, Deposition, John Milican, October 8, Deposition, James H. Morrisson, October 8, Deposition, M. L. Boling, October 8, Deposition, D. L. Lewis, October 8, Deposition, Charles Saunders, October 8, Deposition, Robert K. Brewer, October 9, 1868, in *United States vs. J. W. Marshal, et al.,* copy in H. Sands to C. E. Morse, AAAG, October 15, 1868, LR, Box 12; "Charges . . . against Alfred Drye," March (n.d.), 1868, in H. E. Scott, Post of Sherman, to C. E. Morse, AAAG, March 12, 1868, LR, Box 5, DT, 5MD, RG 393, NA; Ray, *Murder at the Corners.* Other Unionists of the Corners who eventually petitioned the authorities for help against the Lee raiders included George Fowler, Hugh Hudson, I. F. Stinnertt, P. D. Wilson, Ed Lively, Henry Boren, Alexander Boren, John Boren, Hugh Woody, William Pendleton, Hugh Astin, F. J. Thompson, William Levy, O. Crocker, F. Wisdom, C. C. Hearold, C. Batrell, A. Lewis, Henry Taylor, N. Taylor, S. S. Thompson, N. Maddox, George Norris, and still others. See George Fowler, et al., to E. R. S. Canby, January 23, 1869, LR, Box 12, DT, 5MD, RG 393, NA; L. Peacock, "Union men in the Lee-Peacock Feud," Peacock-Crouch-Smallwood Collection, Archives, TAMC Library.

10. William E. Strong to O. O. Howard, January 1, 1866, *House Executive Documents,* 39th Cong., 1st sess., Doc. no. 70, 308–12. And see William L. Richter, *The Army in Texas During Reconstruction, 1865–1870* (College Station: Texas A&M University Press, 1987), 37; James M. Smallwood, *Time of Hope, Time of Despair: Black Texans During Reconstruction* (New York: Kennikat Press, 1981), 35.

11. Strong to Howard, January 1, 1866, *House Executive Documents,* 39th Cong., 1st sess., Doc. No. 70, 308–12; Richter, *The Army in Texas During Reconstruction,* 37; Landrum and Smith, *Grayson County,* 73; Smallwood, *Time of Hope, Time of Despair,* 35.

12. L. Peacock, "Lee-Peacock Feud," 6, 8, Peacock-Crouch-Smallwood Collection, Archives, TAMC Library; Peters, *Mace Bowman,* 42; Landrum and Smith, *Grayson County,* 73.

13. *Sherman Courier,* n.d., quoted in Mattie Davis Lucas and Mita Holsapple Hall, *A History of Grayson County, Texas* (Sherman, Texas: Scruggs Printing Company, 1936), 156; L. Peacock, "Lee-Peacock Feud," 6, 8, Peacock-Crouch-Smallwood Collection, Archives, TAMC Library; Peters, *Mace Bowman,* 42.

14. Anthony Bryant to J. P. Richardson, AAAG, Sub-Assistant Commissioner, Sherman, LS, BRFAL, RG 105, NA.

15. Hunt County, Texas, manuscript census returns, 1860.

16. Ibid.

17. Sonnichsen, *I'll Die Before I'll Run,* 9, 21; Ray, *Murder at the Corners,* 2–5; Stewart Sifakis, *Compendium of the Confederate Armies: Texas* (New York: Facts on File, 1995), 61–63; Landrum and Smith, *Grayson County,* 61; Taylor, "Lee-Peacock Feud," 2; John Gentry, interviewed by L. L. Bowman, July 22, 1931, in "Bob Lee," VF, L. L. Bowman Papers, Archives, TAMC Library.

18. Robert Lee, Military Service Record, Confederacy, NA; Ray, *Murder at the Corners,* 2–5; Sonnichsen, *I'll Die Before I'll Run,* 9; J. John Gentry interviewed by L. L. Bowman, July 22, 1931, in "Bob Lee," VF, L. L. Bowman Papers, Archives, TAMC Library.

19. Robert Lee, Service Record, Confederacy, NA; Sonnichsen, *I'll Die Before I'll Run,* 9; Ray, *Murder at the Corners,* 2–5; for other writers who repeated the myth of "Captain Lee," see Taylor, "Lee-Peacock Feud," 2, Landrum and Smith, *Grayson County,* 72, Leonard Public Library, *History of Leonard,* 14; for the war record of Lee's unit, see Sifakis, *Compendium of the Confederate Armies: Texas,* 61–63. Gwen Short, a member of the extended Lee family, said that Robert "Bob" Lee's middle name was recorded as "Jehu" in the Lee family Bible, Short to L. Peacock, n.d., L. Peacock, "notes," L. Peacock, "Lee-Peacock Feud," 9, Peacock-Crouch-Smallwood Collection, Archives, TAMC Library.

20. Leonard Public Library, *History of Leonard,* 14–17.

21. Landrum and Smith, *Grayson County,* 72.

22. Hunt County, Texas, manuscript census returns, 1860; L. Peacock, "Descendants of Lewis Peacock," 1–2, Peacock-Crouch-Smallwood Collection, John Gentry, interviewed by L. L. Bowman, July 22, 1931, in "Bob Lee," VF, L. L. Bowman Papers, Archives, TAMC Library; Lillian Womack, "Leonard Man Recalls Story of Ancestors, Deadly Feud," newspaper clippings, n.d., No. 35, Peacock-Crouch-Smallwood Collection, Archives, TAMC Library; Leonard Public Library, *History of Leonard,* 17. As late as the 1990s, prospectors were still looking for the gold. They continued to dig in areas in and around the cemetery where Bob Lee was put to rest.

23. Sonnichsen, *I'll Die Before I Run,* 22–23; Leonard Public Library, *History of Leonard,* 17; Womack, "Leonard Man Recalls Story of Ancestors, Deadly Feud," newspaper clipping, No. 35, n.d., Peacock-Crouch-Smallwood Collection, John Gentry interviewed by L. L. Bowman, July 22, 1931, and other Bowman notes, in "Bob Lee," VF, L. L. Bowman Papers, Archives, TAMC Library; and see Ray, *Murder at the Corners.*

24. Ray, *Murder at the Corners,* 10–11; Walter Clay Dixson, *Richland Crossing: A Portrait of Texas Pioneers* (Fort Worth: Peppermill Publishing Company, 1994), 186 (although published as a novel, *Richland Crossing* is based on historical events and includes letters and original documents that are in possession of the author who lives in Fort Worth, Texas); Oleta Morris to "Dear Sir," March 19, 1986, copy in Peacock-Crouch-Smallwood Collection, Archives, TAMC Library.

25. Dixson, *Richland Crossing,* 186; Ray, *Murder at the Corners,* 10–11; Sonnichsen, *I'll Die Before I'll Run,* 22–23; Leonard Public Library, *History of Leonard,* 17–18.

26. Dixson, *Richland Crossing,* 186; Ray, *Murder at the Corners,* 10–12; Morris to "Dear Sir," March 19, 1986, copy in Peacock-Crouch-Smallwood Collection, Archives, TAMC Library.

27. Dixson, *Richland Crossing,* 186; Ray, *Murder at the Corners,* 10–12.

28. Joe W. Chumbley, "Brief Biography of Bill Penn," in *Kentucky-Town and its Baptist Church* (Houston: D. Armstrong, 1975), unnumbered pages; Ray, *Murder at the Corners,* 12–14.

29. Chumbley, "Penn Biography," *Kentucky-Town,* unnumbered pages; Ray, *Murder at the Corners,* 12–14.

30. Penn, quoted in Chumbley, "Penn Biography," *Kentucky-Town,* unnumbered pages.

31. Ibid.; Ray, *Murder at the Corners,* 15–16, 89.

32. Chumbley, "Penn Biography," *Kentucky-Town,* unnumbered pages; Ray, *Murder at the Corners,* 16–17.

33. Floy Crandall Hodge, *A History of Fannin County Featuring Pioneer Families* (Hereford, Texas: Pioneer Publishers, 1966), 122; Ray, *Murder at the Corners;* L. Peacock, "Lee-Peacock Feud," 10, Chuck Parsons to Kerry Ross Boren, n.d., Peacock-Crouch-Smallwood Collection, Archives, TAMC Library; Deposition, Lewis Peacock, October 9, 1868, in *United States vs. J. W. Marshal, et al.,* copy in J. H. Sands to AAAG C. E. Morse, October 15, 1868, LR, Box 12, "Charges and Specifications against J. Alfred Drye," "Charges and Specifications against J. W. Clements," in H. E. Scott, Post of Sherman, to AAAG C. E. Morse, March 12, 1868, LR, Box 5, DT, 5MD, RG 393, NA; Leonard Public Library, *History of Leonard,* 17–18; Jones, "Lee-Peacock Feud," 52; L. L. Bowman, "Notes on Bob Lee," W. R. Adams, interviewed by Bowman, July 22, 1931, John Gentry, interviewed by L. L. Bowman, July 22, 1931, in "Bob Lee," VF, L. L. Bowman Papers, Archives, TAMC Library; Chumbley, "Penn biography," *Kentucky-Town,* unnumbered pages; Morris to "Dear Sir," March 19, 1886, copy in Peacock-Crouch-Smallwood Collection, Archives, TAMC Library.

34. Peters, *Mace Bowman,* 43, 51.

Chapter 4. The "Man Eater" and Other Northeast Texas Desperadoes

1. See "Condition of Affairs in Texas," U.S. House of Representatives, *Executive Documents,* Doc. no. 61, 39th Cong., 2nd sess.; H. E. Scott, Post of Sherman, to C. E. Morse, AAAG,

March 12, 1868, LR, Box 5, DT, 5MD, RG 393, NA. Although Scott wrote Morse in March of 1868, his letter includes a summary of Bob Lee's activities, some of them criminal, from mid–1865 to March of 1868. Primary records do not reveal many details of Bob Lee's misspent postwar life and criminal career from 1865 to 1867, the year that Congress seized control of Reconstruction and wrested power in the South from former Confederates. But information gleaned from primary sources coupled with existing secondary works can be pieced together for an overview.

2. C. S. Roberts to J. P. Richardson, November 12, 1867, Sub-Assistant Commissioner, Clarksville, LS, DeWitt Brown to Roberts, June 1, 1868, Sub-Assistant Commissioner, Paris, LS, BRFAL, RG 105, Scott, Post of Sherman, to Morse, AAAG, March 12, 1868, LR, Box 5, DT, 5MD, NA.

3. Scott, Post of Sherman, to Morse, AAAG, March 12, 1868, LR, Box 5, DT, 5MD, RG 393, NA.

4. Ibid.; G. W. King, interviewed by L. L. Bowman, July 22, 1931, in "Bob Lee," VF, L. L. Bowman Papers, Archives, TAMC Library.

5. Scott, Post of Sherman, to Morse, AAAG, March 12, 1868, LR, Box 5, DT, 5MD, RG 393, NA; for the theft charge, see Case #9180, Box 33, Paper no. 728, Grayson County Courthouse, Sherman, Texas; and see G. W. King, interviewed by L. L. Bowman, July 22, 1931, in "Bob Lee," VF, L. L. Bowman Papers, Archives, TAMC Library.

6. Pauline Wilson, quoted in W. Walworth Harrison, *The History of Greenville and Hunt County, Texas* (Waco: Texian Press, 1976), 134.

7. P. Wilson, quoted in Ibid.

8. For the Black Codes, see, for example, Barry A. Crouch, "All the Vile Passions: The Texas Black Code of 1866," *SWHQ* 97 (July 1993): 13–36 and James M. Smallwood, *Time of Hope, Time of Despair: Blacks in Reconstruction Texas* (New York: Kennikat Press, 1981); David Pickering and Judy Falls, *Brush Men and Vigilantes: Civil War Dissent in Texas* (College Station: Texas A&M University Press, 2000), 118; Richard B. McCaslin, *Tainted Breeze: The Great Hanging at Gainesville, Texas, 1862* (Baton Rouge: Louisiana State University Press, 1994), 170; Dale Baum, *The Shattering of Texas Unionism: Politics in the Lone Star State During the Civil War Era* (Baton Rouge: Louisiana State University Press, 1998), 158–59.

9. Sheridan quoted in Pickering and Falls, *Bush Men and Vigilantes,* 124.

10. The quotes are from McCaslin, *Tainted Breeze,* 173–74, 178.

11. Charles F. Rand to J. S. Kirkman, AAAG, March 4, 1867, "Monthly Report," Sub-Assistant Commissioner, Marshall, Texas, LS, BRFAL, RG 105, NA; Deposition, J. D. Ivey, October 10, 1868, in *United States vs. J. W. Marshal, et al.,* copy in H. Sands to Morse, AAAG, October 15, 1868, LR, Box 12, Scott, Post of Sherman, to AAAG Morse, March 12, 1868, LR, Box 5, DT, 5MD, RG 393, NA; Lillian Womack, "Leonard Man Recalls Deadly Feud," newspaper clipping no. 35, Peacock–Crouch-Smallwood Collection, Archives, TAMC Library.

12. See Allen Trealese, *White Terror: The Ku Klux Klan Conspiracy and Southern Reconstruction* (New York: Harper & Row, 1971); and see James M. Smallwood, "When the Klan Rode: White Terror in Reconstruction Texas," *Journal of the West* 25 (October 1986): 4–13.

13. Randolph B. Campbell, "District Judges of Texas in 1866–1867, an Episode in the Failure of Reconstruction," *SWHQ* 93 (January 1990): 357–77; Pickering and Falls, *Brush Men and Vigilantes,* 125.

14. Scott, Post of Sherman, to AAAG Morse, March 12, 1868, LR, Box 5, DT, 5MD, RG 393, NA; Leonard Public Library, *A History of Leonard, Texas, 1880–1980* (Leonard, Texas: Privately published, n.d.) 17; Denise Maddox, "The Lee-Peacock Feud," internet site.

15. See "Conditions of Affairs in Texas," U.S. House of Representatives, *Executive Documents,* Doc. No. 61, 39th Cong., 2nd Sess.

16. Mrs. L. E. Potts, Lamar County, Texas, to the President (Andrew Johnson), n.d., 1866, in "Conditions of Affairs in Texas," House of Representatives, *House Executive Documents,* Doc. No. 61, 39th Cong., 2nd sess., 1866, 1–4 (this document is replete with examples of murderous violence in Texas); William L. Richter, *The Army in Texas During Reconstruction, 1865–1870* (College Station: Texas A&M University Press, 1987), 145–47; Richter, "'The Revolver Rules the Day!': Colonel DeWitt C. Brown and the Freedmen's Bureau in Paris, Texas, 1867–1868," *SWHQ* 93 (Winter, 1990): 315–16; and see Smallwood, *Time of Hope, Time of Despair;* Scott, Post of Sherman, to AAAG Morse, March 12, 1868, LR, Box 5, DT, 5MD, RG 393, NA.

17. See "Condition of Affairs in Texas," House of Representatives, *Executive Documents,* Doc. No. 61, 39th Cong., 2nd sess., 1866, 1–4; Richter, " 'The Revolver Rules the Day!'," 315–16; Richter, "'Oh God, Let Us Have Revenge': Ben Griffin and His Family during the Civil War and Reconstruction," *Arkansas Historical Quarterly* 67 (Autumn 1998): 271; Roberts to AAAG, August 12, November 12, 1867, endorsement by J. B. Johnson in Adam Desch to A. L. Bennett, Acting Post adjutant, Waco, February 4, 1870, LR, BRFAL, RG 105, NA; and see Richter, *The Army in Texas During Reconstruction,* 145–47; James Stephen Peters, *Mace Bowman: Texas Feudist, Western Lawman* (N.p.: Privately published, 1996), 41; Leonard Public Library, *History of Leonard,* 17.

18. *Weekly Harrison Flag,* January 28, 1869; Smallwood, "Swamp Fox of the Sulphur" *True West* 38 (October 1991), Pt. 1: 21; Barry A. Crouch and Donaly Brice, *Cullen Montgomery Baker: Reconstruction Desperado* (Baton Rouge: Louisiana State University Press, 1997), 36–38.

19. Crouch and Brice, *Cullen Montgomery Baker,* 38.

20. Ibid.

21. Joseph G. Rosa, *Age of the Gunfighter: Men and Weapons on the Frontier, 1840–1900* (Norman: University of Oklahoma Press, 1993), 68–69; Rick Miller, "William Preston Longley," *NHT, 4: 282.* For more on Longley, see Rick Miller, *Bloody Bill Longley: A Biography* (Wolfe City, Texas: Henington Publishing Company, 1996).

22. Lee Pierce, Statement, Federal Writers' Project, "The Slave Narratives: A Folk History of Slavery in the United States From Interviews with Former Slaves, Texas Narratives," Vol. 16, pts. 1–4, Washington, D.C.: Works Progress Administration, 1941, NA.

23. "Titus County," VF, Pickering-Falls Collection, Archives, TAMC Library; Norman C. Russell, "The History of Titus county Since 1860" (M. A. thesis, East Texas State Teachers College, 1937), 39–40.

24. "Titus County," VF, Pickering-Falls Collection, Archives, TAMC Library; *Cleburne Chronicle,* April 10, 17, 1869; Russell, "Titus County Since 1860," 39–40; *Texas Republican,* August 25, September 18, 1868; Jay Robert Nash, *Encyclopedia of Western Lawmen and Outlaws* (New York: Paragon Press, 1992), 37.

25. Rand to AAAG J. S. Kirkman, "Monthly Report," March 4, 1867, Sub-Assistant Commissioner, Marshall, Texas, LS, BRFAL, RG 105, NA; for more on area violence, outlaws, and Klansmen, see *New York Times,* January 28, 1867.

26. DeWitt Brown to AAAG C. S. Roberts, June 1, 1868, Sub-Assistant Commissioner, Paris, Texas, LS, Gregory Barrett to AAAG Vernou, "Monthly Report," August 1, 1868, Sub-Assistant Commissioner, Tyler, Texas, LS, BRFAL, RG 105, NA. See also Crouch and Brice, *Cullen Montgomery Baker;* Peacock, "Lee-Peacock Feud," 10, Peacock-Crouch-Smallwood Collection, Archives, TAMC Library.

27. *New York Tribune,* September 29, 1868; Scott, Post of Sherman, to AAAG Morse, October 15, 1868, LR, Box 12, DT, 5MD, RG 393, NA.

28. *New York Tribune,* September 29, 1868; Scott, Post of Sherman, to AAAG Morse, October 15, 1868, LR, Box 12, DT, 5MD, RG 393, NA.

29. *New York Tribune,* September 29, 1868; Brown to AAAG C. S. Roberts, June 1, 1868, Sub-Assistant Commissioner, Paris, Texas, LS, Gregory Barrett to AAAG Vernou, "Monthly Report," August 1, 1868, Sub-Assistant Commissioner, Tyler, Texas, LS, BRFAL, RG 105, NA; See Crouch and Brice, *Cullen Montgomery Baker;* L. Peacock, "Lee-Peacock Feud," 10, Peacock-Crouch-Smallwood Collection, Archives, TAMC Library; Peters, *Mace Bowman,* 41–42; Smallwood, *Time of Hope, Time of Despair,* 135–36.

30. Brown to AAAG Roberts, June 1, 1868, Sub-Assistant Commissioner, Paris, Texas, LS, BRFAL, RG 105, NA.

31. For more on terrorist groups in the South, see Trelease, *White Terror: The Ku Klux Klan Conspiracy and Southern Reconstruction* (New York: Harper and Row, 1971); also see, Smallwood, "When the Klan Rode," 4–13.

32. Smallwood, "When the Klan Rode, 4–5; *New Orleans Tribune,* September 1, 1866; John E. Thompson to Andrew Jackson Hamilton, October 8, 1865, D. J. Baldwin to Hamiltion, n.d., GP, ARIS/TSL. See also Smallwood, *Time of Hope, Time of Despair.*

32. *New Orleans Tribune,* September 1, 1866; Trelease, *White Terror,* 3–8; Smallwood, "When the Klan Rode," 5; Roy Sylvan Dunn, "The KGC in Texas, 1860–1861," *SWHQ* 70 (April, 1967): 543–73; Susan Lawrence Davis, *The Authentic History: Ku Klux Klan, 1865–1877* (New York: Privately printed, 1924), 254. See also Smallwood, *Time of Hope, Time of Despair.*

33. J. Lee Stambaugh and Lillian J. Stambaugh, *A History of Collin County* [Texas] (Austin: Texas State Historical Association, 1958), 73–74; Barbara Leah Clayton Barnhill, "The Lone Star Conspiracy: Racial Violence and the Ku Klux Klan Terror in Post-Civil War Texas, 1865–1877" (M.A. thesis, Oklahoma State University, 1979), 15, 93–97; *Denton Monitor,* May 30, September 5, 1868; Peters, *Mace Bowman,* 42; Russell, "Titus County Since 1860," 37. And see Crouch and Brice, *Cullen Montgomery Baker.*

34. A. G. Malloy to AAAG Charles Garretson, "Monthly Report," September 30, 1867, Sub-Assistant Commissioner, Marshall, Texas, LS, BRFAL, RG 105, NA; *Denton Monitor,* May 30, September 5, 1868; Stambaugh and Stambaugh, *History of Collin County,* 73–74; Smallwood, "When the Klan Rode," 4–13. See also Barnhill, "The Lone Star Conspiracy."

35. A. G. Malloy to AAAG Charles Garretson, "Monthly Report," September 30, 1867, Sub-Assistant Commissioner, Marshall, Texas, LS; Rand to AAAG J. S. Kirkman, April 20, 1867, Sub-Assistant Commissioner, Marshall, Texas, LS, BRFAL, RG 105, NA.

36. William G. Kirkman to AAAG J. S. Kirkman, September 18, 1868; and see W. Kirkman to AAAG J.S. Kirkman, July 25, 1867, Sub-Assistant Commissioner, Boston, Texas, LS, BRFAL, RG 105, NA.

37. *New York Daily Tribune,* July 30, 1867, September 18, 1868; and see William G. Kirkman

to AAAG J. S. Kirkman, July 25, 1867, Sub-Assistant Commissioner, Boston, Texas, LS, BRFAL, RG 105, NA. For more on William Kirkman's hardships and the problems that the bureau faced in Texas, see James M. Smallwood, "The Freedmen's Bureau Reconsidered: Local Agents and the Black Community," *Texana* 11 (1973): 309–20, and Barry A. Crouch, *The Freedmen's Bureau and Black Texans* (Austin: University of Texas Press, 1992). W. G. Kirkman was later murdered. For another study that looks at the hardships of the bureau men, see James M. Smallwood, "Charles E. Culver: A Reconstruction Agent in Texas: The Work of Local Freedmen's Bureau Agents and the Black Community," *Civil War History* 27 (1981): 350–61. Culver was also later murdered.

38. Claude Elliott, "The Freedmen's Bureau in Texas," *SWHQ* 56 (July 1952): 6.

39. *Bonham Texas News,* June 26, 1868; the story is also reported in several secondary sources including Sonnichsen, *I'll Die Before I'll Run,* 23–25. Modern researchers, however, find fault with Lee's account. For one thing, Lee waited three years to make his statement—and by 1868 he was still being pursued by the law. Thus, his account was self-serving, designed to sway the populace in the hope that they would continue to give him refuge and even more help. Second, it was unlikely that either Lee or his family members had $2,000 or his father Daniel would not have been forced to make money by becoming a horse thief who was later killed for just such an offense. Third, researchers scoured the Fannin County courthouse records and found no "civil suit" brought by Lee against Peacock or any other Unionist. Researchers did, however, turn up indictments against Lee and others in his gang—indictments for robbery and murder. One must conclude that just as Lee lied about his Confederate military record, he also lied about the supposed events of his unlikely "arrest" of 1865. Coauthor Larry Peacock found several indictments against Lee for robbery and murder—see, for example, Case 810, Sixth Judicial District, Fannin County Courthouse, Bonham, Texas. Smallwood searched in the courthouses of Collin, Grayson, and Hunt and found nothing that would support Lee's claims.

40. Commissioner of the Freedmen's Bureau, "Report for 1867," U.S. House of Representatives, *House Executive Documents,* Doc. No. 1, 40th Cong., 2nd Sess., 1867 (serial 1324), Vol. 3, pt, 1: 683; O. O. Howard to Charles Griffin, April 3, 1867, Educational Division, LR, BRFAL, RG 105, NA; Smallwood, *Time of Hope, Time of Despair,* 136.

Chapter 5. The Devil Stalks the Corners

1. Gladys B. Ray, *Murder at the Corners* (San Antonio: Naylor Press, 1957), 9–10; James Stephen Peters, *Mace Bowman: Texas Feudist, Western Lawman* (N.p.: Privately published, 1996), 44; C. L. Sonnichsen, *I'll Die Before I'll Run: The Story of the Great Feuds of Texas* (New York: Harper and Brothers, 1951), 29; Leonard Public Library, *A History of Leonard, Texas, 1880–1980* (Leonard, Texas: Privately published, n.d.), 14.

2. See James M. Smallwood, "When the Klan Rode: White Terror in Reconstruction Texas," *Journal of the West* 25 (October 1986): 4–13. See also James M. Smallwood, *Time of Hope, Time of Despair: Black Texans During Reconstruction* (New York: Kennikat Press, 1981).

3. W. R. Adams, interviewed by L. L. Bowman, July 22, 1931, in "Bob Lee," VF, L. L. Bowman Papers, Archives, TAMC Library; Nick Jones, "Lee-Peacock Feud," *Real West: True Tales of the American Frontier* (January 1979): 52–53; Ray, *Murder at the Corners,* 26–28; Denise Maddox, "The Lee-Peacock Feud," article on Internet site; Leonard Public Library, *History of Leonard,* 14; *Bonham Texas News,* late June or July, 1868, quoted in Sonnichsen,

I'll Die Before I'll Run, 26; Walter Clay Dixson, *Richland Crossing: A Portrait of Texas Pioneers* (Fort Worth: Peppermill Publishing Company, 1994), 195.

4. See Ray, *Murder at the Corners,* 26–28; Jones, "Lee-Peacock Feud," 51–52; Peters, *Mace Bowman,* 42–43.

5. For examples, see Ray, *Murder at the Corners,* 26–28; Jones, "Lee-Peacock Feud," 52–53; Leonard Public Library, *History of Leonard,* 14; Maddox, "Feud," article on Internet site; U. T. Taylor, "The Lee-Peacock Feud," *Frontier Times* 3 (May 1926): 3; Sonnichsen, *I'll Die Before I'll Run,* 26. Given the different versions, historic confusion reigns. Bob Lee's later reminiscence of the incident that he sent to the *Bonham Texas News* in the summer of 1868 is unreliable, even spurious, for Lee gave details about Jim's actions that Lee could not have known, including a statement about where the unarmed Maddox got a gun. Moreover, no one who investigated the incident ever thought to ask the obvious question. If Maddox—the evil Unionist—hated Lee with the intensity that both contemporary observers and later partisan pro-Southern historians asserted, why did not the Unionist just finish the job while Lee was unconscious in the street? Maddox could have walked up close to the prone gunman and, with but one more shot, killed him. Bob Lee was already an outlaw on the run from the authorities with warrants out for his arrest. Whoever killed him might face an investigation but would likely never be convicted by any court.

   Maddox knew that he could kill Lee and walk away from a courtroom a free man. Yet, Jim took no action except to leave. Could it have been that the fight, if there was one, was fair and that Jim was satisfied and did not believe he needed to kill the captain? Additionally, Dr. Pierce was a known Lee man and a Lost Cause sympathizer, and some sources maintained that Lee's wound was not really that serious. With the law already looking for him, Lee probably stayed those few days at the Pierce home just to hide rather than convalesce. About the shooting itself, so many conflicting stories exist that one must acknowledge that Maddox indeed wounded Lee—that is a fact, but no accurate account exists about the exact details of the incident. *Bonham Texas News,* late June or early July, 1868, quoted in Sonnichsen, *I'll Die before I'll Run,* 23–26; Ray, *Murder at the Corners,* 26–28; Jones, Lee-Peacock Feud," 52–53; Leonard Public Library, *History of Leonard,* 14; Maddox, "Feud," article on Internet site; Taylor, "Lee-Peacock Feud," 3.

6. G. W. King, interviewed by L. L. Bowman, in "Bob Lee," VF, L. L. Bowman Papers, newspaper clipping, n.d., Peacock-Crouch-Smallwood Collection, Archives, TAMC Library; Sonnichsen, *I'll Die Before I'll Run,* 26.

7. Albert Evans to AAAG J. T. Kirkman, February 1, 1867, Sub-Assistant Commissioner, Sherman, LS, BRFAL, RG 105, NA.

8. Ibid.

9. Ibid.; Anthony Bryant to AAAG Richardson, August 31, 1867, Sub-Assistant Commissioner, Sherman, LS, BRFAL, RG 105, NA.

10. A. Evans to AAAG J. T. Kirkman, February 1, 1867; A. Bryant to AAAG Richardson, August 31, 1867, Sub-Assistant Commissioner, Sherman, LS, BRFAL, RG 105, NA.

11. A. Evans to AAAG J. T. Kirkman, February 1, 1867, A. Bryant to AAAG Richardson, August 31, 1867, Sub-Assistant Commissioner, Sherman, LS, BRFAL, RG 105, NA.

12. *Dallas Weekly Herald,* April 20, 1867; Ray, *Murder at the Corners,* 29–30; Sonnichsen, *I'll Die Before I'll Run,* 27; Peters, *Mace Bowman,* 44–45; Deposition, Lewis Peacock, October 9, 1868, in *United States vs. J. W. Marshal, et al.,* copy in J. H. Sands, Post of Sherman, to C. E. Morse, AAAG, October 15, 1868, LR, Box 12, DT, 5MD, RG 393, NA.

13. Bryant to AAAG Richardson, August 31, 1867, Sub-Assistant Commissioner, Sherman, LR, BRFAL, RG 105, NA; James M. Smallwood, "The Perpetuation of Caste: Black Agricultural Workers in Reconstruction Texas," *Mid-America* 61 (January 1979): 5–23.

14. William H. Sinclair to AAAG J. T. Kirkman, July 2, 1867, Texas Assistant Commissioner, LR, BRFAL, RG 105, NA; also see William L. Richter, "Who was the Real Head of the Texas Freedmen's Bureau," *Military History of the Southwest* 20 (Fall 1990): 121–56; for more on black sharecroppers, see Smallwood, "The Perpetuation of Caste," 5–23.

15. *Flake's Semi-Weekly Bulletin,* July 24,1867; Sinclair to AAAG J. Kirkman, July 2, 1867, Texas Assistant Commissioner, LR, BRFAL, RG 105, NA. Both the *Bulletin* and Sinclair reported the details on Guest's gruesome disemboweling of the pregnant freedwoman.

16. *Flake's Semi-Weekly Bulletin,* July 24, 1867.

17. Sinclair to AAAG J. Kirkman, July 2, 1867, Texas Assistant Commissioner, LR, BRFAL, RG 105, NA; Dale Baum, *The Shattering of Texas Unionism: Politics in the Lone Star State During the Civil War Era* (Baton Rouge: Louisiana State University Press, 1988) 177, 179.

18. C,. S. Roberts to J. P. Richardson, Sub-Assistant Commissioner, Clarksville, n.d., LS, BRFAL, RG 105, Roberts to AAAG J. T. Kirkman, July 27, 1867, LR, Box 5, DT, 5MD, RG 393, NA.

19. J. T. Kirkman to AAAG A. H. M. Tayler, LR, BRFAL, RG 105, NA; W. Walworth Harrison, "Hardin Hart," unpublished paper, Harrison to Lutie Brown, August 1966, "Hardin Hart" VF, W. Walworth Harrison Collection, Archives, Greenville Public Library, Greenville, Texas; David Pickering and Judy Falls, *Brush Men and Vigilantes: Civil War Dissent in Texas* (College Station: Texas A&M University Press, 2000), 69: and see William E. Sawyer, "Martin Hart, Civil War Guerrilla," *Texas Military History* 3 (fall 1963): 146–53; V. W. Grubbs, "Hunt County Pioneer: Judge Hardin Hart," *Greenville Banner,* April 12, 1911. Also see Randolph B. Campbell, "Scalawag District Judges: The E. J. Davis Appointees, 1870–1873," *Houston Review* 14 (1992): 75–88.

20. For more detail on the Hart brothers, see W. Harrison, "Hardin Hart," unpublished paper, in "Hardin Hart," VF, W. Harrison Collection, Archives, Greenville Public Library; Pickering and Falls, *Brush Men and Vigilantes,* 72–79; Grubbs, "Judge Hardin Hart, *Greenville Banner,* April 12, 1911; Sawyer, "Martin Hart," 146–57; William E. Sawyer, "The Martin Hart Conspiracy," *Arkansas Historical Quarterly* 23 (Summer 1964): 154–65; Thomas E. Jordon, "Captain Martin Hart's Date with Death," *Civil War Times* 36 (May 1997): 40–46; Graham Landrum and Allan Smith, *An Illustrated History of Grayson County, Texas* (2d ed.; Fort Worth Historical Publishers, 1967), 70–71; Cecil Harper, "Martin D. Hart," *NHT,* 3: 491; Tom Scott, "Fannin County: Two Centuries of Texas Legend," *Bonham Daily Favorite,* September 1, 1985.

21. *Marshall Texas Republican,* January 29, 1863; J. T. Kirkman to AAAG A. H. M. Taylor, May 2, 1867, LS, BRFAL, RG 105, NA; W. Harrison, "Hardin Hart," unpublished paper, in "Hardin Hart, VF, W. Harrison Collection, Archives, Greenville Public Library.

22. William Sinclair, Inspector General, to Charles Griffin, Assistant Commissioner, June 30, 1867, J. T. Kirkman to AAAG A. H. M. Taylor, July 12, 1867, LS, BRFAL, RG105, NA; W. Sinclair to AAAG J. T. Kirkman, July 18, 1867, LR, Box 3, DT, 5MD, RG 393, NA.

23. Sinclair to Griffin, July 5,1867, LR, Box 3, Sinclair to W. Paine, July 5, 1867, LR, Box 2, DT, 5MD, RG 393, NA.

24. "Charges and specifications against J. Alfred Drye," March 7, 1868, in H. E. Scott, Post of Sherman, to AAAG C. E. Morse, March 12, 1868, LR, Box 5, DT, 5MD, RG 393, NA.

25. G. E. Ramey to H. Torbett, April 1, 1869, LR, Post of Greenville, Box 16, DT, 5MD, RG 393, NA.

26. W. R. Adams, interviewed by L. L. Bowman, summer of 1931, notes in "Bob Lee," VF, L. L. Bowman Papers, Archives, TAMC Library.

27. Ramey, Statement, in J. W. Thomas to E. M. Pease, October 23, 1867, LS, Box 3, DT, 5MD, RG 393, NA.

28. John Scott, Statement, Ramey, Statement, R. C. White, Statement, in Thomas to E. Pease, October 23, 1867, LS, Box 3, DT, 5MD, RG 393, NA.

29. Ibid.

30. Scott, Statement, Ramey, Statement, White, Statement, petition, J. W. Thockmorton, et al., November 11, 1867, in Thomas to E. Pease, October 23, 1867, LR, Box 3, DT, 5MD, RG 393, NA.

31. E. Pease to E. R. S. Canby, February 5, 1869, GP, ARIS/TSL; Ramey to Thomas, January 29, 1869, in LR, Box 9, DT, 5MD, RG 393, NA.

32. S. H. Starr to AAAG C. E. Morse, February 9, 1868, LR, Box 4, DT, 5MD, RG 393, NA.

33. Ray, *Murder at the Corners,* 33–35; and see Sonnichsen, *I'll Die Before I'll Run.*

34. Sonnichsen, *I'll Die Before I'll Run,* 27; Ray, *Murder at the Corners,* 33–35.

35. Ray, *Murder at the Corners,* 35–36; Sonnichsen, *I'll Die Before I'll Run,* 27.

36. Petition, Pilot Grove, to Scott, March 9, 1868, LR, Box 5, DT, 5MD, RG 393, NA.

37. Scott to AAAG Morse, March 12, 1868, LR, Box 5, DT, 5MD, RG 393, NA.

38. Deposition, Lewis Peacock, October 9, 1868, in *United States vs. John W. Marshal,* copy in J. H. Sands to AAAG Morse, October 15, 1868, LR, Box 12, Scott to AAAG Morse, March 12, 1868, LR, Box 5, DT, 5MD, RG 393, NA.

39. G. W. King, interviewed by L. L. Bowman, July 22, 1931, in "Bob Lee," VF, L. L. Bowman Papers, Archives, TAMC Library; Ray, *Murder at the Corners,* 37; Sonnichsen, *I'll Die Before I'll Run,* 27–28.

40. *Bonham Texas News,* late June or early July, 1868, quoted in Sonnichsen, *I'll Die Before I'll Run,* 23–25; and see G. W. King, interviewed by L. L. Bowman, July 22, 1931, in "Bob Lee," VF, L. L. Bowman Papers, Archives, TAMC Library.

41. G. W. King, interviewed by L. L. Bowman, July 22, 1931, in "Bob Lee," VF, L. L. Bowman Papers, Archives, TAMC Library; Gladys B. Ray, one of the Lee family's most formidable historical apologists, one who never questioned the Lee version of the struggle with Peacock, did indeed question Bob's account of Billy's demise, apparently believing none of it. In *Murder at the Corners,* Ray concocted a story about Billy and Charlie being on the Jefferson Road but having to stop to repair a wagon wheel. Then, while they were still working, a posse of about a dozen troopers showed up. With Peacock present, they gave Billy a swift, fair trial, found him guilty of murder, and executed him. The soldiers forced Billy, with hands up, to march ten paces. On step seven, while Billy's back was still turned, one army man fired a lone shot, killing Billy instantly. Charlie? The men let him go. He was Billy's first cousin, but he had never joined the ex-Confederate-Unionist struggle and had nothing

to do with Lige Clark's death. See Ray, *Murder at the Corners,* 37–39. C. L. Sonnichsen in *I'll Die Before I'll Run* quoted Bob Lee's letter but he did not believe it, either. Instead, he cited Ray's version but the lone bullet became bullets, and Charlie turned out to be Billy's brother, not cousin. In an article that appeared in *Real West,* historian Nick Jones generally followed Sonnichsen and erroneously confirmed that Charlie was Billy's older brother, not first cousin (which was correct). Jones also has both boys tied to wagon wheels and beaten unmercifully before the detachment killed Billy. Historical confusion reigns. Sonnichsen, *I'll Die Before I'll Run,* 27–28. See also Jones, "Lee-Peacock Feud."

42. Jones, "Lee-Peacock Feud," 52.

43. "Charges and Specifications against J. Alfred Drye," and "Charges of Specifications against J. W. Clements," March 7, 1868, in Scott, Post of Sherman, to AAAG Morse, LR, Box 5, DT, 5MD, RG 393, NA; and see G. W. King, interviewed by L. L. Bowman, July 22, 1931, in "Bob Lee," VF, L. L. Bowman Papers, Archives, TAMC Library.

44. Deposition, Lewis Peacock, in *United States vs. J. W. Marshal,* October 9, 1868, copy in J. H. Sands to AAAG Morris, LR, Box 12, DT, 5MD, RG 393, NA.

45. Deposition, James H. Morrisson, Deposition, William McCallom, Deposition, M. L. Boling, October 8, 1868, in *United States vs. John W. Marshal, et al.,* copy in Sands to AAAG Morse, October 15, 1868, LR, Box 12, DT, 5MD, RG 393, NA.

46. Deposition, Charles Saunders, October 8, 1868, ibid.

47. Deposition, D. L. Lewis, October 8, 1868, ibid.

48. Jesse A. Ashberry to J. J. Reynolds, April 9, 1868, LR, Box 4, DT, 5MD, RG 393, NA.

49. *Bonham Texas News,* June 26, 1868, quoted in Sonnichsen, *I'll Die Before I'll Run,* 23–25.

50. Deposition, D. L. Lewis, October 8, 1868, in *United States vs. J. W. Marshal, et al.,* copy in Sands to AAAG Morse, October 15, 1868, LR, Box 12, Asberry to Reynolds, April 9, 1868, LR, Box 4, 5MD, RG 393, NA; *Sherman Courier,* April 25, 1868; C. M. Wilcox to "Dear Sir" [Governor Pease] June 4, 1868, GP, ARIS/TSL; L. Peacock, "Reconstruction in Texas," 1–7, Peacock-CrouchSmallwood Collection; G. W. King, interviewed by L. L. Bowman, July 22, 1931, in "Bob Lee," VF, L. L. Bowman Papers, Archives, TAMC Library.

51. Wilcox to "Dear Sir" [Governor E. Pease], June 4, 1868, GP, ARIS/TSL, copy in Peacock–Crouch–Smallwood Collection, Archives, TAMC Library; *Sherman Courier,* April 25, 1868; *Flakes Semi-Weekly Bulletin,* May 6, 1868; Asberry to Reynolds, April 9, 1868, LR, Box 4, DT, 5MD, RG 393, NA.

52. Wilcox to "Dear Sir" [Governor E. Pease], June 4, 1868, GP, ARIS/TSL; *Sherman Courier,* April 25, 1868; *Flakes Semi-Weekly Bulletin,* May 6, 1868; Asberry to Reynolds, April 9, 1868, LR, Box 4, DT, 5MD, RG 393, NA; Bill O'Neal, *Encyclopedia of Western Gunfighters* (Norman: University of Oklahoma Press, 1979), 253; Sonnichsen, *I'll Die Before I'll Run,* 28; Ray, *Murder at the Corners,* 40–41.

53. Wilcox to "Dear Sir" [Governor E. Pease], June 4, 1868, GP, ARIS/TSL.

54. Sonnichsen, *I'll Die Before I'll Run,* 28; Ray, *Murder at the Corners,* 40–41.

55. *Dallas Weekly Herald,* July 4, 1868; *Galveston News,* June 27, 1868; Ray, *Murder at the Corners,* 40–41; Jones, "Lee-Peacock Feud," 52; Peters, *Mace Bowman,* 51; O'Neal, *Gunfighters,* 253; U. T. Taylor, "More About Bob Lee," *Frontier Times* 5 (March 1928): 252; L. Peacock, "Notes on Lewis Peacock," Peacock-Crouch-Smallwood Collection, Archives, TAMC Library.

56. *Dallas Weekly Herald,* July 4, 1868; *Galveston News,* June 27, 1868; Ray, *Murder at the Corners,* 40–41; Jones, "Lee-Peacock Feud," 52; Peters, *Mace Bowman,* 51; O'Neal, *Gunfighters,* 253; Taylor, "More About Bob Lee," 252.

57. *Dallas Weekly Herald,* July 4, 1868; *Galveston News,* June 27, 1868; Ray, *Murder at the Corners,* 40–41; Jones, "Lee-Peacock Feud," 52; Peters, *Mace Bowman,* 51; O'Neal, *Gunfighters,* 253; Taylor, "More About Bob Lee," 252; *Bonham Texas News,* June 26, 1868, quoted in Sonnichsen, *I'll Die Before I'll Run,* 23–25.

58. Deposition, J. D. Ivey, October 10, 1868, in *United States vs. J. W. Marshal, et al.,* copy in Sands to AAAG Morse, October 15, 1868, LR, Box 12, DT, 5MD, RG 393, NA; G. W. King, interviewed by L. L. Bowman, July 22, 1931, in "Bob Lee," VF, L. L. Bowman Papers, Archives, TAMC Library.

59. Deposition, J. D. Ivey, October 10, 1868, in *United States vs. J. W. Marshal, et al.,* copy in Sands to AAAG Morse, October 15, 1868, LR, Box 12, DT, 5MD, RG 393, NA.

60. DeWitt Brown to AAAG Roberts, June 1, 1868, Sub-Assistant Commissioner, Paris, LS, BRFAL, RG 105, NA.

61. *Bonham Texas News,* June 26, 1868, quoted in Sonnichsen, *I'll Die Before I'll Run,* 23–25; G. W. King, interviewed by L. L. Bowman, in "Bob Lee," VF, L. L. Bowman Papers, Archives, TAMC Library.

62. Brown to AAAG Roberts, June 1, 1868, Sub-Assistant Commissioner, Paris, LS, BRFAL, RG 105, NA.

63. Brown to AAAG Vernou, June 8, 1868, "Monthly Report," Sub-Assistant Commissioner, Paris, LS, BRFAL, RG 105, NA; Barry A. Crouch and Donaly Brice, *Cullen Montgomery Baker: Reconstruction Desperado* (Baton Rouge: Louisiana State University Press, 1997), 113–15; David Pickering and Judy Falls, *Brush Men and Vigilantes: Civil War Dissent in Texas* (College Station: Texas A&M University Press, 2000), 116; William L. Richter, "'The Revolver Rules the Day!' Colonel DeWitt Brown and the Freedmen's Bureau in Paris, Texas," *SWHQ* 93 (January 1990): 329.

64. Brown to AAAG Vernou, June 8, 1868, "Monthly Report," Sub-Assistant Commissioner, Paris, LS, BRFAL, RG 105, NA; Crouch and Brice, *Cullen Montgomery Baker,* 113–15; Pickering and Falls, *Brush Men and Vigilantes,* 116; Richter, "The Revolver Rules the Day," 329.

65. Brown to AAAG Vernou, June 8, 1868, "Monthly Report," Sub-Assistant Commissioner, Paris, LS, BRFAL, RG 105, NA; Crouch and Brice, *Cullen Montgomery Baker,* 113–115; Richter, "The Revolver Rules the Day," 329; *New York Daily Tribune,* July 30, September 18, 1868.

66. Sinclair to Roberts, August 18, 1868, Assistant Commissioner, Texas, LR, BRFAL, RG 105, NA; and see State of Texas, *Report of Special Committee on Lawlessness and Violence in Texas* (Austin: n.p., 1868); Baum, *Shattering Texas Unionism,* 223, 225.

67. *Galveston Daily News,* July 4, 1868.

68. Fannin County Grand Jury indictment, January 8, 1869, of Bob Lee and Simp Dixon for murder of Ruben Hogue, unserved warrant to arrest Bob Lee and Simp Dixon for murder with the constable's notations listed on the warrant, Fannin County Courthouse, Bonham, Texas, copy in Peacock-Crouch-Smallwood Collection, Archives, TAMC Library.

Chapter 6. Chaffee's Guerrillas and the Federal Crackdown

1. Charles F. Rand to AAAG J. P. Richardson, July 21, July 28, 1868, Sub-Assistant Commissioner, Clarksville, LS, BRFAL, RG 105, NA; William L. Richter, "'Oh God, Let Us Have Revenge': Ben Griffin and his Family During the Civil War and Reconstruction," *Arkansas Historical Quarterly* 67 (Autumn 1998): 273–74.

2. Rand to AAAG Richardson, July 21, 28, 1868, Sub-Assistant Commissioner, Clarksville, LS, BRFAL, RG 105, NA; Richter, "Oh God, Let Us Have Revenge," 273–74.

3. *Clarksville Standard,* August 15, 1868; *Marshall Texas Republican,* August 21, 1868; "Guard Report," Post of Sulphur Springs, December 31, 1868, LR, Box 14, DT, 5MD, RG 393, NA; Richter, "Oh God, Let Us Have Revenge," 274.

4. *Marshall Texas Republican,* August 21, 1868.

5. H. E. Scott, Post of Sherman, to AAAG C. E. Morse, March 12, 1868, LR, Box 5, DT, 5MD, RG 393, NA.

6. J. J. Reynolds, Special Order No. 16, August 27, 1868, DT, 5MD, RG 393, NA. Reynolds's reward offer was printed in many Texas newspapers, including the *Marshall Texas Republican,* September 11, 1868; and see File 849M1868, AGO, RG 94, NA; James E. Sefton, *The United States Army and Reconstruction, 1865–1877* (Baton Rouge: Louisiana State University Press, 1967), 191. Also see Barry A. Crouch and Donaly Brice, *Cullen Montgomery Baker: Reconstruction Desperado* (Baton Rouge: Louisiana State University Press, 1997).

7. *Marshall Texas Republican,* August 7, 1868; *New York Times,* August 31, 1868; *Daily Austin Republican,* August 4, 1868; *Galveston Daily News,* July 4, 1868; Gregory Barrett to AAAG Charles Vernou, "Monthly Report," August 1, 1868, Sub-Assistant Commissioner, Tyler, Texas, LS, BRFAL, RG 105, NA; James M. Smallwood, *Time of Hope, Time of Despair: Black Texans During Reconsruction* (New York: Kennikat Press, 1981), 144–45.

8. Smallwood, *Time of Hope, Time of Despair,* 144–45; also see Crouch and Brice, *Cullen Montgomery Baker.*

9. D. W. Stedham to Reynolds, September 1, 1868, AGO, RG 94, NA.

10. G. A. Evarts to AAAG Vernou, n.d., Sub-Assistant Commissioner, Sherman, LS, BRFAL, RG 105, NA. Sherman's Mayor John Dorchester, County Court Clerk W. L. Taylor, and Judge Solomon Bostick endorsed Evarts appraisal of the conditions in Grayson County; also see A. B. Norton to E. Pease, December 9, 1868, GP, ARIS/TSL.

11. *Paris Vindicator,* n.d., quoted in *Marshall Texas Republican,* September 4, 1868.

12. [?] to AAG, December 24, 1868 [?], to Louis V. Caziarc, January 14, 1869, Jefferson Post Records, LR, Thomas M. Tolman to AAAG, August 15, 1868, LR, Box 16, Reynolds to A. R. Chaffee, September 1, 1868, LS, Reynolds to Secretary of War, September 3, 1868, LS, DT, 5MD, RG 393, NA; Crouch and Brice, *Cullen Montgomery Baker,* 97, 118–119; Sefton, *The United States Army and Reconstruction,* 191.

13. [?] to AAG, December 24, 1868, [?] to Caziarc, January 14, 1869, Jefferson Post Records, LR, Tolman to AAAG, August 15, 1868, LR, Box 16, Reynolds to Secretary of War, September 3, 1868, LS, DT, 5MD, RG 393, NA; Crouch and Brice, *Cullen Montgomery Baker* 97, 118–119; Sefton, *The United States Army and Reconstruction,* 191.

14. [?] to AAG, December 24, 1868 [?], to Caziarc, January 14, 1869, Jefferson post records, LR,

Tolman to AAAG, August 15, 1868, LR, Box 16, Reynolds to Secretary of War, September 3, 1868, endorsements attached, LS, DT, 5MD, RG 393, NA; Crouch and Brice, *Cullen Montgomery Baker,* 97, 118–19; Sefton, *The United States Army and Reconstruction,* 191.

15. Richter, "Oh God, Let Us Have Revenge," 274; and see Crouch and Brice, *Cullen Montgomery Baker.*

16. William H. Carter, "6th Regiment of Cavalry," in *The Army of the United States* (Washington: Government Printing Office, 1894), 241; and see Crouch and Brice, *Cullen Montgomery Baker.*

17. Carter, "6th Cavalry," 241.

18. Ibid.

19. Tolman to AAAG C. E. Morse, August 14, 15, 1868, Post of Sulphur Springs, LR, Reynolds to Secretary of War, with endorsements, September 3, 1868, LS, DT, 5MD, RG 393, NA.

20. Tolman to AAAG Morse, August 15, 1868, Post of Sulphur Springs, LR, Reynolds to Secretary of War, with endorsements, September 3, 1868, LS, DT, 5MD, RG 393, NA.

21. Reynolds to Secretary of War, with endorsements, September 3, 1868, LS, [?] to AAG, December 24, 1868, [?] to Caziarc, January 14, 1869, Tolman to AAAG, August 15, 1868, Vernou to AAAG Morse, September 3, 1868, LR, ADG and AAAG to J. H. Sands, September 16, 1868 (microfilm, reel 1165), Sands to AAAG C. E. Morse, September 9, 1868, LR, DT, 5MD, RG 393, NA.

22. Gladys St. Clair, *A History of Hopkins County, Texas* (Waco: Texian Press, 1965), 32.

23. Tolman to AAAG, August 15, 1868, LR, Box 16, DT, 5MD, RG 393, NA.

24. Ibid.

25. Sands to AAAG Morse, September 9, 1868, Vernou to AAAG C. E. Morse, September 3, 1868, LR, Box 6, DT, 5MD, RG 393, NA.

26. Sands to AAAG Morse, September 9, 1868, Vernou to AAAG Morse, September 3, 1868, LR, DT, Box 6, 5MD, RG 393, NA.

27. Sands to AAAG Morse, September 9, 1868, LR, Box 6, ADG and AAAG Morse to Sands, LS, September 16, 1868 (microfilm, reel 1165), Vernou to AAAG Morse, September 3, 1868, LR, Box 6, DT, 5MD, RG 393, NA.

28. Sands to AAAG C. E. Morse, September 9, 1868, LR, Box 6, ADG and AAA, Morse to Sands, LS, September 16, 1868 (microfilm, reel 1165); Vernou to AAAG Morse, September 3, 1868, LR, Box 6, DT, 5MD, RG 393, NA.

29. Sands to AAAG Morse, September 9, 1868, LR, Box 6, DT, 5MD, RG 393, NA.

30. C. C. Binkley, endorsement by Judge J. D. Gurge, to Vernou, Post of Sherman, September 1, 1868, LR, Box 6, DT, 5MD, RG 393, NA.

31. *Paris Vindicator,* quoted in *Marshall Texas Republican,* September 4, 1868.

32. Ibid.

33. Binkley, endorsement by Judge Gurge, to Vernou, Post of Sherman, September 1, 1868, LR, Box 6, DT, 5MD, RG 393, NA; and see D. W. Stedham to J. J. Reynolds, September 1, 1868, LR, AGO, RG 94, NA. For more on politics, see Dale Baum, *The Shattering of*

Texas Unionism: Politics in the Lone Star State During the Civil War Era (Baton Rouge: Louisiana State University Press, 1998).

34. Binkley, endorsement by Judge Gurge to Vernou, Post of Sherman, September 1, 1868, LR, Box 6, DT, 5MD, RG 393, NA; and see D. W. Stedham to J. J. Reynolds, September 1, 1868, LR, AGO, RG 94, NA.

35. See Dale Baum's "Chicanery and Intimidation in the 1869 Texas Gubernatorial Race," *SWHQ* 97 (July 1993): 37–54, and his *Shattering Texas Unionism.*

36. Hardin Hart to E. Pease, September 17, 1868, E. Pease to E. R. S. Canby, February 10, 1869, GP, ARIS/TSL.

37. Hardin Hart to E. Pease, September 17, 1868, E. Pease to E. R. S. Canby, February 10, 1869, GP, ARIS/TSL.

38. E. Pease to Reynolds, September 22, 1868, LR, Box 6, DT, 5MD, RG 393, NA.

39. Evarts to Vernou, September 1, 1868, LR, Box 6, DT. 5MD, RG 393, NA.

40. Ibid.

41. Vernou to AAAG C. E. Morse, September 3, 1868, LR, Box 6, DT, 5MD, RG 393, NA.

42. Ibid.

43. Ibid.

44. Special Order No. 40, September 24, 1868, in LR, Box 15, DT, 5MD, RG 393, NA.

45. Sinclair to AAAG Roberts, August 18, 1868, LR, Box 5, DT, 5MD, RG 393, NA.; see State of Texas, *Report of Special Committee on Lawlessness and Violence in Texas* (Austin, n.p., 1868); Richter, "Oh God, Let Us Have Revenge," 275; Richter, *The Army in Texas During Reconstruction, 1865–1870* (College Station: Texas A&M University Press, 1987), 146–47.

46. Tolman to AAAG, August 15, 1868 [?], to AAG, December 24, 1868, [?] to L. V. Caziarc, January 14, 1869, Jefferson Post records, LS, Box 6, DT, 5MD, RG 393, NA; Richter, "Oh God, Let Us Have Revenge," 275; Richter, *The Army in Texas,* 146–47. Papers relating to Tolman's court martial are in the files of the Office of the Judge Advocate General, "General Courts Martial, 1812–1938, 728, Box 1577, RG 153, NA.

47. Deposition, William Edwards, October 11, 1868, in *United States vs. J. W. Marshal, et al.,* copy in Sands to AAAG Morse, October 15, 1868, LR, Box 12, DT, 5MD, RG 393, NA.

48. Ibid.

49. Ibid.

50. Deposition, Martin Gentry, October 8, 1868, ibid.

51. "Guard Report," Post of Sulpfur Springs, December 31, 1868, LR, Box 14, DT, RG 393, NA.

52. Jones, "Lee-Peacock Feud," 52; Binkley to Vernou, September 14, 1868, LR, BRFAL, RG 105, NA.

53. Nick Jones, "The Lee-Peacock Feud," *Real West: True Tales of the American Frontier* (January 1979): 52; Binkley to Vernou, September 14, 1868, LR, BRFAL, RG 105, NA; Denise Maddox, "The Lee-Peacock Feud," article at Internet site, Gladys B. Ray, *Murder at the Corners* (San Antonio: Naylor Press, 1957), 46; Graham Landrum and Allan Smith, *An Illustrated History of Grayson County, Texas* (2nd ed.; Fort Worth: Historical Publishers, 1967), 73.

54. W. B. Pease, Post of Sulphur Springs, to AAAG Morse, October 3, 1868, LR, Box 13, DT, 5MD, RG 393, NA; and see G. W. King, interviewed by L. L. Bowman, July 22, 1931, in "Bob Lee," VF, L. L. Bowman Papers, Archives, TAMC Library.

55. W. B. Pease, Post of Sulphur Springs, to AAAG Morse, October 3, 1868, LR, Box 13, DT, 5MD, RG 393, NA.

56. Ibid.

57. Ibid.

58. Ibid.; W. G. King, interviewed by L. L. Bowman, July 22, 1931, in "Bob Lee," VF, L. L. Bowman Papers, Archives, TAMC Library.

59. W. B. Pease, Post of Sulphur Springs, to AAAG Morse, October 3, 1868, LR, Box 13, DT, 5MD, RG 393, NA.

60. Ibid.

61. Tolman to J. M. Burns, Post adjutant, Sulphur Springs, November 5, 1868, LR, Box 13, DT, 5MD, RG 393, NA.

62. Deposition, Lewis Peacock, October 9, 1868, in *United States vs. John W. Marshal,* enclosed in Sands to AAAG Morse, LR, Box 12, DT, 5MD, RG 393, NA.

63. ADG and AAAG Roberts to H. P. Eakin, November 25, 1868 (microfilm reel 1165), LS, DT, 5MD, RG 393, NA.

64. Eakin to ADG and AAAG Cariarc, February 8, 1869, LR, Box 16, DT, 5MD, RG 393, NA.

65. A. R. Chaffee to AAAG Caziarc, January 21, 1869, LR, Box 16, DT, 5MD, RG 393, NA.

66. L A. Abbott to AAAG Morse, November 5, 1868 (microfilm reel 1193), LR, DT, 5MD, RG 393, NA.

67. F. Maytheny to AAAG, November 22, 1868, LR, Box 12, DT, 5MD, RG 393, NA; G. W. King, interviewed by L. L. Bowman, July 22, 1931, in "Bob Lee," VF, L. L. Bowman Papers, Archives, TAMC Library.

68. F. Maytheny to AAAG, November 22, 1868, LR, Box 12, DT, 5MD, RG 393, NA.

69. *Galveston News,* December 31, 1868; James Stephen Peters, *Mace Bowman: Texas Feudist, Western Lawman* (n.p.: Privately published, 1996), 46; Ray, *Murder at the Corners,* 46; Bill O'Neal, *Encyclopedia of Western Gunfighters* (Norman: University of Oklahoma Press, 1979), 253.

70. H. C. Mack, *Texas: Information for Emigrants* (Franklin, Tennessee: Haynes & Figures, Publishers, 1869), 141–43; Crouch and Brice, *Cullen Montgomery Baker,* 18.

71. *The State of Texas vs. Robert Lee and Simp Dixon,* a true bill, No. 838, March 1, 1869, Fannin County Courthouse, Bonham, Texas. For more on Baker's death, see Crouch and Brice *Cullen Montgomery Baker,* the best, most reliable study of Baker in life and death; for a brief account of Baker's career of crime, see James M. Smallwood, "Cullen Baker: Swamp Fox of the Sulfur," *True West* 38 (October 1991), pt. 1: 20–23, 39 and (November 1991), pt. 2: 38–41.

72. A. R. Chaffee to AAAG Caziarc, January 21, 1869, LR, Box 16, DT, 5MD, RG 393, NA.

73. Ibid.

74. Ibid.

Chapter 7. Continuing Warfare and the End of the "Man Eater"

1. G. E. Ramey to J. H. Thomas, January 29, 1869, LR, Box 9, DT. 5MD, RG 393, NA; *McKinney Weekly Enquirer,* February 6, 1869.

2. *McKinney Messenger,* January, n.d., 1869, clipping in LR, Box 9, DT, 5MD, RG 393, NA.

3. Ibid.

4. Ibid.; *McKinney Weekly Enquirer,* February 6, 1869.

5. Ibid.; Ramey to Thomas, January 29, 1869, H. P. Eakin to H. Torbett, Adjutant, Post of Greenville, March 9, 1869, LR, Box 9, DT, 5MD, RG 393, NA.

6. Ramey to Thomas, January 29, 1869, LR, Box 9, DT, 5MD, RG 393, NA.

7. Ibid.

8. L. Bowlbey to E. Pease, January 30, 1869, GP, ARIS/TSL.

9. *McKinney Weekly Express,* February 6, 1869; Gladys B. Ray, *Murder at the Corners* (San Antonio: Naylor Press, 1957), 53–56. Ray includes quotes from the *Sherman Courier* in the matter of Thompson and Blackmore.

10. Charles Campbell, Post of Pilot Grove, to AAAG, June 2, 1869, LR, Box 6, DT, 5MD, RG 393, NA; *McKinney Weekly Express,* February 6, 15, 1869.

11. H. P. Eakin to ADG and AAAG Louis V. Caziarc, February 8, 1869, LR, Box 12, DT, 5MD, RG 393, NA.

12. Hugh Hudson, Henry Boren, A. Lewis, Henry Taylor, et al., January 23, 1869, petition, LR, Box 12, DT, 5MD, RG 393, NA.

13. Ibid.

14. T. Maytheny to AAAG Cariarc, February 1, 1869, LR, Box 12, DT, 5MD, RG 393, NA.

15. Ibid.

16. Campbell, Post of Pilot Grove, to AAAG, June 2, 1869, LR, Box 6, DT, 5MD, RG 393, NA; *McKinney Weekly Express,* February 15, *1869.*

17. *Campbell, Post of Pilot Grove, to AAAG, June 2, 1869, LR, Box 6, DT, 5MD, RG 393, NA; McKinney Weekly Express,* February 15, 1869.

18. Campbell, Post of Pilot Grove, to AAAG, June 2, 1869, LR, Box 6, DT, 5MD, RG 393, NA; *McKinney Weekly Express,* February 15, 1869.

19. E. Pease to E. R. S. Canby, April 2, 1869, LS, copies of Hunt County Grand Jury Indictments, Hardin Hart to E. Pease, March 25, 1869, LR, Box 15, DT, MD, RG 393, NA.

20. Eakin to ADG and AAAG Caziarc, February 8, 1869, LR, Box 12, DT, 5MD, RG 393, NA.

21. Ibid.

22. Sands, quoted in James E. Sefton, *The United States Army in Reconstruction, 1865–1877* (Baton Rouge: Louisiana State University Press, 1967), 193.

23. Ibid.

24. A. M. Bryant to Rev. Thadeous McKae [private secretary of Governor E. Pease], March 1,

1869, GP, ARIS/TSL. For more detail on Bryant, see William L. Richter, *Overreached on all Sides: The Freedmen's Bureau Administrators in Texas, 1865–1868* (College Station: Texas A&M University Press, 1991), 158, 194–95, 241–42.

25. Bryant to McKee, March 1, 1869, E. Pease to Canby, March 16, 1869, GP, ARIS/TSL.

26. Bryant to McKae, March 1, 1869, E. Pease to Canby, March 16, 1869, GP, ARIS/TSL.

27. Bryant to McKae, March 1, 1869, E. Pease to Canby, March 16, 1869, GP, ARIS/TSL.

28. Bryant to McKae, March 1, 1869, E. Pease to Canby, March 16, 1869, GP, ARIS/TSL; *Harrison Flag,* February 6, 13, 1869; Smallwood, *Time of Hope, Time of Despair,* 139–140; Reconstruction Convention, *Journal of the Reconstruction Convention of 1868–1869* (2 vols.; Austin, 1870).

29. Eakin to ADG and AAAG Caziarc, March 1, 1869, LR, Box 12, DT, 5MD, RG 393, NA.

30. E. Pease to Canby, February 10, 1869, GP, ARIS/TSL; Special Order, No. 40, September 24, 1868, Special Order No. 42, February 24, 1869, in LR, Box 15, DT, 5MD, RG 393, NA.

31. AAAG Caziarc to Commanding Officer, Post of Greenville, LS, copy in LR, Box 16, DT, 5MD, RG 393, NA.

32. Ramey to H. W. Torbett, April 1, 1869, LR, Box 16, George A. Wilson to Torbett, April 16, 1869, LR, Box 24, William McGraw to Commanding Officer, Post of Greenville, April 2, 1869, LR, Box 16, DT, 5MD, RG 393, NA; Denise Maddox, "Lee-Peacock Feud," article at Internet site; Ray, *Murder at the Corners,* 57–58.

33. Wilson to Torbett, April 16, 1869, LR, Box 24, McGraw to Commanding Officer, Post of Greenville, April 2, 1869, Ramey to Torbett, Post of Greenville, April 1, 1869, LR, Box 16, DT, 5MD, RG 393, NA; James Stephen Peters, *Mace Bowman: Texas Feudist, Western Lawman* (N.p.: Privately published, 1996), 46; Ray, *Murder at the Corners,* 57–59.

34. Peters, *Mace Bowman,* 46; Maddox, Maddox, "Lee-Peacock Feud," article at Internet site; Ray, *Murder at the Corners,* 58–59; Wilson to Torbett, April 16, 1869, LR, Box 24, McCraw to Commanding Officer, Post of Greenville, Ramey to Torbett, Adj., Post of Greenville, April 1, 1869, LR, Box 16, DT, 5MD, RG 393, NA; Joe W. Chumbley, "Brief Biography of Bill Penn," in *Kentucky-Town and Its Baptist Church* (Houston: D. Armstrong, 1975), two unnumbered pages. None of the pages in Chumbley's book are numbered.

35. *McKinney Enquirer,* n.d., quoted in Ray, *Murder at the Corners,* 59.

36. Ramey to Torbett, April 1, 1869, LR, Box 16, DT, 5MD, RG 393, NA.

37. McGraw to Commanding Officer, Post of Greenville, April 1, 1869, Ramey to H. Torbett, April 1, 1869, LR, Box 16, DT, 5MD, RG 393, NA; Maddox, "Lee-Peacock Feud," article at Internet site; Ray, *Murder at the Corners,* 59.

38. McGraw to Commanding Officer, Post of Greenville, April 1, 1869, Ramey to Torbett, April 1, 1869, LR, box 16, DT, 5MD, RG 393, NA; Maddox, "Lee-Peacock Feud," article at Internet site; Ray, *Murder at the Corners,* 59.

39. McGraw to Commanding Officer, Post of Greenville, April 1, 1869, Ramey to Torbett, April 1, 1869, LR, Box 16, DT, 5MD, RG 393, NA; Maddox, "Lee-Peacock Feud," at Internet site; Ray, *Murder at the Corners,* 59.

40. McGraw to Commanding Officer, Post of Greenville, April 1, 1869, Ramey to Torbett,

April 1, 1869, LR, Box 16, DT, 5MD, RG 393, NA; Peters, *Mace Bowman,* 46; Maddox, "Lee-Peacock Feud," article at Internet site; Ray, *Murder at the Corners,* 59.

41. McGraw to Commanding Officer, Post of Greenville, April 1, 1869, Ramey to Torbett, April 1, 1869, LR, Box 16, DT, 5MD, RG 393, NA.

42. *Waco Register,* n.d., quoted by *Weekly Austin Republican,* April 21, 1869; *Waxahachie Argus Extra,* April 6, 1869.

43. *Marshall Texas Republican,* April 30, 1869.

44. *Waxahachie Argus Extra,* April 6, 1869.

45. [?] to AAG, December 24, 1868, [?] to AAAG Caziarc, January 14, 1869, Post of Jefferson, LS, DT, 5MD, RG 393, NA; *Marshall Texas Republican,* April 30, 1869; Smallwood, *Time of Hope, Time of Despair,* 144–45.

46. H. H. Sneed to E. Pease, April 12, 1869, Pease, GP, ARIS/TSL; *Marshall Texas* Republican, April 30, 1869; *Waxahachie Argus, Extra,* April 6, 1869; Smallwood, *Time of Hope, Time of Despair,* 144–46.

47. Sneed to E. Pease, April 12, 1869, Pease, GP, ARIS/TSL; *Marshall Texas Republican,* April 30, 1869.

48. [?] to AAG, December 24, 1868, [?] to AAAG Caziarc, January 14, 1869, Post of Jefferson, LS, DT, 5MD, RG 393, Gregory Barrett to Charles Vernou, "Monthly Report," August 1, 1868, LS, Sub-Assistant Commissioner, Tyler, Texas, BRFAL, RG 105, NA; Smallwood, *Time of Hope, Time of Despair,* 144–46; Sneed to E. Pease, April 12, 1869, GP, ARIS/TSL; *Marshall Texas Republican,* April 30, 1869; *Waxahachie Argus, Extra,* April 6, 1869.

49. [?] to AAG, December 24, 1868, [?] to AAAG Caziarc, January 14, 1869, Post of Jefferson, LS, DT, 5MD, RG 393, NA; *Waxahachie Argus Extra,* April 6, 1969; *Clarksville Northern Standard,* April 17, 1869; Jay Robert Nash, *Encyclopedia of Western Lawmen and Outlaws* (New York: Paragon Press, 1992), 37. For more on Lee, see *Texas Republican,* August 7, 1868; *New York Times,* August 31, 1868; *Daily Austin Republican,* August 4, 26, 1868; Sneed to E. Pease, April 12, 1869, GP, ARIS/TSL; Barrett to Vernou, "Monthly Report," August 1, 1868, Sub-Assistant Commissioner, Tyler, Texas, LS, BRFAL, RG 105, NA; Smallwood, *Time of Hope, Time of Despair,* 144–45.

50. Sneed to E. Pease, April 12, 1869, GP, ARIS/TSL; M. P. Hunnicutt to AAAG, April 7, 1869, LR, Box 12, DT, 5MD, RG 393, NA. For the fate of Bickerstaff's head, see Stephen Mills, Samuel Milliken, and other members of the Alvorado Vigilance Committee to J. B. Johnson, Post of Waco, April 30, 1869, J. B. Johnson, Post of Waco to Mills and Milliken, April 30, 1869, LR, Box 16, DT, RG 393, NA; *Marshall Texas Republican,* April 30, 1869.

51. *Waxahachie Argus Extra,* April 6, 1869.

52. Ramey to Torbett, April 1, 1869, LR, Box 16, DT, 5MD, RG 393, NA.

53. Chumbley, "Penn Biography," *Kentucky-Town,* two unnumbered pages.

54. Deputy Sheriff John Hunter, W. A. Salmen, et al., to George E. Head, Post of Greenville, April 23, 1869, LR, Box 16, DT, 5MD, RG 393, NA; Chumbley, "Penn biography," *Kentucky-Town,* two unnumbered pages.

55. Hunter, Salmen, et al., to Head, Post of Greenville, April 23, 1869, LR, Box 16, DT, 5MD, RG 105, NA; Chumbley, "Penn Biography," *Kentucky-Town,* two unnumbered pages.

56. Hunter, Salmen, et al., to Head, Post of Greenville, April 23, 1869, LR, Campbell to Lemuel Pettee, Post of Greenville, April 26, 1869, LR, Box 16, DT, 5MD, RG 393, NA; Peters, *Mace Bowman,* 46; Ray, *Murder at the Corners,* 62–63; Graham Landrum and Allan Smith, *An Illustrated History of Grayson County, Texas* (2d ed.; Fort Worth: Historical Publishers, 1967), 73.

57. M. W. Bledsoe to Torbett, Post of Greenville, n.d., LR, Box 9, DT, 5MD, RG 393, NA.

58. A. C. Pettee, Post of Greenville, to Commanding Officer, Post of Waco, April 27, 1869, LR, Box 9, DT, 5MD, RG 393, NA.

59. Peters, *Mace Bowman,* 46–47; Ray, *Murder at the Corners,* 66–68; Landrum and Smith, *Grayson County,* 73.

60. Ray, *Murder at the Corners,* 67.

61. Peters, *Mace Bowman,* 46–47; Ray, *Murder at the Corners,* 66–68; Landrum and Smith, *Grayson County,* 73.

62. Leonard Public Library, *A History of Leonard, Texas, 1880–1980* (Leonard, Texas: Privately printed, n.d.), 17.

63. G. W. King, interviewed by L. L. Bowman, Mrs. W. C. Lee, interviewed by L. L. Bowman, July 22, 1931, in "Bob Lee, VF, L. L. Bowman Papers, Archives, TAMC; Campbell to H. Corbett, May 30, 1869, LR, Box 16, DT, 5MD, RG 393, NA; Peters, *Mace Bowman,* 47; Ray, *Murder at the Corners,* 68–71.

64. Campbell to Corbett, May 30, 1869, LR, box 16, 5MD, RG 393, NA; Peters, *Mace Bowman,* 47; Ray, *Murder at the Corners,* 68–71; Lillian Womack, "Leonard Man Recalls Story of Ancestors, Deadly Feud," newspaper clipping no. 35, Peacock-Crouch-Smallwood Collection, Archives, TAMC Library; Landrum and Smith, *Grayson County,* 73.

65. Peters, *Mace Bowman,* 47; Ray, *Murder at the Corners,* 68–71; Womack, "Leonard man," newspaper clipping no. 35, Kerry Ross Boren to Chuck Parsons, January 19, 1974, Peacock-Crouch-Smallwood Collection, Archives, TAMC Library; G. W. King, interviewed by L. L. Bowman, Mrs. W. C. Lee, interviewed by L. L. Bowman, July 22, 1931, in "Bob Lee," VF, L. L. Bowman Papers, Archives, TAMC Library; Campbell to Corbett, May 30, 1869, Roberts to Campbell, May 30, 1869, LR, Box 16, DT, 5MD, RG 393, NA; Landrum and Smith, *Grayson County,* 73; Leonard Public Library, *History of Leonard,* 15, 17; Stephen Marshall, Affidavit, October 18, 1869. Hunt County Clerk, Hunt County Courthouse, copy on Reel 21, M 1188, DT, 5MD, RG 393, NA.

66. Joseph A. Wright to A. T. Monroe, January 3, 1868, copy, accompanied by documents, in LR, Box 6, DT, 5MD, RG 393, NA.

67. C. G. Gordon to Post Adjutant Thomas Merit, May 16, 1869, A. B. Norton to Reynolds, August 21, 1869, accompanied by a civilian petition of August 4, E. B. Spilman, Benjamin Long, J. J. Boyer, et al., to W. S. Hancock, February 15, 1868, LR, Box 6, DT, 5MD, RG 393, NA.

68. G. A. Evarts to Vernou, September 1868, AGO Records, RG 94, Spilman, Long, Boyer, et al., to Hancock, February 15, 1868, LR, Box 4, Mason Jackson, Post of Greenville, to AAAG C. E. Morse, August 30, 1869, LR, Box 16, DT, 5MD, RG 393, NA; *Clarksville Standard,* July 31, 1869; G. W. King, interviewed by L. L. Bowman, July 22, 1931, in "Bob Lee," VF, L. L. Bowman Papers, Archives, TAMC. Hart's shootout in the yard is mentioned by Richter, *Overreached on All Sides,* 194.

69. James Thomas to E. Pease, September 7, 1869, LR, GP, ARIS/TSL; *McKinney Messenger,* September 11, 1869; David Pickering and Judy Falls, *Brushmen and Vigilantes: Civil War Dissent in Texas* (College Station: Texas A&M University Press, 2000), 106; W. Walworth Harrison, *History of Greenville and Hunt County, Texas* (Waco, Texas: Texian Press, 1976), 134–35; Charles Whiting, Post of Greenville, to headquarters, September 8, 1869, LR, Box 16, DT, 5MD, RG 393, NA. More than forty years after the gang's ambush of Hart, Major John Kirk reminisced in print about the attack—see John Kirk, "Hardin Hart's Ambush by Eye-Witness," *Greenville Banner, November 28,* 1913. See also J. E. Carraway, "When the Yankee Soldiers Made a Run for Safety," unpublished paper in "Bowman and Hart," VF, Pickering-Falls Collection, G. W. King, interviewed by L. L. Bowman, July 22, 1931, in "Bob Lee," VF, L. L. Bowman Papers, Archives, TAMC Library.

70. *McKinney Messenger,* September 11, 1869; W. Whiting, Post of Greenville, to headquarters, September 8, 1869, LR, Box 16, DT, 5MD, RG 393, NA.

71. J. Thomas to E. Pease, September 7, 1869, GP, ARIS/TSL; *McKinney Messenger,* September 11, 1869; *Greenville Banner,* November 26, 1913; *Austin Republican,* July 25, 1868; Harrison, *History of Greenville and Hunt County, Texas,* 134–35; Evarts to Vernou, September 1868, AGO Records, RG 94, C. B. McLellan, Post of Greenville, to Fannin County District Clerk, March 17, 1870, LR, Box 26, DT, 5MD, RG 393, NA; Richter, *Freedmen's Bureau Administrators in Texas,* 194.

72. Thomas to E. Pease, September 7, 1869, GP, ARIS/TSL, copy also in LR, Box 26, DT, 5MD, RG 393, NA; *McKinney Messenger,* September 11, 1869; *Greenville Banner,* November 26, 1913; *Austin Republican,* July 25, 1868; Harrison, *Greenville and Hunt County,* 134–135; Evarts to Vernou, September 1868, AGO Records, RG 94, NA; Richter, *Freedmen's Bureau Administrators in Texas,* 194; Pickering and Falls, *Brush men and Vigilantes,* 106.

73. *McKinney Messenger,* September 11, 1869.

74. Thomas to E. Pease, September 7, 1869, GP, ARIS/TSL, copy also in LR, Box 26, DT, 5MD, RG 393, NA.

75. *McKinney Messenger,* September 11, 1869.

76. L. F. Smith to Reynolds, March 18, 1870, S. B. Maxey to J. Throckmorton, March 19, 1870 (Maxey's letter is attached to Smith's), LR, Box 26, DT, 5MD, RG 393, NA.

77. William Hoffman, Post of Greenville, to Charles J. Whiting, Commanding, July 27, 1869, LR, Box 16, DT, 5MD, RG 393, NA.

Chapter 8. The Lee-Peacock Struggle Plays Out

1. Kerry Ross Boren to Chuck Parsons, January 19, 1974, November 27, 1975, Peacock-Crouch-Smallwood Collection, Archives, TAMC Library; Gladys B. Ray, *Murder at the Corners* (San Antonio: Naylor Press, 1957), 72–74.

2. Bill Boren to Dick Boren, n.d., 1870s, Peacock-Crouch-Smallwood Collection, Archives, TAMC Library.

3. Ibid.

4. Leonard Public Library, *A History of Leonard, Texas, 1880–1980* (Leonard, Texas: Privately

published, n.d.), 18; W. G. King, interviewed by L. L. Bowman, July 22, 1931, in "Bob Lee," VF, L. L. Bowman Papers, Archives, TAMC Library.

5. Walter Clay Dixson, *Richland Crossing: A Portrait of Texas Pioneers* (Fort Worth: Peppermill Publishing Company, 1994), 214; also see Richard C. Marohn, *The Last Gunfighter: John Wesley Hardin* (College Station: Creative Publishing Company, 1995) and Leon Metz, *John Wesley Hardin: Dark Angel of Texas* (El Paso: Mangan Books, 1996).

6. Dixson, *Richland Crossing,* 214.

7. *Waxahachie Argus* quoted in *Dallas Herald,* September 4, 1869.

8. T. U. Taylor, "The Lee-Peacock Feud," *Frontier Times* 3 (May 1926), 12.

9. *Dallas Herald,* September 25, 1869; Ray, *Murder at the Corners,* 73–74.

10. *Dallas Herald,* September 25, 1869; Ray, *Murder at the Corners,* 75.

11. A. Bledsoe to J. J. Reynolds, July 1, 1869, LR, Box 6, DT, 5MD, RG 393, NA.

12. *McKinney Messenger,* September 18, 1869.

13. Ibid.

14. Ibid.

15. David Medlock to E. J. Davis, February 17, 1870, GP, ARIS/TSL; Walter Cotton, *History of the Negroes of Limestone County* (Mexia, Texas: Privately printed, 1939), 28; James M. Smallwood, *Time of Hope, Time of Despair: Black Texans During Reconsruction* (New York: Kennikat Press, 1981), 126; Dixson, *Richland Crossing,* 220; *Flakes Daily Bulletin,* February 6, 1870.

16. Cotton, *History of the Negroes of Limestone County,* 28; Smallwood, *Time of Hope, Time of Despair,* 126; Dixson, *Richland Crossing,* 220.

17. *Corsicana Observer,* quoted in *Galveston Tri-Weekly News,* February 14, 1870; Dixson, *Richland Crossing,* 221, 223; Leonard Public Library, *History of Leonard,* 18; for more on Culver, see James M. Smallwood, "Charles E. Culver: A Reconstruction Agent in Texas: The Work of Local Freedmen's Bureau Agents and the Black Community," *Civil War History* 27 (1981): 350–61. Culver was later murdered.

18. W. A. Borthwick to C. E. Morse, secretary for civil affairs, January 26, 1870, LR, Box 24, DT, 5MD, RG 393, NA.

19. Medlock to Davis, February 17, 1870, GP, ARIS/TSL.

20. Ibid.

21. Ibid.; Adam Desch to A. Bennett, Acting Post Adjutant, Post of Waco, February 4, 1870, LR, Box 26, DT, 5MD, RG 393, NA; *Waco Register,* quoted in *Flake's Daily Bulletin,* February 6, 1870.

22. Desch to Bennett, Acting Post Adjutant, Post of Waco, February 4, 1870, LR, Box 26, RG 393, NA; *Waco Register,* quoted in *Flake's Daily Bulletin,* February 6, 1870; Dixson, *Richland Crossing,* 219; *Dallas Morning News,* January 9, 1873.

23. Medlock to Davis, February 17, 1870, Davis, GP, ARIS/TSL; Desch to Bennett, Acting Post Adjutant, Post of Waco, February 4, 1870, LR, Box 26, DT, 5MD, RG 393, NA; *Waco Register,* quoted in *Flake's Daily Bulletin,* February 6, 1870; Dixson, *Richland Crossing,* 219; Odie Minatra, "J. S. Burdette, Minute Man and Soldier," *Frontier Times,* 6–7, uniden-

tified newspaper clipping, Peacock-Couch-Smallwood Collection, Archives, TAMC Library; *Dallas Morning News,* January 9, 1973; Barry A. Crouch, "The Texas State Police," unpublished manuscript, 41, copy in Smallwood-Crouch-Peacock Collection, Archives, TAMC Library.

24. Desch to Bennett, February 4, 1870, LR, Box 26, DT, RG 393, NA; C. L. Sonnichsen, *I'll Die Before I'll Run: The Story of the Great Feuds of Texas* (New York: Harper and Brothers, 1951), 32; Dixson, *Richland Crossing,* 220, 223; Cotton, *Negroes of Limestone County,* 18; *Dallas Morning News,* January 9, 1973. Although Cotton's chronology is questionable, his account of "Dixie," when compared to material from Sonnichsen, Dixson, and primary sources in the National Archives create strong evidence that leaves no doubt. Indeed, "Dixie" was Simp. For ex-Confederate views of the killing of Trammell, see *Austin Daily Democratic Statesman,* June 1, 1875, and *Galveston Daily News,* June 18, 1875. For Unionist accounts, see *San Antonio Daily Express,* June 19, 1875, and Crouch, "Texas State Police," 42–43, unpublished manuscript, Pecock-Crouch-Smallwood Collection, Archives, TAMC; also see Mollie Kirkland, Statement, Federal Writers Project, "Texas Narratives," "A Folk History of Slavery in the United States from Interviews with Former Slaves," vol. 16, pt. 2: 18, NA; *Brenham Banner,* November 19, 1875.

25. Medlock to Davis, February 17, 1870, Davis, E. J. Davis, GP, ARIS/TSL.

26. Marohn, *The Last Gunfighter,* 86–90; Metz, *Dark Angel of Texas,* 135–47; Mollie Moore Godbold, "Comanche and the Hardin Gang," *SWHQ* 67 (July 1963), Pt. 1: 55–77 and (October 1963), Pt 2: 247–66. Marohn seems to believe that John Wesley was "unjustly treated" in this entire affair. Considering Wes's exploits, this interpretation is rather dubious.

27. Sonnichsen, *I'll Die Before I'll Run,* 31–32; Nick Jones, "The Lee-Peacock Feud," *Real West: True Tales of the American Frontier* (January 1979): 53.

28. Dixson, *Richland Crossing,* 222. Ray perpetuates the Lee myth surrounding Simp's death. See Ray, *Murder at the Corners,* 87; and see Lillian Womack, "Leonard Man Recalls Story of Ancestors, Deadly Feud," newspaper clipping no. 35, Peacock-Crouch-Smallwood Collection, Archives, TAMC Library; also see Desch to Bennett, Acting Post Adjutant, Post of Waco, February 4, 1870, LR, Box 26, DT, 5MD, RG 393, NA; *Waco Register,* quoted in *Flake's Daily Bulletin,* February 6, 1870.

29. Milam County, manuscript census returns, 1870; Texas ballots, 1869, DT 5MD, RG 393, NA; Larry Peacock, "notes on the Lee Peacock Feud," Peacock-Crouch-Smallwood Collection, Archives, TAMC Library; for the troubles in Milam County, see Dale Baum, *The Shattering of Texas Unionism: Politics in the Lone Star State During the Civil War Era* (Baton Rouge: Louisiana State University Press, 1998), 197, 201, 204–05.

30. Dixson, *Richland Crossing,* 222; *Fannin County Plus,* March 29, 1992.

31. A. B. Norton to J. J. Reynolds, August 21, 1869, LR, Box 6, DT, 5MD, RG 393, NA; Sonnichsen, *I'll Die Before I'll Run,* 33.

32. Norton to Reynolds, August 21, 1869, W. H. Stark to Reynolds (petition attached), August 4, 1869, LR, Box 6, DT, 5MD, RG 393, NA.

33. *Paris Vindicator,* September 27, 1871; *Flakes Daily Bulletin,* October 7, 1871; Ray, *Murder at the Corners,* 97; Dixson, *Richland Crossing,* 236; Sonnichsen, *I'll Die Before I'll Run,* 33; U. T. Taylor, "The Lee-Peacock Feud," *Frontier Times* 3 (May 1926): 11; James Stephen Peters, *Mace Bowman: Texas Feudist, Western Lawman* (N.p.: Privately printed, 1996), 48.

34. *Paris Vindicator,* September 27, 1871; Ray, *Murder at the Corners,* 97; Dixson, *Richland Crossing,* 235; Sonnichsen, *I'll Die Before I'll Run,* 33; *Flakes Daily Bulletin,* October 7, 1871.

35. *Galveston Daily News,* June 11, 1876.

36. *Paris Vindicator,* September 27, 1871; Ray, *Murder at the Corners,* 97; Dixson, *Richland Crossing,* 236; Sonnichsen, *I'll Die Before I'll Run,* 33; *Galveston Daily News,* June 11, 1876; Taylor, "The Lee-Peacock Feud," 11.

37. *Flake's Daily Bulletin,* June 28, 1871.

38. *Bonham Texas News,* June 16, 1871.

Epilogue

1. James Stephen Peters, *Mace Bowman: Texas Feudist, Western Lawman* (N.p.: Privately printed, 1996) 44; and see Lea Lawlis, "Feud Leader Grave Gets Marker," newspaper clipping no. 36, Lillian Womack, "Leonard Man Recalls Deadly Feud," newspaper clipping no. 35, L. Peacock, "Casualties of the Lee-Peacock Feud," Peacock-Crouch-Smallwood Collection, Archives, TAMC Library.

2. Nick Jones, "The Lee-Peacock Feud," *Real West: True Tales of the American Frontier* (January 1979): 53.

3. Mrs. Carl Stripling, "110-Year-Old Peacock Grave Marked," newspaper clipping, n. d., Lawlis, "Feud Leader Grave Gets Marker," newspaper clipping no. 36, Peacock-Crouch-Smallwood Collection, Archives, TAMC LIbrary. Charles, Larry, and Loyd Peacock placed the marble slab on the grave on October 28, 1998.

4. *Dallas Morning News,* n. d., newspaper clipping, Peacock-Crouch-Smallwood Collection, Archives, TAMC Library.

5. Ibid.

6. Ibid.

7. Ibid.; Stripling, "110-Year-Old Peacock Grave Marked," Ibid.

8. Kent Biffle, "Bitter North Texas Feud Dogged Rebel to his Grave," *Dallas Morning News,* August 17, 1986.

9. David Pickering and Judy Falls, *Brush men and Vigilantes: Civil War Dissent in Texas* (College Station: Texas A&M University Press, 2000), 139; and for violence in the wider South, see George C. Rable, *But There was no Peace: The Role of Violence in the Politics of Reconstruction* (Athens: University of Georgia Press, 1984).

10. Edgar P. Sneed, "A Historiography of Reconstruction in Texas: Some Myths and Problems," *SWHQ* 72 (April 1969): 436.

11. Ibid., 437.

12. Ibid., 436.

13. Barry A. Crouch, "'Unmanacling Texas Reconstruction: A Twenty-Year Perspective," *SWHQ* 93 (January 1990): 302.

Essay on Sources

The Reconstruction years in Texas and the events that occurred during the turbulent era have not generally been well-served by historians. In the popular imagination, the decade following the Civil War is often viewed as one where carpetbaggers, scalawags, ignorant African Americans, and unscrupulous and corrupt politicians controlled the state. Nothing could be further from the truth. And violent episodes such as the Lee-Peacock War have been distressingly distorted, mostly because individuals relied upon the faulty memories of people instead of doing the necessary research to find the truth that would replace legend and lore. Unfortunately, this has been the pattern for too much of Texas Reconstruction history.

Almost every past account of the Lee-Peacock struggle has been pro-Lee and anti-Peacock. The majority of chroniclers of this conflict accept old, worn viewpoints of Reconstruction or do not understand the era at all. They simply see the period as one where the hated North attempted to further crush the South's spirit. Lee is praised as a returning hero who killed in self-defense, guarded the values of Southern culture, and attempted to prevent the occupation Union Army from imposing a dreaded, despotic regime upon the citizens of the Corners region. In addition, he fought against the Republican ideal of political equality for the newly freed slaves and through his violent efforts maintained the old social order where African Americans remained on the bottom.

Traditional accounts of the Lee-Peacock clash, which follow the above interpretation include Gladys B. Ray's *Murder at the Corners* (San Antonio: Naylor Press, 1957) and Nick Jones's "The Lee-Peacock Feud," *Real West: True Tales of the American Frontier* (January 1979), pp. 12–14, 52–53. Perhaps the most influential and widely read expositions of the bitterness is C. L. Sonnichsen, *I'll Die Before I'll Run: The Story of the Great Feuds of Texas* (New York: Harper and Brothers, 1951), which relies heavily upon oral recollections that are too often wrong. In a similar vein is T. U. Taylor's "The Lee-Peacock Feud," *Frontier Times* 3 (May 1926): pp. 1–10.

County histories are also an important source although they tend to accept out-of-date interpretations and perpetuate past myths. All four counties that converged at the Corners have their historians but their works must be used with caution. The most balanced county study used in this study is probably W. Walworth Harrison's *History of Greenville and Hunt County* (Waco: Texian Press,

1976). Also especially valuable was J. Lee Stambaugh's and Lillian J. Stambaugh's *A History of Collin County* (Austin: Texas State Historical Association, 1958).

Newer works that discuss the North Texas region in the post-Civil War era are significant and bring new perspectives to the historical background. They include David Pickering and Judy Falls, *Brush Men and Vigilantes: Civil War Dissent in Texas* (College Station: Texas A&M University Press, 2000); Richard B. McCaslin, *Tainted Breeze: The Great Hanging at Gainesville, Texas, 1862* (Baton Rouge: Louisiana State University Press, 1994), an outstanding study; James Marten, *Texas Divided: Loyalty and Dissent in the Lone Star State, 1865–1874* (Lexington: University of Kentucky Press, 1990); and the excellent *Frontier Defense in the Civil War: Texas' Rangers and Rebels* by David Paul Smith (College Station: Texas A&M University Press, 1992).

What is missing from previous accounts of the Lee-Peacock clash is research into primary materials that enhance the circumstances surrounding the events. Essential for understanding the context of these violent episodes are four major Record Groups at the National Archives in Washington, D.C. Perhaps most important are the Records of the United States Army Continental Commands, 1821–1900 and the Army Post Records in RG 393. They are voluminous, not all have been microfilmed, and we have used the original manuscripts whenever possible. Perhaps equally important are the papers of the Bureau of Refugees, Freedmen, and Abandoned Lands (the Freedmen's Bureau), in RG 105. They had much additional information that is not available in any other depository. Less significant, but still worth investigation, are the files of the Adjutant General's Office, RG 94, and those of the Judge Advocate General, RG 153.

Worthy local records that need to be ferreted out can be found in the county courthouses of the four respective counties discussed in the text. In addition, primary sources in the archives at Texas A&M at Commerce and at the Greenville Public Library also help to explain many of the horrific events of this period in North Texas. The Governor's Papers in the archives section of the Archives and Information Services at the Texas State Library in Austin are essential sources. At the Center for American History, University of Texas at Austin, are various collections that broaden the scope of the Lee-Peacock imbroglio. Contemporary newspapers that covered aspects of the Second Civil War in Texas are also invaluable. We may have missed material, but we have attempted to be most thorough in our coverage of local, county, state, and national sources. For specific citations as we moved through the study, readers are invited to review the notes section.

Index